D1624839

Jesus Daily®

Jesus Daily®

365 Interactive Devotions

Inspired by the over 27 million
fans on Facebook

Faith
Words

Aaron Tabor, MD
Founder of the *Jesus Daily* Fan Page

Jesus Daily is not endorsed, approved, connected, or supported by Facebook.

Editing and design: Koechel Peterson & Associates, Inc., Minneapolis, Minnesota.

FaithWords
Hachette Book Group USA
237 Park Avenue, New York, NY 10017
www.faithwords.com.

Printed in the United States of America

First Edition: October 2014

10 9 8 7 6 5 4 3 2 1

FaithWords is a division of Hachette Book Group, Inc. The FaithWords name and logo are trademarks of Hachette Book Group, Inc.

The Hachette Speakers Bureau provides a wide range of authors for speaking events. To find out more, go to www.hachettespeakersbureau.com or call (866) 376-6591.

The publisher is not responsible for websites (or their content) that are not owned by the publisher.

Library of Congress Control Number: 2014934602

ISBN: 978-1-4555-7723-1

Introduction

"Give us each day our daily bread."
LUKE 11:2

Before I created the Jesus Daily Page on Facebook, I felt that I wasn't really doing enough for Christ on a daily basis. Sure, I read my Bible and other materials daily, but as a medical doctor, my time was consumed by breast cancer research and gene therapy for wound and skin regeneration. So it seemed too out of reach to do something positive *every* single day as a disciple of Jesus.

However, then I realized the incredible opportunity right at my fingertips and the Jesus Daily Page was born. To say its popularity has shocked me is an understatement! The numbers continue to astound and amaze me. As I write this, Jesus Daily is the number one most active page on Facebook with 27 million fans and in 20 different countries! When you think about the dozens of sites devoted to celebrities, pop singers, world leaders, and other belief systems, it's really extraordinary. Over one billion likes, comments, and shares were posted on the Jesus Daily Wall last year. On average, Jesus Daily now reaches almost 200 million unique people each month, sometimes reaching over 300 million.

The web and social media have now created the largest "Roman Road" in history and empowered each of us to boldly share the love, forgiveness, and salvation of Jesus with a few simple clicks and keystrokes daily! As the early Christians used the Romans' roads to carry the gospel to the unsaved in the farthest parts of the world, each of us can now read about God in our daily devotionals as well as *do* more. Every single day after your devotion, you can share the gospel with a long-distance friend by email, type in a prayer for cancer patients, sign a petition to save abused pets, comfort an anxious new Christian overseas who could be killed for her faith, and share with others the peace of God that passes all human understanding.

I created the *Jesus Daily® 365 Interactive Devotional* to make it quick and easy to stop just reflecting upon your love and relationship with Jesus and to start bearing real-life fruit on a daily basis. Every devotional includes a daily **CONNECT** short web mission that takes only seconds of your time, enabling you to obey Jesus when he said to "love your neighbor." I promise that if you love Jesus enough to complete all 365 interactive devotions and each daily web mission, you will be closer to God

—— DAILY INTERACTION ▾ ——

 CONNECT: Post a picture on JesusDaily.com that depicts how God's grace makes you feel.

than ever before. Helping others enjoy the saving grace and comforts of our Lord and Savior Jesus Christ is the best way to grow spiritually.

I challenge you not only to start reading and reflecting about Jesus, but also **CONNECT** with others by sharing the love and comfort of God. While many fine devotional books help you think and reflect on Jesus, this book empowers and motivates you to share and defend our Savior boldly and lovingly. You will be blessed in more ways than you can imagine, even in the midst of life's inevitable storms.

Finally, I urge you to create other disciples to multiply our global impact. Jesus was the Master of the viral message! This book allows you to easily emulate the actions of Christ as part of the largest connected Body of Christ at www.Facebook.com/JesusDaily—with just a few simple clicks and keystrokes every day. So come out of your quiet Christian prayer closet and let's "roar" like the Lion of Judah who has saved our sinful souls!

Daily blessings,
Dr. Aaron Tabor, M.D.

JANUARY

And my God will meet all your needs according to his glorious riches in Christ Jesus.

Philippians 4:19

January 1

> *Therefore, if anyone is in Christ, he is a new creation;*
> *the old has gone, the new is here!*
> 2 CORINTHIANS 5:17

——— DEVOTION ▼ ———

Good News

A blank page, a clear space, a fresh start.

With a new year, we often feel pressure to make resolutions and finally become the best version of ourselves that we can muster. While it's a good time to make changes as the calendar turns a new page, it's also good to know that there's really only one thing that can transform us. The grace of God is freely given to us regardless of how many calories we count or how many workouts we complete. We don't have to watch less television and eat more vegetables. We only have to ask our Father to forgive us and accept the grace that he so freely gives.

And the good news is that this fresh start is available every day, not just New Year's Day. God's forgiveness changes us from the inside out. What better way to begin again than to remember who we are in Christ!

——— DAILY INTERACTION ▼ ———

 CONNECT: Post a picture on JesusDaily.com that depicts how God's grace makes you feel.

"For I know the plans I have for you," declares the LORD,
"plans to prosper you and not to harm you,
plans to give you hope and a future."

JEREMIAH 29:11

▼ **DEVOTION**

He Is in Control

As we fill in our appointments and line up our schedules, we must remember that God ultimately controls our calendar. Each day we think we know what's ahead—and often our routine holds to the same pattern. But when it doesn't, we may feel disappointed, worried, or afraid of how quickly our lives can change in the course of a day. Our friend betrays us, the test results scare us, or our boss undermines our performance. So much can change in a matter of seconds.

But in his Word, God tells us that he's the same yesterday, today, and tomorrow. Not only does he remain the only constant in an ever-changing world, but he also has a plan for our lives. We may not always be able to see what he's up to, but we can rest in the security of knowing our future rests in our Father's hands.

DAILY INTERACTION ▼

 CONNECT: Arrange a time to chat or video conference with a long-distance friend and tell them one thing you really miss about them.

 ## January 3

DEVOTION ▼

He Is with Us

Often at the beginning of a new year, you're faced with lots of decisions. Whether it's scheduling meetings, trips, and events, or choosing how you'll spend your time and money, you cast a vision for how you'd like the next twelve months to go. You can plan all you want, but if the Lord isn't the compass at the heart of your choices, you're bound to get lost.

When we turn to God and ask for his guidance, he delights in leading us to fulfill our purpose. We may still face obstacles and challenges, but we can persevere knowing that he is leading the way before us. Even when suffering painful circumstances, we can experience joy, because we know that God is with us, directing our paths and protecting our heart.

DAILY INTERACTION ▼

 CONNECT: Visit JesusDaily.com, register to receive email updates and encouragement, and explore ways to connect with other believers.

*Look to the LORD and his strength; seek his face always.
Remember the wonders he has done, his miracles,
and the judgments he pronounced.*

1 CHRONICLES 16:11–12

▼ DEVOTION

He Is Ahead of Us

As you begin a new year, it's often a great time to reflect on the past year and where you are now. You can trace your path over the prior twelve months and catch glimpses of God's presence in your experiences. Whether it's the memory of a stunning sunset at the beach or the connection you felt with a loved one, God reveals himself in so many beautiful and unexpected ways.

He's also there for us during the hard times, the moments last year when we felt disappointed, hurt, and afraid. Sometimes these experiences provide more strength for us than the pleasant ones. When we look back and see how God provided for us, strengthened us, and protected us, we're reminded that he will do the same for us this year. We may feel apprehensive about what the next months hold, but God is already ahead of us, clearing a path for us.

DAILY INTERACTION ▼

CONNECT: Share something from your gratitude list with a friend online. Ask them to share one of their own gratitudes with you.

January 5

The LORD is my strength and my shield; my heart trusts in him, and I am helped. My heart leaps for joy and I will give thanks to him in song.
PSALM 28:7

He Is Strong

How many resolutions did you make for this new year? One that seems on most people's list is to exercise more. As we embrace a fresh start, we often commit to working out and being more deliberate about taking care of our bodies.

This is a wonderful goal—after all, your body is indeed the temple of the Lord, the sacred place where his Spirit dwells. When you respect and revere your body as a gift from God, you're saying thank you. If you're able to read these words, your eyes are working. If you're able to log on to the Jesus Daily page, your fingers must be able to type. If you enjoyed a good night's sleep or the taste of your breakfast, thank the Lord.

Regardless of the condition of your body, the closer you grow in your relationship with God, the stronger you become—often on the outside, but always on the inside.

 CONNECT: Go for a twenty-minute walk with a coworker, neighbor, or family member. Share with this person one thing you know would make your body stronger.

Now to him who is able to do immeasurably more than all we ask or imagine, according to his power that is at work within us, to him be glory in the church and in Christ Jesus...

EPHESIANS 3:20–21

▼ DEVOTION

He Is Able

You serve a God who is able to do so much more than you can even imagine. Often we may feel afraid to ask God for what we need, let alone what we think we want. But if you approach him with the highest expectations—hoping beyond what we can even imagine—you might realize how often he fulfills your requests.

Sometimes your faith may feel limited simply because you're not praying expectantly and paying attention. Jesus tells us that we don't have because we don't ask. We shouldn't feel self-conscious, guilty, or greedy when we ask our Father for what we need. He delights in giving us good gifts, surpassing far beyond anything we can imagine for ourselves. But we have to allow him the opportunity by turning our hearts toward him. When we practice this habit, we discover that his mercies are truly fresh every morning.

DAILY INTERACTION ▼

CONNECT: Look for an opportunity to meet the need of someone else by scanning message boards, blogs, and websites that list opportunities to serve God's kingdom.

Surely he will never be shaken; a righteous man will be remembered forever. He will have no fear of bad news; his heart is steadfast, trusting in the LORD.
PSALM 112:6–7

DEVOTION ▼

Run to Him

Now that you've lived an entire week in this new year, you may find yourself slipping into old patterns. Your goals to change were well-intentioned, and you'll keep trying when you think of it. But there's just so much that has to get done and so many hours in the day. It seems so hard to stay connected to God when everything and everyone around you is constantly pushing and pulling you.

God is training you to be steady on your feet. So many things interrupt you, distract you, and interrupt your awareness of his presence in your life. With so many voices clamoring for our attention, with smart phones and social media always at our fingertips, you may lose your focus and lose sight of your true priority.

Don't lose hope. When you find yourself distracted, just ask God to anchor your heart to him. When troubles come your way, run to him and ask for guidance and protection. Stay the course no matter what happens.

DAILY INTERACTION ▼

CONNECT: Encourage a friend who is also trying to make some changes this new year and who might be feeling discouraged about now.

The LORD is good, a refuge in times of trouble.
He cares for those who trust in him.

NAHUM 1:7

▼ DEVOTION

He Can Handle It

When your heart is troubled, it can be hard to sort out all that you're feeling. And it can be harder still to know what to do with those emotions. You don't want to unleash them on those around you, the people you care about. But you know you can't keep them bottled up inside. And God doesn't want you to bury them—that's how bitterness, jealousy, and envy sprout into your life.

Whatever it is, God wants you to share it with him. Lay down your burden before him, knowing that he can always handle what you can't. If you're willing to face your feelings and examine the people and events to which they're connected, it's easier to be honest before God.

On the other hand, when you stuff them, ignore them, or deny them, you're setting yourself up for much greater problems. So turn your cares over to God today. Feel today's weight lifted from your shoulders.

DAILY INTERACTION ▼

 CONNECT: Visit JesusDaily.com and post a prayer request. If possible, connect with a new regular prayer partner.

> *Then Peter got down out of the boat, walked on the water and came toward Jesus. But when he saw the wind, he was afraid and, beginning to sink, cried out, "Lord, save me!"*
> MATTHEW 14:29–30

— DEVOTION ▼ —

Walk on Water

When Peter and the disciples were out on the Sea of Galilee, they didn't anticipate the storm that blew in around them. And they certainly didn't expect to see someone walking toward them across the waves! Although Jesus identified himself, Peter wanted proof.

"If you're really the Master," Peter yelled, "tell me to come meet you!" So, of course, Jesus did just that. And without thinking about it, Peter got out of the little boat and put one foot in front of the other. He took a step and then another—until suddenly his faith gave way to logic, reason, and fear. How in the world could he be *walking on water*?

Christ makes it clear to Peter and to us that faith sustains us, taking us far beyond what we believe possible. Even when we fall and find ourselves foundering and sputtering in deep waters, Jesus rescues us and gets us back on our feet.

— DAILY INTERACTION ▼ —

 CONNECT: Video conference with someone who displays the kind of faith you admire the most, a Christian willing to get out of the boat and obey the Master's voice.

> *Godliness with contentment is great gain.*
> 1 TIMOTHY 6:6

▼ DEVOTION

Finding Contentment

When was the last time you let out a sigh of contentment? Paul tells us to give thanks in all circumstances and to discover a joy that goes far beyond how we feel about our circumstances. And he certainly knew a thing or two about hard circumstances. He was shipwrecked, arrested, beaten, placed in jail, and impoverished. You may have a hard time imagining how anyone in such bleak circumstances could ever be content.

But you can. When we tether our hope to Christ, we don't have to rely on our circumstances and moods for satisfaction. We can relax, knowing that our lives have meaning when we're living out the purpose for which we were created.

DAILY INTERACTION ▼

 CONNECT: Post a prayer request on JesusDaily.com and also commit to praying for someone else's need that you see there.

> *Now it is God who makes both us*
> *and you stand firm in Christ.*
> 2 CORINTHIANS 1:21

His Grace Transforms

More than ever, we feel pressured to have it together in all areas of our lives. Sometimes it's tempting to compare ourselves to friends and others we see on Facebook and other social media sites. We want to change our lives and be just as happy and successful as they seem.

But we don't have to change ourselves to earn God's love. He loves us, and our experience of his grace transforms us from the inside out. You may never lose those extra pounds or keep all your resolutions. And the good news is that you don't have to!

You will naturally become more like Christ when you draw closer to him, enjoy getting to know him better, and serve him out of gratitude, not obligation. Sometimes the best way to grow in our faith is to stop trying so hard to be a better person.

 CONNECT: Post a photo or illustration of a caterpillar becoming a butterfly and use it as your personal page status.

*Carry each other's burdens, and in this way
you will fulfill the law of Christ.*

GALATIANS 6:2

▼ DEVOTION

Remain Connected

Who knows your secrets? Who do you trust when you're in real trouble? Who helps you when you can't help yourself? Friends, family, and confidants are wonderful blessings—and God uses them in our lives in so many wonderful ways. Sometimes we get so busy that we end up isolating ourselves without realizing it. We remain connected to others by texting or sending an email, dashing off a twitter or posting a selfie on Instagram. But rarely do those connections satisfy our souls.

God created us to be in relationship with other people. Ask him to guide you to the relationships he wants to deepen in your life. Look for others who share your faith and commitment to God. And then see how you can bless and encourage one another in the faith. God doesn't want you to be alone.

DAILY INTERACTION ▼

 CONNECT: Request prayer for an area of struggle from three close Christian friends or members of your faith community.

January 13

> *For you created my inmost being; you knit me together in my mother's womb. I praise you because I am fearfully and wonderfully made.*
>
> PSALM 139:13–14

Be Who You Are

It can be so tempting to want to be someone other than who we are. We're conditioned to compare ourselves, and most of the time, we tend to come up short. We know people who are smarter, richer, more successful—even more mature in their faith—than we will ever be. We live in a virtual world in which we can continually find someone online who appears to be living the good life.

And it's not that we shouldn't pursue excellence and success; it's simply that imitating someone else's journey can never replace blazing our own trail. God knew who he wanted us to be long before we were even born. He invested exactly what we needed for our life, nothing more and nothing less. We can trust him in designing us to be original.

You're one of a kind, a special Designer original!

 CONNECT: Look for images of your favorite things and form an e-collage of them. Share your flash art online with someone whom you hope to get to know better.

> *And my God will meet all your needs according*
> *to his glorious riches in Christ Jesus.*
>
> PHILIPPIANS 4:19

▼ DEVOTION

He Will Provide

You pursue so many tasks and measure yourself in so many ways throughout the day. At work, you hope you do a good job that meets the approval of your boss. At home, you try to keep up with chores and the needs of your family so you can feel like an anchor for them. At church and in the neighborhood, you're trying to help others and serve them in the name of the Lord. But in the midst of all these momentary evaluations and personal judgments, you may feel as though you don't have enough—enough time, enough energy, enough compassion, enough of anything.

Don't forget that God has promised to meet all our needs according to his glorious riches in Christ. Sometimes in pursuit of tackling so many goals, chores, and responsibilities, we forget our primary needs. But God doesn't—he ensures we have everything we need.

DAILY INTERACTION ▼

 CONNECT: Surprise someone with unsolicited praise. It could be a coworker for a job well done or a family member who's struggling. Tell them you appreciate them.

January 15

For God did not give us a spirit of timidity,
but a spirit of power, of love and of self-discipline.
2 Timothy 1:7

DEVOTION ▼

Rely upon Him

We expend so much effort trying to have our lives run smoothly. We plan and schedule how we want our time to be spent, we buy gadgets to create shortcuts for all we want to accomplish, and we constantly revise this plateau of perfection where we want to live. As a result, we make each day conditional on how well it conforms to these images of success that dwell in our expectations.

But God makes it clear that our lives will never be without problems. Jesus told us that the closer we grow to him, the more we'll be at odds with the world. We don't have to live up to anyone else's standards—including our own—as we go through each day. We only have to stay in constant communication with God, allowing him to point out what needs to be done and letting go of our own unrealistic expectations.

You can rely on God for whatever you're facing today.

DAILY INTERACTION ▼

 CONNECT: Go to JesusDaily.com and post your favorite Bible verse of encouragement.

> *The name of the LORD is a strong tower;*
> *the righteous run to it and are safe.*
>
> PROVERBS 18:10

▼ DEVOTION

Our Firm Foundation

More than ever, your world changes not just daily but hourly. Relationships come and go, and new opportunities flash before you while other doors close. Information assaults you from the multitude of media sources constantly competing to attract attention. Disasters strike and tragedies unfold, along with an occasional unexpected surprise. With so much change, it's hard to feel as though you're on solid ground. The world can feel like a strange and unfamiliar place from one day to the next.

This is why you can't survive without the firmest foundation for your life. God remains the same regardless of what the stock market does or how many companies downsize. You can rest in the knowledge that no matter how chaotic and unstable the rest of your life may feel, your relationship with your Father is rock solid.

DAILY INTERACTION ▼

 CONNECT: Explore JesusDaily.com for examples of the ways others are placing their trust in God during difficult times.

> *A cheerful heart is good medicine,*
> *but a crushed spirit dries up the bones.*
>
> PROVERBS 17:22

— DEVOTION ▾

Laugh Regularly

When was the last time you laughed until tears streamed down your face? Maybe it was watching a funny movie with family, sharing a joke with coworkers, or cracking up over one of your own mistakes. Regardless of what led you to laugh, we see in God's Word that laughter is good medicine for our souls. When we can lighten our load by seeing a different perspective or celebrate the silliness in an unexpected situation, we're often reminded of our own limitations and God's power and sovereignty.

Sometimes we become so burdened by the weight of all we carry. Pressured by the demands of our many responsibilities, we forget to laugh. Our heart becomes hardened and our joy dries up. But laughing regularly and frequently restores a wellspring of joy and gratitude in our lives. We pause and realize that we don't have to be responsible for every detail today. God is in control.

— DAILY INTERACTION ▾

CONNECT: Post a humorous story or favorite joke on the Jesus Daily wall today, taking time to read what others have shared and laugh with them.

We wait in hope for the LORD;
he is our help and our shield.

PSALM 33:20

▼ DEVOTION

Trust Him

It's not easy to ask for help, whether we're asking for directions, assistance with completing a task, or resources that we need. Maybe it's our human pride or desire to be independent and self-sufficient. It probably has something to do with being vulnerable to others and acknowledging that we need them. And, finally, we probably don't like asking for help because we don't want to be disappointed, because sometimes we ask only to be denied.

We may be disappointed by God's response to our requests, too. But he will never turn us down without providing what we need more in its place. This is where we have to trust him and depend on him in ways that go beyond our comfort zones. This is the essence of faith: trusting the Lord to provide all that we need, even if he chooses to do so in ways different than we requested.

DAILY INTERACTION ▼

 CONNECT: Offer your assistance to others on a community or church bulletin board. Or share a need that you have requiring another's assistance.

The testing of your faith develops perseverance.
JAMES 1:3

Finish the Race

Some days it's not easy to keep going. Whether it feels like a bad day where nothing goes right, or just another boring repeat of the same routine, we struggle to stay the course. We begin to feel insecure and inadequate, unsure if we can maintain the pace we've been going. We don't have all the answers or feel in control. We get tired and don't know how we'll make it through the day.

These are the times when we must cry out to God, acknowledging our pain and weakness and asking for his power and strength to carry us. We know we can't do it on our own and can't imagine how we can finish the race. And that's okay—it's not up to us. We simply have to keep living day by day, stepping out in faith moment by moment.

CONNECT: Encourage someone online to keep going beyond their own limits. Share a favorite verse or time from your own life.

> *Forgive as the Lord forgave you.*
> COLOSSIANS 3:13

▼ DEVOTION

Live as Forgiven

Who offended you this week? Maybe a friend forgot to call or a family member said something hurtful. You might have been slighted by a coworker or cut off by an aggressive driver on the highway. These nicks and cuts add up over time, taking a toll on our own ability to forgive others and to ask their forgiveness for the ways we hurt them.

You probably have some more serious injuries you're carrying around as well. Lifelong wounds of betrayal, abuse, loss, and addiction do not heal overnight. They require you to seek the Lord's healing as you work through the process of recovery and restoration. While the consequences may continue to clutter your life, you can advance your healing dramatically by forgiving the people who have hurt you.

Forgiveness restores those lines that have been crossed and enables us to appreciate how God forgives us.

DAILY INTERACTION ▼

 CONNECT: Forgive someone who has posted a message or image that offends you. Offer them a message of hope instead of hurt.

> *"Our Father in heaven, hallowed be your name,*
> *your kingdom come, your will be done on earth*
> *as it is in heaven."*
> MATTHEW 6:9–10

— DEVOTION ▾ —

Be a Bridge

When we consider the way Jesus taught us to pray, so many lessons emerge. One of the most basic is that we stick with it, diving below the surface of life each day to reconnect with our Father at a base level. The repetition is important not because God's counting how many times we talk to him, but because talking to him—and listening—strengthen and deepen our relationship.

"Our Father in heaven" immediately reminds us of our relationship with him. We, his children, are here on earth in mortal bodies. Our Creator and Abba Father maintains his kingdom from the realm of heaven. We have the opportunity to bridge heaven and earth as we follow Christ and share God's goodness with those around us. We cannot make earth as perfect as heaven, but God can—by dwelling in us and shining through to everyone around us.

— **DAILY** INTERACTION ▾ —

 CONNECT: Send an e-card to someone who needs the Lord.

> *Be at rest once more, O my soul,*
> *for the LORD has been good to you.*
>
> PSALM 116:7

▼ DEVOTION

Schedule Rest

Texts, emails, video calls, meetings, phone conferences, driving here and there. In our nano-paced mega-world, it's hard to find real downtime when you're unplugged from your cares and responsibilities both literally and mentally. But it's essential, not just for your mind and body but also for your soul. We need time away from all the usual demands and distractions so we can simply still ourselves before the Lord and quiet the chatter in our minds.

One of the best ways to ensure we get the rest we need is to schedule it. Just like any other appointment, we often need to pencil in time to do nothing! When we carve out the time and space to rest, God refreshes us and renews our energy for the tasks to be done later.

DAILY INTERACTION ▼

 CONNECT: Stay offline today! Or choose a day this week when you will unplug and use the time to experience sacred rest.

> *If any of you lacks wisdom, he should ask God,*
> *who gives generously to all without finding fault,*
> *and it will be given to him.*
>
> JAMES 1:5

— DEVOTION ▾ —

Ask for Wisdom

Wisdom is different from knowledge, because wisdom has been seasoned by experience. It accrues based on the trials and temptations you've endured and overcome, not from how many books you've read or the number of degrees you've earned. When we lack wisdom, we usually lack the ability to suffer through hard times while depending on God.

We're told to ask God for wisdom if we don't have it. But keep in mind that we may be asking him to allow us to endure a trial or suffer a hardship. Wisdom can certainly be gleaned in other ways, including as a supernatural gift bestowed immediately upon us by the Lord. But usually wisdom accumulates over time, layer upon layer, as we trust God to provide for our needs and to see us through challenges.

— DAILY INTERACTION ▾ —

 CONNECT: Make a list of five things God has taught you in the past week and share one of the items on your list as a comment on the Jesus Daily page.

> *Who is wise and understanding among you?*
> *Let him show it by his good life, by deeds done*
> *in the humility that comes from wisdom.*
>
> JAMES 3:13

▼ DEVOTION

Share Your Struggles

So often when we follow Jesus daily, we forget that we don't have to appear perfect to those around us. Obviously, we want to set a good example and share God's love with others in ways that will draw them to want him. But just as wisdom is gained by suffering some of life's hard knocks, living a "good life" includes showing some of our struggles, needs, and mistakes.

When other people see us going through trials without giving up, when they witness us turning to God to see us through, they realize that we're not trying to do it alone. Those around us need to see our limitations from time to time so that they can appreciate the miraculous ways that God intervenes in our lives.

DAILY INTERACTION ▼

 CONNECT: Post a picture on Instagram or Pinterest that illustrates humility.

> [Jesus said,] "I am the vine; you are the branches.
> If a man remains in me and I in him, he will
> bear much fruit; apart from me you can do nothing."
>
> JOHN 15:5

DEVOTION ▼

Do Some Pruning

We tend to think of pruning as painful, and while it may be at times, it's also very refreshing to your soul. There's something very liberating about making space for more of God in your life. With the priorities of your faith as your guide, you get back to basics, remembering how you want to spend your time and resources rather than allowing them to be consumed by everyone else's demands.

Gardeners know that trees require pruning if they're to remain healthy and grow straight. We're the same way. We need to get rid of the possessions, relationships, and responsibilities that aren't working, especially the ones that pull us away from God. As we "clean house" within our lives, we may discover new rooms where God is waiting to meet us.

DAILY INTERACTION ▼

CONNECT: Sort through your personal emails, deleting "spiritual spam," messages that are no longer relevant to who you are in Christ.

> *Now faith is being sure of what we hope for
> and certain of what we do not see.*
>
> HEBREWS 11:1

▼ DEVOTION

God's Profile Never Changes

Since we have millions of sources online, sometimes it's hard to know who to believe. Years ago, we might have believed most things we saw on the "information superhighway." But with such a growing, global online community, it's clear that not everyone can be trusted. From dating sites to start-up business opportunities, many individuals hide behind their virtual identity and deceive others about who they are and what they have to offer. We literally can't accept everyone online at face value because we cannot see them. They might have selfies, profiles, likes and dislikes, but unfortunately, they may not accurately reveal who the online user really is as a person.

Our faith in God also requires us to make decisions based on limited information. Often we have to risk stepping out in faith, uncertain of the result because of our limited vision. Regardless of the outcome, we can trust that God's profile never changes.

DAILY INTERACTION ▼

 CONNECT: Update your profile or status by sharing the latest truth you've learned about God.

> *Stand firm. Let nothing move you. Always give yourselves fully to the work of the Lord, because you know that your labor in the Lord is not in vain.*
>
> 1 Corinthians 15:58

— DEVOTION ▼ —

Stand Firm

Some days it feels as though nothing goes right. You oversleep, your car breaks down, and you miss the big meeting at work. Even when your day goes smoothly, it can still seem monotonous and tiring. You get caught up in all kinds of busyness, but then at the end of the day, you wonder what you've actually accomplished.

People tend to assess their day based on what they produce, complete, resolve, and check off their lists. However, when we focus on God, we can stand firm when change comes our way and blocks our paths. We can know that everything we do contributes to our Father's master plan, his holy purpose for our lives. Even when we feel as though we didn't accomplish anything on our to-do lists, we are part of something bigger and more meaningful than we can see.

— DAILY INTERACTION ▼ —

 CONNECT: Post a note or verse of encouragement to someone on the Jesus Daily page who needs to know that what they do matters.

> *The LORD gives strength to his people.*
> PSALM 29:11

▼ DEVOTION

Spiritual Conditioning

When you exercise your body, you push yourself beyond what is comfortable so that your muscles become stronger. Stretching, flexing, and taxing your body's muscles produce pain, but their recovery results in harder, leaner tissue that has more density and power. It's never easy, but knowing the outcome—a stronger, healthier body—motivates us to exercise.

We rarely approach spiritual conditioning the same way, but we might be surprised that the training principle is similar. No one deliberately rushes into a crisis with a calm, peaceful focus unless they have been through hard times before and experienced the power of the Lord. Reflecting on the past and the ways you've grown can help you realize that you're more than able to conquer anything you face today.

We know that God empowers us beyond the limitations of our own abilities. He knows what we can bear and, like a good coach, only pushes us to make us stronger.

DAILY INTERACTION ▼

CONNECT: Download a podcast from a favorite Christian pastor or teacher to listen to during your lunch or coffee time today.

> *This is what the LORD says, "…you are precious and honored in my sight, and because I love you…"*
> ISAIAH 43:1, 4

Unconditional Love

Love notes keep the romance alive when you're dating as well as after you're married. Similarly, an email from a parent or sibling, a text from a dear friend, or a card from your children can make your whole day seem extra special. Knowing that your beloved took the time to write down their feelings makes you feel uniquely loved and reminds you how much they care about you.

God's Word provides the same kind of encouragement to us as his beloved children. Throughout its pages, he reveals his passionate pursuit of his sons and daughters, even when we turn away from him or struggle to under-stand our life's events. The Lord comforts us, embraces us, and encourages us as the loving Father he is. When we view the Bible as being filled with love notes from our Dad, we can't wait to explore its pages.

 CONNECT: Share one of your favorite verses about God's love with someone you secretly admire.

Continue to work out your salvation with fear and trembling, for it is God who works in you to will and to act in order to fulfill his good purpose.

PHILIPPIANS 2:12–13

▼ DEVOTION

A Work in Progress

Even after you encounter the love of God and give your heart to Christ, accepting the gift of salvation through his death on the cross, you will continue to discover new dimensions of what it means to be saved. When you accepted Jesus into your life, the Holy Spirit came to dwell inside you, and his presence guides and directs you, comforts and encourages you.

But we still have choices to make and must learn to allow our love for God to be at the center of our decisions. Our obedience to God is for our own good, not because we have to work our way to heaven or because he's going to leave us if our work isn't good enough. Working out our salvation with fear and trembling means that we remain humble, teachable, and open to what God is doing in our lives. Salvation is a process, a work in progress, as we become transformed into the image of Jesus.

DAILY INTERACTION ▼

CONNECT: Choose an artist's portrayal of the crucifixion from the many websites with sacred art and post it on your Facebook, Pinterest, or Snapchat main page.

We are God's workmanship, created in Christ Jesus to do good works, which God prepared in advance for us to do.
EPHESIANS 2:10

—————— DEVOTION ▼ ——————

The Master's Handiwork

One of the things we love about the artwork of children is the open, sincere way it expresses their emotions. Maybe we enjoy their artwork so much because it's not perfect in the way it's done, but it still expresses enormous beauty.

God's work in our lives reflects the same kind of tension that we see in the artwork of children. We're certainly not perfect people yet, but because of what God is doing in us, we reveal our Creator's holiness and love for his creation and the other people around us. We don't have to have our lives together or every area under control to know that we are divine masterpieces, works in progress that reveal the Master's gentle, beautiful handiwork.

Today, spend less time worrying about living up to someone else's—or even your own—impossible standard of perfection. Instead, simply enjoy being your unique, authentic self—the one-of-a-kind living art being shaped by the Potter to be used as his vessel.

—————— DAILY INTERACTION ▼ ——————

CONNECT: Make a collage online—drawing from pictures, digital techniques, and the artwork of others—that reflects what God is doing in your life. Share it with friends online.

Worry
Job
Death
Broken Heart
Loneliness
Divorce
Depressed
JESUS
IS
THE
ANSWER
Anxiety
Money
Addiction
Bullying
Cancer

FEBRUARY

Surely goodness and love will follow me all the days of my life, and I will dwell in the house of the LORD forever.

Psalm 23:6

You will keep in perfect peace him whose mind is steadfast, because he trusts in you.
Isaiah 26:3

—————————————————— DEVOTION ▼ ——————

Perfect Peace

What does "perfect peace" look like to you? Many people believe the false idea that peace is the absence of trouble, conflict, or anxiety in their lives. They think that in order to feel content, calm, and relaxed, everything must go according to schedule, smoothly following their own plans and expectations.

Life doesn't work this way, though, and neither does peace. Just as your body can be healthy even when you're hungry, hot, cold, or tired, you can experience peace in your life regardless of life's circumstances. When you focus on loving the Lord and serving others out of this love, you can know peace no matter what else happens today.

This kind of calm center remains unruffled by the winds of change and storms of unexpected trouble. This kind of peace provides a permanent shelter against anything you face today.

—————————————————— **DAILY** INTERACTION ▼ ——————

 CONNECT: Surf photographers' websites and other online sources and find a beautiful landscape that illustrates your vision of God's perfect peace.

> *"The joy of the LORD is your strength."*
> NEHEMIAH 8:10

▼ DEVOTION

Real Joy

Have you ever watched a hard rain fall, noticing the way it fills up puddles, creeks, streams, and rivers? Sometimes, of course, rains cause flooding that wreaks havoc as it destroys buildings and claims lives. But most rains bring new life to everything. Plants grow, water sources are replenished, and living creatures have plenty to drink.

When you're going through a tough day or a hard season, it can feel like a drought. Your joy seems to have dried up with no hope for showers in sight. Your heart feels parched and your spirit is so thirsty for the life-giving power of real joy. You go through the motions of your day, but inside the well is dry.

God's love provides the constant light we need to grow, and our joy in him produces the refreshment that replenishes and sustains us. Joy is the rain for the soil of our spirit. Watered by his love, we grow stronger.

DAILY INTERACTION ▼

 CONNECT: Video conference or cam with someone whose presence brings you joy.

> *[Jesus said,] "Give, and it will be given to you."*
> LUKE 6:38

Give of Yourself

God gave us the gift of his Son, the ultimate present for our salvation. His gift enables us to enjoy the closest of relationships with him, our Father. Because he loves us so much, he regularly blesses us with gifts of friendship, beauty, and provision. There are no strings attached; we simply have to accept them in order to enjoy them.

God provides our model for giving. With Christ, we see this model in the flesh. Jesus was never too busy to listen to a child, a leper, a tax collector, a prostitute, or even a Pharisee, the hypocritical religious leaders of his day. He gave of himself to everyone he encountered, healing them, feeding them, transforming them by the power of his truth.

Today, give of yourself to those around you the same way Jesus did—with selflessness, compassion, and acceptance.

 CONNECT: Go to JesusDaily.com and give encouragement to three people by posting hopeful comments in response to their prayer requests.

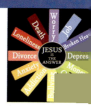

> *Weeping may remain for a night,*
> *but rejoicing comes with the morning.*
>
> Psalm 30:5

▼ DEVOTION

Joy Restored

All of us have faced disappointment and failure. Usually during these times we feel very alone, sometimes even abandoned by the ones who are closest to us. God feels distant. All we want is for someone to take us by the hand and tell us, "Things will not always be this way. You are going to be okay. You are going to feel happy again." We want someone to offer us hope for something beyond what we can see and feel at this moment.

God offers us this kind of comfort directly through his Word. In Psalm 30, David praises God for lifting him up and saving his soul, restoring him and bestowing favor. He said these things to God after experiencing his own dark night of the soul, when he felt that he was as low as he could go. God came to him and restored his joy.

He will do the same for you.

DAILY INTERACTION ▼

 CONNECT: Email words of encouragement to someone whom you know is hurting. Let them know they are not alone.

Set a guard over my mouth, O LORD;
keep watch over the door of my lips.

PSALM 141:3

--- DEVOTION ▼ ---

Check Your Words

Often we think back over recent conversations and wince. "I can't believe I said that!" "I think I hurt her feelings." "I was just trying to be funny and it backfired." We all have many cringe-worthy moments that we wish we could relive. We look behind our words and we can see that our comment had everything to do with our own insecurity, selfishness, anger, and pain.

Did you know that God could help you control what you say? If you ask him to help you, you will be surprised by its effect on your speech. There will be a moment before you speak when you pause to think. You will not be able to find the right words without thinking first. You may just become unusually quiet. Soon, your inner conversation of praise and peace will emerge in what you say.

God wants your words to bless and build up those around you.

--- DAILY INTERACTION ▼ ---

 CONNECT: Before you text with someone today, take a moment and think about your response. Be thoughtful and check your words.

> *"My grace is sufficient for you, for my power is made perfect in weakness." Therefore I will boast all the more gladly about my weaknesses, so that Christ's power may rest on me.*
>
> 2 Corinthians 12:9

▼ DEVOTION

In Your Weaknesses

Every day some of us wake up and wonder if we have what it takes to face the day. We may have a busy day ahead of us, or it might be a pretty empty day. The demands that we face may range from huge one-of-a-kind challenges to absolute boredom.

The apostle Paul felt this way some of the time. He asked God to take his weaknesses from him. We aren't told exactly what they were, but his answer from God told him what to do. "Be glad for your weaknesses! Brag about them! This is the way I will show myself through you!"

We may feel broken, but God's power shines through us and brightens the world around us. If we could do everything ourselves, we wouldn't need to rely on God. Today, give thanks for the way God meets you in your struggles.

DAILY INTERACTION ▼

 CONNECT: Text "My grace is sufficient for you" to yourself and a friend whom you know struggles with a weakness.

Don't you know that you yourselves are God's temple and that God's Spirit lives in you?

1 Corinthians 3:16

DEVOTION ▾

For His Glory

What are you putting in your temple today?

The apostle Paul tells us that our bodies are made for worship as a place where God lives, as vessels where the Holy Spirit dwells. The problems come up because we don't believe this about ourselves. God sees us as *holy*—a word we do not often use to describe ourselves. It matters what we allow to come inside our "temples."

When we participate in unhealthy eating, drinking, entertainment, and relationships, we are choosing to defile God's temple and tarnish our vessel. Having this perspective on our bodies, minds, and hearts may help make better choices. We can honor God in our bodies if we see ourselves as his temple.

Today, consider what you eat, what you watch, where you go. Do they honor and build up your temple for God's glory?

DAILY INTERACTION ▾

 CONNECT: Take some time to research healthier habits or better alternatives.

> *He makes me lie down in green pastures, he leads me*
> *beside quiet waters, he restores my soul.*
>
> PSALM 23:2–3

▼ DEVOTION

Unplug

Do you grab your cell phone or your computer the first thing every morning? Do you panic when you can't immediately lay your hands on your phone? We twenty-first-century citizens have become reliant on these devices to help us feel connected to the world. We are "wired" much of the time, and it contributes to our stress.

We may be connected with the world, but it is hard to find God in the midst of all that media. God has made us for deep connection with him. He made us to rest in his presence. But we feel guilty when we rest, when we do not seem to be busy at something.

When we slow down and spend time quietly with God, we are telling him that we are weak and that we need him. We cannot connect with him unless we are still and listening. It is an admission that we cannot live our lives apart from him.

Today, unplug and allow yourself to receive the peace of the Lord.

DAILY INTERACTION ▼

 CONNECT: Unplug from all electronic devices for at least one hour today.

February 9

> *She gave this name to the LORD who spoke to her:*
> *"You are the God who sees me," for she said,*
> *"I have now seen the One who sees me."*
>
> GENESIS 16:13

He Sees

You stand and look out your window, and you may see traffic or trees or other houses or people, and a thought runs through your mind. *No one knows what my life is like. No one knows what goes on inside me.* You feel alone. If you entertain the thought, self-pity elbows itself in—*and no one cares.* Even if you have close relationships with friends and family, sometimes in moments of quiet, of solitude, we can feel isolated in the world.

And the truth is, we are.

We were created by God and for God, in his image. That means that there are places inside of us that only he can reach. As good as life can be at times, there's nowhere as good as closeness to God, because he knows us. He knows *all* of us. He knows that sometimes you don't enjoy being with your children. He knows that the special people in your life don't always "get" you. He knows that some days you may not talk to anyone at all and you feel forgotten. He sees you.

And he loves you.

 CONNECT: Share one item from your prayer journal with someone who might be feeling lonely today.

> *For I am convinced that neither death nor life, neither angels*
> *nor demons...nor anything else in all creation, will be able to*
> *separate us from the love of God that is in Christ Jesus our Lord.*
>
> ROMANS 8:38–39

▾ DEVOTION

The Power of His Love

The biggest lie that we believe is that God can't love us the way we are. We have never been loved perfectly. Our families and friends have done the best they can, but they are limited by their own wounds and feelings of not being loved. Some of us, unfortunately, have been hurt deeply, and we have started to believe lies as a result. "I am unlovable." "I have to be good in order to be loved." "Love hurts." We carry these beliefs with us, and they form our abilities to give and receive love and acceptance.

How can we change this belief? We can't do it by ourselves.

Only God can show us how much he loves us. Through his Word, through the words and actions of others, and through his whispers to our heart, our Father wants his love to permeate us through and through. The enemy's lies melt away in the power of God's love.

DAILY INTERACTION ▾

 CONNECT: Encourage a friend by telling them that you love them. You may be God's message of love to them today.

For as in Adam all die, so in Christ all will be made alive.
1 CORINTHIANS 15:22

—————————— DEVOTION ▼ ——————————

Abundant Life

The new life we receive through Christ is not a makeover of our outward appearance and wardrobe. It's not a special feeling or physical sensation we experience while it's taking place. It's not winning the lottery and having all our problems go away.

The life we gain when we give our hearts to Jesus is eternal life—the promise of being with our Lord in heaven—but also an abundant life of purpose, joy, and contentment in our earthly existence. We have the two best reasons possible to rejoice over the enormous gifts God extends to us through salvation in his Son. Even though our mortal bodies will perish just as Adam's did, our spirits will not die but will complete our transformation.

Today, enjoy the gifts of the new life you've been given.

—————————— DAILY INTERACTION ▼ ——————————

 CONNECT: Post a message on the Jesus Daily page, praising God for your salvation and abundant life.

Surely goodness and love will follow me all the days of my life, and I will dwell in the house of the LORD forever.

PSALM 23:6

▼ **DEVOTION**

His Goodness and Love

Sometimes when we're on a road trip, we follow someone we know driving the car ahead of us. We keep each other's vehicles within sight and stop at the same time for gas and meals. Usually, we travel this way out of necessity, since everyone going might not fit in just one car. But we also follow each other because it's safer, ensuring if one car breaks down, the other could offer assistance.

When we look at the rearview mirror of our lives, we will notice someone who always follows us closely. God has pursued us and continues to travel with us, offering his mercy, guidance, and protection wherever we go. We never travel alone on life's journey, because our Father's goodness paves the way.

DAILY INTERACTION ▼

 CONNECT: Do a little surfing and choose someone who inspires your faith and follow them on social media.

 **February 13**

Praise be to the Lord, to God our Savior,
who daily bears our burdens.
PSALM 68:19

— DEVOTION ▼ —

Divine Relief

If you've ever carried a full backpack, armful of grocery bags, or heavy package to mail, you know the relief that comes when you release your burden. Your muscles relax, your arms tingle, and you can catch your breath. If you've ever been carrying a heavy load and someone came along to help lighten it, you know the kind of gratitude you feel for such assistance.

God provides us with the same kind of relief each day. From the laundry list of cares and concerns we continually seem to carry to the new items we'll add today, he can lift them all. We don't have to strain, strive, and struggle alone. In his power, sovereignty, and wisdom, he knows the leverage points that will help us lift our part of the burden. As Jesus also reminds us, it's light and easy to carry.

Today, rest in the knowledge that God bears your burdens.

— **DAILY** INTERACTION ▼ —

 CONNECT: Email a friend or loved one and offer to help them deal with a burden currently weighing them down.

> *"The LORD does not look at the things man looks at. Man looks at the outward appearance, but the LORD looks at the heart."*
>
> 1 SAMUEL 16:7

▼ DEVOTION

The Most Precious Valentine

Romance and hearts abound today, and you may or may not feel like participating in the traditional celebrations. Either way, it's okay, because the love you celebrate every day has a source that lasts longer than roses and tastes sweeter than any chocolates. God knows what you're feeling and going through today, and his love envelops you completely.

He loved you so much that he gave you the most precious valentine imaginable—the living-word love letter of his Son, Jesus. And Christ's love compelled him to make the supreme sacrifice and lay down his life. As he tells us, there is no greater gift a person can give. We have a God who demonstrated his love on the cross and continues to demonstrate it through his many blessings each day of our lives.

So today, amidst the candy and flowers, remember that the love you have knows no end and requires no gift other than your own heart. Your Father's love is unconditional!

DAILY INTERACTION ▼

 CONNECT: Extend the love of Christ to three people today online—use Valentine's Day as an excuse and be creative!

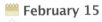

O LORD, be gracious to us; we long for you.
Be our strength every morning, our salvation
in time of distress.

ISAIAH 33:2

———— DEVOTION ▼ ————

Who We Know

Strength remains a commodity we desire whether it's physical, emotional, or spiritual. And in most cases, we know that the kind of strength we desire won't happen overnight. We lift weights and exercise, knowing that we won't be looking like a superhero for some time, if ever. We push through painful disappointments and grieve private losses, feeling our emotions but not allowing them to overpower us. And spiritually, we strengthen our faith by praying, spending time in God's Word, and serving others.

Our spiritual strength, however, isn't built on what we do but who we know. God is the source of our strength, and it's our relationship with him that increases our strength, not any spiritual disciplines by themselves. Many people can do "spiritual exercises" for the wrong reasons. If we're committed to loving God, they are natural ways to flex the muscles of our heart.

———— **DAILY** INTERACTION ▼ ————

 CONNECT: Friend someone online and link them to JesusDaily.com, emphasizing the features you enjoy most.

[Jesus said,] "Whoever serves me must follow me; and where I am, my servant also will be. My Father will honor the one who serves me."

JOHN 12:26

▼ DEVOTION

Serve Those in Need

Sometimes you feel as though no one understands you or can appreciate your faith. You want to talk about Jesus more—at home, at work, at school, in the neighborhood—but you don't want to be misunderstood as a religious fanatic or someone driven by a political axe to grind. You want to do more than share your perspective or exchange words with other people.

The solution is simple.

Allow others to see Jesus in you by what you do, not by anything you say. Christ's actions shouted his Father's love to those around him—feeding the hungry, healing the sick, helping outsiders. Today, go out of your way to serve those in need, to surprise those alongside you, and to honor those in a position of authority above you. Humble yourself the way Jesus humbled himself.

DAILY INTERACTION ▼

 CONNECT: Message someone who models a servant's heart and tell them how much you can see Jesus by what they do.

 **February 17**

*Peacemakers who sow in peace raise
a harvest of righteousness.*
James 3:18

DEVOTION ▼

Be His Peacemaker

While conflict is unavoidable in daily life, God still wants you to be his peacemaker. In fact, *because* conflicts are unavoidable, he needs you to bring his peace into the world around you. Whether it's a problem at work, an argument with your family, or different points of view with a friend, you must learn to access your Father's supernatural peace in order to access it and share with others.

Being a peacemaker does not mean rolling over, dodging a disagreement, or avoiding a problem. It won't be easy, but God wants us to present a larger perspective to the situation, a holy and eternal point of view. He wants us to be farmers plant-

ing seeds of unity, harmony, love, and reconciliation so that our harvest will produce relationships and results that honor him.

Peacemaking is not about anger management; it's about growing righteous fruit.

DAILY INTERACTION ▼

 CONNECT: Reconnect with someone from whom you've drifted because of differing opinions. Let them know you still care about connecting with them.

> *Let us hold unswervingly to the hope we profess,*
> *for he who promised is faithful.*
>
> HEBREWS 10:23

▼ DEVOTION

His Promises Are Unshakable

Promises seem to have lost their value as currency—probably because there's often nothing to back them up. Political candidates make promises, knowing that even if they win they won't be able to hold to their word. Companies make promises about their products and employees, but we still see product recalls and frequent layoffs. Couples promise undying love to each other, and yet our divorce rate remains more than fifty percent.

Living in a culture that expects promises to be broken, we become jaded and even cynical when someone gives us their word. They say they'll be on time, but end up late. They promise to deliver the terms of our agreement, but then make excuses for failing. They offer a warranty for products and services, but find hidden loopholes to justify their broken promise.

All the more reason we must realize that God's promises are bedrock—unmovable, unshakable, eternal. Our hope has a foundation in the only One who has never broken a promise. He is always faithful.

DAILY INTERACTION ▼

 CONNECT: Post one of your favorite promises from God's Word on the Jesus Daily page.

> *Do everything without complaining or arguing, so that*
> *you may become blameless and pure, children of God.*
> PHILIPPIANS 2:14–15

DEVOTION ▾

Be Honest as Children

Children often bicker or squabble over things, but they usually don't harbor a grudge. Whether disagreeing on the rules of a game, divvying up treats, or fighting over time on the tablet, kids usually express their emotions right in the moment.

Adults, on the other hand, learn to be polite, "nice," and socially acceptable. We become conditioned to withhold our unpleasant emotions and instead work out amicable, at least on the surface, solutions. However, many times we might be better off being as honest as children. When we're honest with our emotions, we don't allow anger, resentment, and conflict to fester into bitterness, jealousy, and envy.

Self-discipline is important. And no one enjoys a complainer or whiner. So if we want to represent God's love and compassion to those around us, maybe we have to strike a balance between honesty and empathy.

DAILY INTERACTION ▾

 CONNECT: Friend someone you know who holds different faith beliefs than you do.

> *Live a life of love, just as Christ loved us and gave himself up for us as a fragrant offering and sacrifice to God.*
>
> EPHESIANS 5:2

▼ **DEVOTION**

A Sweet Fragrance

The sense of smell encompasses one of our most powerful sensory experiences. Scientists tell us we usually have more memories associated with smells than any other sense. And if you've inhaled the scent of cookies baking, a freshly mown lawn, or gasoline lately, you know this is true.

No wonder then that most companies have been deliberate about including a pleasant scent as part of their products. From perfume, cologne, candles, air freshener, soap, shampoo, lotion, window cleaner—more and more scents surround us every day.

The makers of these products know that a nice smell can be powerful. Sweeter than the scent of any rose, more fragrant than jasmine, the essence of Christ's sacrifice reminds us of his unfathomable love. We have the privilege to carry this same sweet smell to those around us.

DAILY INTERACTION ▼

 CONNECT: Text or chat with someone and thank them for the pleasant aroma of their attitude.

It is required that those who have been given a trust must prove faithful.

1 CORINTHIANS 4:2

DEVOTION ▼

Living Proof

When a detective solves a crime, he looks for evidence. When a lawyer represents a defendant, they examine all the evidence gathered to make the case. When a judge or jury determines a verdict, they sort through all the evidence to see the pattern that emerges.

What evidence are you leaving behind that ensures others know you are a follower of Jesus? Are your words kind and considerate? Your actions selfless and diligent? Your attitude compassionate and authentic? If someone tried to "prove" you are a Christian, would there be enough evidence today?

Fortunately, whether they could or not, God's grace sustains us and reminds us that we have been forgiven. We don't have to prove anything to anyone. Christ has established all the proof we need to live as forgiven people.

DAILY INTERACTION ▼

 CONNECT: Encourage a friend online who recently demonstrated the love of Christ to you.

*Be very careful, then, how you live—
not as unwise but as wise.*

EPHESIANS 5:15

▼ **DEVOTION**

Follow His Wisdom

When cooking you follow a recipe, when traveling you follow the directions from your GPS or map, when assembling a new cabinet you follow the instructions. Reading through these sequential steps and acting on the information provided allows us to achieve the results we desire: a delicious cake, a pleasant journey to our destination, and a sturdy piece of furniture.

Too often, however, we forget or overlook the instructions that God has provided for us in his Word. There we find the most important directions for our life's journey. These aren't just rules and regulations or pleasant suggestions to make us feel better. These are principles of truth about ultimate reality—who we are, how we're made, our purpose in life, the character of God, the power of grace, and so much more.

If we want to please our Father, we will follow the wisdom that he has provided.

DAILY INTERACTION ▼

 CONNECT: Visit JesusDaily.com and post one thing you've recently learned in God's Word.

> *Jesus came to them and said, "…go and make disciples of all nations … teaching them to obey everything I have commanded you."*
>
> MATTHEW 28:18–20

DEVOTION ▼

Be His Hands and Feet

In the global community, it's easier than ever to share information, exchange emails, and correspond electronically with video calls. While these technological advances allow us to share the gospel in new ways, we must never overlook the power of our example. Certainly, God's Spirit works in amazing and miraculous ways, but we have more to share with others around the world.

God can reach people anywhere at any time, but it's clear from his Word that he wants us living and loving in community together.

People were transformed when they encountered Jesus during his lifetime; we have the opportunity now to be Christ's hands and feet, eyes and ears all over the world.

Today, consider what it means for you to share your faith with people in other cultures, other countries, and other continents.

DAILY INTERACTION ▼

CONNECT: Choose someone from another country on the Jesus Daily page and become their electronic pen pal.

We have not stopped praying for you and asking God to fill you with the knowledge of his will through all spiritual wisdom and understanding.

Colossians 1:9

▼ DEVOTION

Committed to Prayer

Praying with another person can be a very intimate experience. You're not just sharing words and information with them. You're revealing your beliefs, doubts, struggles, needs, dreams, and desires—well, maybe not all at once! But prayer has a way of bonding individuals and knitting their hearts together toward common goals for God's kingdom.

When we commit to pray for someone else's needs, we're sharing their burden and offering to intercede on their behalf before our Father. He already knows their needs, of course, but our participation through prayer is for our benefit as much as theirs. We are changed when we share at a prayer-level sightline.

Prayer provides us access to the most powerful Force in the world. But it also opens a connection of compassion between us.

— DAILY INTERACTION ▼

 CONNECT: Post a request asking others to pray for a specific need you have today.

"For my thoughts are not your thoughts, neither are your ways my ways," declares the LORD.

ISAIAH 55:8

———— DEVOTION ▼ ————

Speaking God's Language

Sometimes people speak the same language, but still can't communicate. It may be because of different beliefs, backgrounds, or agendas. They hear each other, but neither seems able to listen. If they can't persevere and find a way to communicate, they fail to connect in any meaningful way.

Sometimes our words, prayers, and actions must seem just as challenging to God. Not because he doesn't understand us—he does, of course—but because of our limitations. We only see what's visible and therefore tend to rely on it for a sense of reality. With this concrete basis of comparison, we can only imagine a limited number of options, possibilities, and directions to take.

God, on the other hand, sees what is visible to us and what is invisible. He can see all of time, history, and space in the time we blink an eye. We must rely on faith if we want to speak God's language, trusting that his thoughts truly are higher and best.

———— DAILY INTERACTION ▼ ————

CONNECT: Go online and find a favorite Bible verse that is in another language. Post this as a reminder of our limited ability to understand God.

> *Keep yourself pure.*
> 1 Timothy 5:22

▼ DEVOTION

White as Snow

After a long trip, especially if you're camping or hiking, there's nothing like a hot bath or shower. Warm water never felt so good on your skin. The clean scent of soap washing away layers of dirt refreshes you like nothing else. Scrubbing your hair with shampoo makes you feel reborn.

This same sensation of cleansing is possible if we're willing to follow God's guidelines and keep our bodies and hearts pure. The two go together, so we have to make sure that we're eliminating the harmful pollutants that we encounter in the world. We also have to make sure we're immersing ourselves in God's Word, confessing our sins in prayer, receiving God's forgiveness, and serving others.

By God's grace, we are washed as white as snow, forgiven our sins, and purified through the love of Christ.

DAILY INTERACTION ▼

 CONNECT: Ask someone you've offended to forgive you and then show them that you mean it.

Defend the rights of the poor and needy.
PROVERBS 31:9

Care for the Needy

We love stories about underdogs defeating more powerful opponents. And we love heroes who willingly sacrifice their resources to defend, save, and protect others. But what we may not realize is that we, as followers of Jesus, are called to be defenders of the weak and protectors of those in need.

Christ set an example for us to follow that makes our role clear. We don't have to give away a lot of money, avert our eyes out of shame, or fix all of another person's problems. We simply have to open our hearts and engage in the struggle the other person faces. It may be meeting a physical need—providing food to the hungry, water to the thirsty, shelter to the homeless. But it may also be listening, praying, crying, and laughing with the lonely, the grieving, the sick.

We don't have to have super powers to care for the underdogs around us. We simply have to love them the way Christ loves us.

CONNECT: Explore sites that minister to the poor and needy; choose one and commit to praying and possibly serving with this ministry.

> *Encourage the oppressed. Defend the cause of*
> *the fatherless, plead the case of the widow.*
>
> ISAIAH 1:17

▼ DEVOTION

Be His Voice

When Jesus returned to heaven after his resurrection, he left us with the gift of the Holy Spirit. Christ explained that the Spirit dwells in us and is our advocate and comforter, the divine presence of God communicating on our behalf.

With this kind of advocacy as our model, we are called to speak out for those who may not have a voice, or those whose voice cannot be heard. This may be challenging and painful. Others may not like the fact that we're defending those who can't defend themselves. But God gives us strength to stand before those who would harm those weaker than themselves. It's not about violence as much as it's about reminding others of God's peace, power, and protection.

Today, look for opportunities to take a stand for God's truth against those who would oppress others.

DAILY INTERACTION ▼

 CONNECT: Go to JesusDaily.com and make your opinion known about an injustice in our world today.

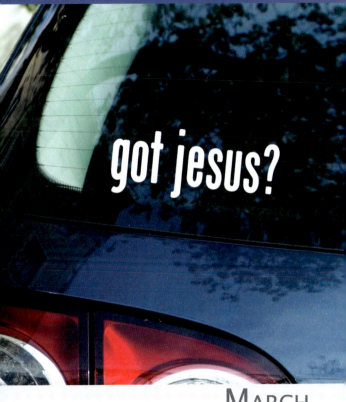

MARCH

What does the LORD require of you?
To act justly and to love mercy and
to walk humbly with your God.

Micah 6:8

📅 **March 1**

> *The LORD replied, "My Presence will go with you, and I will give you rest."*
> EXODUS 33:14

True Rest

We often schedule time for rest or vacation and then wonder why we don't feel more refreshed. Rest does not always come from lack of activity. Sleepless nights remind us that it takes more than simply lying down and closing our eyes. Anxious thoughts spinning through our mind while we try to relax make it clear that we can't just flip a switch and turn our minds off.

True rest comes when we experience God's presence in our lives. Our day may be filled with activities, meetings, and conversations, but if we've invited God into the center of our schedule, we can trust his timing and let go of the stress that comes from trying to control everything.

God is in control of your life and will give you the rest you need.

 CONNECT: Share with others on the Jesus Daily page how you've experienced the deep peaceful rest that can only come from God.

> *In my integrity you uphold me and*
> *set me in your presence forever.*
> PSALM 41:12

▼ DEVOTION

Integrity Grows

Y ou don't have to be a perfect person to have integrity. You simply have to be focused on God's truth. The word *integrity* means wholeness as well as virtue. When we're singularly committed to loving and serving the Lord in every area of our lives, we can count on him to uphold us and guide us. Even when we're distracted and lose sight of our priorities at times, we can know that God remains with us and wants to empower us to advance his kingdom.

With all the voices, sound bites, and information assaulting us each day, it can be hard to focus on our relationship with the Lord. All the more reason why we need to take time throughout our day to pray and invite his presence into all areas of our lives. Integrity grows over time as you become more and more transformed into the likeness of Christ.

Stay focused on what matters most, ignoring the many distractions throughout your day.

DAILY INTERACTION ▼

CONNECT: At the end of the day, review your history online—the sites, blogs, and searches you've visited. Are there any that are outside of God's best for you?

got jesus?

> *[Jesus said,] "Blessed are the merciful,*
> *for they will be shown mercy."*
> MATTHEW 5:7

DEVOTION ▼

Pass His Mercy On

Some days it feels as though everything goes your way: the sun is shining, your schedule runs smoothly, and an unexpected check arrives in the mail. On these days, it's easy to feel as though you experience mercy—undeserved kindness. Like a gift from a stranger or a police officer's warning instead of a ticket, mercy reminds you that you're getting something much better than you deserve.

Jesus tells us to be merciful, just like his Father, in order to be shown mercy. Each day we have the opportunity to surprise those around us with a taste of God's goodness. Both in our attitude and our actions, we can demonstrate our gratitude for his grace and forgiveness.

No matter what challenges you face today, God's mercy—his compassion and kindness—will go ahead of you. In light of this gift, you have the opportunity to pass it along to everyone you encounter.

DAILY INTERACTION ▼

CONNECT: Visit JesusDaily.com and post a message of encouragement for those struggling to show mercy today.

> *Humble yourselves, therefore, under God's mighty hand,*
> *that he may lift you up in due time.*
>
> 1 PETER 5:6

▾ **DEVOTION**

True Humility

The line between humility and humiliation sometimes gets blurred. When we humble ourselves, we acknowledge our lack of self-sufficiency, pride, and power. We make it clear that we can't accomplish anything by ourselves and that we won't take undeserved credit for our contributions to what does get accomplished.

Humiliation, on the other hand, poisons humility with a sense of shame and contempt. Whether we humiliate ourselves or someone else, the sense of inadequacy and unworthiness comes across much the same.

When we're truly humble, there's no sense of putting ourselves—or anyone else—down. In fact, just the opposite: we acknowledge our true worth in Christ alone and make it clear that we depend on God's goodness and power to sustain us. The more we remember our source, the more he empowers us to accomplish mighty deeds for his kingdom.

DAILY INTERACTION ▾

CONNECT: Go to JesusDaily.com and give God the credit for something he allowed you to achieve today, something you clearly could not have done on your own power.

got jesus?

📓 March 5

I will instruct you and teach you in the way you should go;
I will counsel you and watch over you.
PSALM 32:8

New Insights

Each day provides us with new learning opportunities. We don't have to be in school or training for a new career in order to experience the life lessons all around us. God delights in teaching us his truth. Through his Word, we have the opportunity to study his many lessons, each day discovering a new insight or a fresh angle to the only certainty that endures forever.

God also reveals his instructions to us through prayer and our relationships with one another. While we may not have the answer we want when we want it, or the wisdom to see the perspective our Father sees, we can still know that he will guide us. Like a hiker lost in the woods discovering her compass, we don't have to rely on our own knowledge alone.

Today, notice what God is trying to teach you—about yourself, your life, and his character.

 CONNECT: Forward a Jesus Daily post or another post or blog entry that has revealed something fresh about God's love.

> *[Jesus said,] "Blessed are those who mourn,*
> *for they will be comforted."*
>
> Matthew 5:4

A Time to Mourn

No one chooses to be sad. It happens naturally enough when we experience loss or face the pain of difficult circumstances. And most days, in the global village of our world today, we can find plenty to be sad about. So much, in fact, that we may have short-circuited our ability to mourn.

When we mourn, we don't have to wear black clothes, cry all day, or even feel sad. Mourning is more about our ability to recognize injustice, acknowledge imperfection, and spot the distance between our shattered world and God's perfect holiness. It's not up to us to close this gap—Christ has already provided the bridge between our sin and God's love.

Mourning involves bringing our recognition of what's broken before God and asking for his healing, comfort, and restoration. Today, you don't have to be sad—although you may be—as you reflect on areas and individuals who need the love of Jesus.

CONNECT: Research an issue, struggle, or area of brokenness in our world today. Inquire online about ways you can help minister in this area of need.

The LORD is close to the brokenhearted and saves those who are crushed in spirit.

PSALM 34:18

— DEVOTION ▼ —

Healing Our Hurts

When we were children, it only took a moment in our parent's arms to get over a scraped knee or spilled cup of juice. The sense of closeness provided a tangible comfort to our distress. We felt safe and secure, aware that our painful problem bothered us but that our mother's or father's loving presence was bigger than any problem we encountered.

As we grow up, we learn to handle our painful losses and disappointments by ourselves—to tough it out and push through. But often these injuries never heal. They linger only to ache even more acutely.

We still need our Father's embrace when we stumble and fall. Whether it's a day where nothing goes right or a major life loss, we must remember that Someone is bigger than even the largest obstacle we may face. Even when we feel broken and crushed, God comforts us with his care.

— DAILY INTERACTION ▼ —

 CONNECT: Offer a verse that has comforted you to someone you know who needs reassurance.

The LORD is good, a refuge in times of trouble.
He cares for those who trust in him.

NAHUM 1:7

▼ DEVOTION

He Is Our Shelter

In a rainstorm, we take refuge wherever we can find a safe, dry shelter that covers us. Most of the time, we like to be in a house or building to escape the storm, but sometimes a doorway, bus stop, or cave keeps us out of harm's way. We may still get a little wet, but we're safe from the brunt of the storm.

During the storms of life, God wants to cover us the same way. When we run to him, we can experience his care and compassion, a safe shelter from all the harsh words, hurtful actions, and hateful harassment of a bad day. Like warming before a fireplace after getting soaked by the rain, we can experience the renewed energy to venture out again the next day.

Regardless of the kind of weather you experience today, God is there for you.

DAILY INTERACTION ▼

 CONNECT: Chat, text, or video conference with a friend today, encouraging each other to push through current struggles.

got jesus?

*Set an example for the believers in speech,
in life, in love, in faith and in purity.*
1 TIMOTHY 4:12

DEVOTION ▼

What They See

You may not be aware of how many people are watching you, but there are many. Now more than ever, others notice what you do and say in person and online. A careless comment, mean-spirited tweet, or prideful page-status might send the wrong signal to others who look to you as an example.

With so many people expressing opinions, especially online, it's tempting to think that no one will notice your presence—or lack of it. But they will. Many people who don't know God base their understanding of the gospel on what they see in your life.

This responsibility should not add undue pressure to what you say and do. Rather, you should consider what a privilege it is to represent the love of God and truth of Christ to those around you. You don't have to be perfect; you just have to be present to the needs of others.

DAILY INTERACTION ▼

CONNECT: Pick out someone you follow online whose faith inspires you. Write them a brief note of thanks for setting such a Christlike example.

The LORD is righteous, he loves justice;
upright men will see his face.

PSALM 11:7

▼ DEVOTION

Clarity in a Gray World

So many standards, traditions, and customs that once seemed like permanent fixtures have now crumbled with the changes of our current culture. While some of these may have a positive impact, many of them simply indicate how selfish and fickle human beings can be. We want absolutes for the security they provide, but we want to be the exception to the rules they require.

God provides the standard by which all things just, righteous, and holy are measured. And people all fall short of his standard—we're naturally inclined to focus on our own selfish and sinful desires, incapable of living a perfect life. In fact, only one person lived a perfect life—Jesus. Because we could never live up to God's standard of holiness, he sent his Son to live among us, provide an example, and offer us eternal life through the gift of salvation.

Even if we live in a gray world, God provides the clarity and definition we need in black and white.

DAILY INTERACTION ▼

 CONNECT: Explore various opinions on a cultural or moral issue on which Christians seem to disagree. Begin an online dialogue with someone from such a forum.

got jesus?

📅 March 11

Do not repay evil with evil or insult with insult,
but with blessing, because to this you were called
so that you may inherit a blessing.
1 Peter 3:9

Turn the Other Cheek

So much of our daily lives is based on action and reaction, need and reward. We go to work to earn a paycheck. We need that paycheck to have money to live on. We talk with a friend and ask for a favor. Our friend grants the favor, and we know that we now owe her one. It's a kind of reciprocal cycle in which the natural give-and-take of life becomes the predominant law of survival.

The same principle seems to apply to when we suffer injury, insult, or indiscretion. Our coworker snubs us, so we snub them back. Our spouse picks an argument, so we defend ourselves and pick on them. Our friend is discovered to be the source of a cruel rumor about us, so we carefully plant a seed of juicy gossip about her. We retaliate and assume this is how we survive.

But this is not God's way. Through his Word and the example of his Son, we're reminded that grace is irrational, illogical, and unwarranted. Grace breaks the this-for-that, tit-for-tat cycle by which much of the world operates. Today, turn the other cheek and bless someone who insults you.

CONNECT: Avoid making any critical comments online or sending any retaliatory emails.

> *Blessed is he who comes in the name of the LORD.*
> *From the house of the LORD we bless you.*
>
> PSALM 118:26

▼ DEVOTION

Messenger of Hope

You may have heard the expression "don't shoot the messenger," which means that we should not hold the deliverer of bad news responsible for the message itself. On the other hand, everyone loves to deliver good news—whether it's the announcement of a new promotion, excitement over a new addition to the family, or positive results from another's exam. While we can't always take credit for the good news, we can celebrate with the recipient.

When we live by faith as followers of Jesus, we bring good news wherever we go. It may not always be what others around us want to hear, but ultimately it's what each and every one of us longs to hear. We want to believe there's meaning in life and hope for the future. We want to experience the deep, abiding love of God in ways that transform our lives.

There's no better news we can share with anyone than the love of God through the gift of his Son, Jesus Christ.

DAILY INTERACTION ▼

CONNECT: Who needs to hear the good news you can share with them? Email, text, or chat with someone who needs to know Christ.

March 13

Jesus told him, "Because you have seen me, you have believed; blessed are those who have not seen and yet have believed."
JOHN 20:29

Step Out in Faith

These days we can order most anything online: clothes, food, appliances, computers, even cars and houses. But usually, the greater the purchase price, the more we want to see what we're getting for our money before we invest. While some people are comfortable buying a car online, sight unseen, most of us want to see it, touch it, drive it, before we spend our hard-earned dollars to buy it.

Faith requires us to invest in our relationship with God in ways that sometimes seem cloudy and unclear. We can't see what's ahead

or understand why God allows certain events to happen. And yet we're called to step out in faith, trusting that our Father will guide us each step of the way, regardless of how clearly we can see the path.

Today, don't worry about how clearly you can see what God's up to—just take the next step.

 CONNECT: Research the life of someone you admire as a pillar of the faith, such as Billy Graham or Mother Teresa. How did they step out in faith in obedience to God?

> *"Whoever serves me must follow me;*
> *and where I am, my servant also will be.*
> *My Father will honor the one who serves me."*
>
> JOHN 12:26

▼ DEVOTION

Loving Service

The notion of servants usually conjures up images of maids and butlers in black-and-white uniforms waiting on wealthy people in fancy estates. The relationship may go beyond employer and employee, but historically these roles were maintained with a strict decorum. Servants waited on their masters and mistresses without question, while their employers didn't attempt to become their friends.

Through the example we see in the life of Christ, we know that serving others reflects the love of God. Service keeps us humble and reminds us that we are all equals, no matter our income, status, education, or title. We are all God's children, sinful and needy, transformed only by his grace through the gift of salvation.

When we let go of the old-fashioned mindset of superior and inferior roles toward one another, we glimpse the way God sees us—as his sons and daughters, eternal beings created in his image.

DAILY INTERACTION ▼

CONNECT: Review the message board at your local church or favorite ministry website. Choose one need that you can address in some way today.

> *Without faith it is impossible to please God, because anyone who comes to him must believe that he exists and that he rewards those who earnestly seek him.*
>
> HEBREWS 11:6

—— DEVOTION ▼ ——

Pleasing God

No matter how hard you try to please God, you can never do enough to earn his favor. You can give all your money to the church, work in a mission for the homeless, and read your Bible daily. While good if motivated by love and not legalism, these activities are useless when it comes to pleasing God unless you have faith.

When you trust someone, you naturally rely on them for comfort, connection, and collaboration. Our relationship with God works the same way; it's a relationship, not a business transaction, career opportunity, or magic lamp. No matter what we do, if we do it unto the Lord with a sincere faith, he will be pleased. But he does want us to grow and mature in our faith. A father cherishes the crayon-drawn picture his toddler draws him, but he expects more when the child grows into an adult.

The good news is that we can't force ourselves to grow—it happens naturally as we become more deeply acquainted with the love of our heavenly Father.

—— **DAILY** INTERACTION ▼ ——

 CONNECT: Reaffirm a friend's growth as a believer by telling them how you've seen them progress in the past year.

> *What does the LORD require of you? To act justly and*
> *to love mercy and to walk humbly with your God.*
>
> MICAH 6:8

▼ DEVOTION

Walk the Talk

Job requirements often determine whether we're qualified to apply for a particular position. Sometimes employers want a certain educational degree or years of experience in the field. They may want us to have training with certain software or knowledge of industry systems. When someone first begins their career, it can be frustrating because everyone wants you to have experience but no one gives you the opportunity.

We don't have to apply for a position with God. He adopts us as his sons and daughters when we accept Christ into our hearts and commit to following him. This doesn't mean that God doesn't require anything from us, but it does reassure us that he takes us just as we are. We don't need certain prerequisites to be saved by his grace.

In our walk with him, God wants us to "walk the talk," literally. If our focus is truly on knowing, loving, and serving him, then what we think, say, and do will reflect his goodness.

DAILY INTERACTION ▼

 CONNECT: Post a Bible verse at JesusDaily.com that illustrates where you are in your relationship with God today.

got jesus?

> *God is our God for ever and ever; he will be our guide even to the end.*
> PSALM 48:14

—— DEVOTION ▼

He Will Guide

We don't have to worry much about directions anymore. We have lots of gadgets, apps, and programs to help us navigate to our destinations. Most of them get us there by the most direct route possible, occasionally factoring in variables such as traffic, construction, and weather. Sometimes, though, mapping systems aren't up to date or contain a glitch that sends us on a tangent or, worse, gets us lost.

Similarly, our lives rarely seem to take the direct route from one milestone to another. While we might like the predictability that comes from knowing exactly where we're going at all times and how we'll get there, much of the time we don't. This doesn't mean we don't have a reliable guide, however.

God constantly provides us with his guidance and direction. When we trust him with each decision we make and each step we take, we can rest in his sovereignty.

—— DAILY INTERACTION ▼

CONNECT: Make a list of the biggest milestones in your life—maybe the top ten or twelve. Reflect on how God has guided you from each one to the next.

> *If our hearts do not condemn us, we have confidence before God and receive from him anything we ask.*
>
> 1 John 3:21–22

▼ **DEVOTION**

No Condemnation

You know the person who criticizes you the most quite intimately. This critic's voice is always in your ear, pointing out what you should have done, mocking what you have done, and ignoring your rebuttals. While others may contribute to the criticism, usually we are our own worst critic. We hold ourselves to an impossible standard that keeps us scrambling on a cycle of trying harder, failing, feeling ashamed, on and on. Throw in constant comparisons to others and the ups and downs we're bound to experience each day, and it's no wonder that we often struggle in our faith.

When we accept the free gift of salvation and embrace God's loving forgiveness through Christ, we no longer face condemnation from any source. Even when it seems easier to believe that God has forgiven us than it is to forgive ourselves, we must learn to quiet our critic. As we grow in our faith, we become more aware of our true identity, God's child created in his image for good works.

God says you are worthy. Confidence comes from swimming in the depths of God's love. Don't believe what anyone else—including yourself—may try to tell you.

DAILY INTERACTION ▼

 CONNECT: Email someone you love and remind them of the truth about who they are—not who they think they should be.

> *"I am the LORD, your God, who takes hold of your right hand and says to you, Do not fear; I will help you."*
> ISAIAH 41:13

Release Your Fears

Most of our fears come from our perception that something is dangerous, uncertain, and unpredictable. Lightning may or may not strike our house, so we may buy insurance and attach lightning rods to minimize the damage if we are hit. Illness is more likely to develop if we don't exercise, eat nutritious food, and get adequate rest. We do what we can to dispel and control our fears, but no matter how old we are or how mature in our faith, we still get scared sometimes.

Like a child walking through the woods on a moonless night, we stumble and fall, frightened by what we can't see. Our imaginations pick up on every little sound and wonder if it's a wild animal stalking us—or worse, another person. The rumble of thunder or the rustle of branches sends us running, even though we're engulfed by total darkness.

When we're afraid, our Father holds our hand and leads the way through anything we may face. We have nothing to fear.

DAILY INTERACTION ▼

CONNECT: Share one of your fears with someone online and ask them to pray for you to experience God's peace. Then do the same for them.

> *We are more than conquerors*
> *through him who loved us.*
> Romans 8:37

▼ DEVOTION

His Love Is Constant

In the dead of winter, beneath the frozen ground, it's hard to believe that life still resides, buried there in darkness. But it does, of course, as the beauty of spring assures us. Ice and snow melt, tender shoots break the ground, and buds tease us with a blush of colored branches. The days grow longer, and the sun brings new life to everything in nature, resurrecting the promise of hot summer days.

Often we cannot see beyond the spiritual season of winter in which we sometimes find ourselves. Our faith feels lifeless and flat, our interest in spending time in prayer or Bible study seems to have evaporated, and our hope of ever moving through our present troubles seems impossible. But even during these times—especially during these times—we must remember that God's love is constant. It does not waver and increase and decrease based on our feelings.

You will get through your present struggles as sure as spring will bring new life.

DAILY INTERACTION ▼

 CONNECT: Plant a seed of hope in someone you know by reminding them that God's love is not seasonal.

got jesus?

> *[Jesus said,]* "I tell you the truth, whoever hears my word and believes him who sent me has eternal life and will not be condemned; he has crossed over from death to life."
>
> JOHN 5:24

———— DEVOTION ▼ ————

Run the Race

Like a runner with sore feet, we often struggle to keep putting one foot in front of the other. During these moments, we're tempted to quit the race of faith and just go our own way. We want to pursue selfish pleasures that provide instant gratification instead of resisting temptation by trusting God. Often, the enemy of our souls knows that we're vulnerable and weak, weary and overwhelmed. He may try to lure us away from the path of God's righteousness by throwing sinful comforts and addictive idols in front of us.

Running away from the struggles of life never provides relief for long, especially after we've experienced God's goodness. Temptations may appeal to our senses or offer an illusion of rest and comfort. But ultimately, they just distract us from what matters most. If we want to run the race of faith, we must be prepared to keep going. And when we can't, we must trust God to carry us.

We've already crossed the finish line from death to life. God will sustain us as we keep running.

———— DAILY INTERACTION ▼ ————

 CONNECT: Watch a video clip on YouTube of a marathon runner or Ironman triathlete finishing a race. Think about what they can teach you about running the race of faith.

> *For as high as the heavens are above the earth, so great is his love for those who fear him; as far as the east is from the west, so far has he removed our transgressions from us.*
>
> PSALM 103:11–12

▼ DEVOTION

So Great a Love

In the middle of a vast body of water, the ocean or a large lake or river, it can be disorienting. If you can't see the shore in any direction, it's tough to know what's what. And if the sun isn't out to help with some east-to-west clues, it's really tough. The horizon looks the same from every angle. We look from one corner of our line of sight to another and only see the dark blue water. We can't imagine the distance from one side to the other.

Similarly, with stars, it's hard to imagine the distance between them even when we read the scientific data with miles and light years. How much farther then must it be between planet earth and galaxies billions of miles away? Even if we find out, this distance still seems small when we consider how far God removes our sins from us.

He removes our transgressions beyond our ability to imagine. He forgives us wholly and completely. He loves us unconditionally.

DAILY INTERACTION ▼

 CONNECT: Start a thread and ask others why they think we struggle to live as forgiven sons and daughters of the King.

> [Jesus said,] *"Come to me, all you who are weary and burdened, and I will give you rest."*
>
> MATTHEW 11:28

—— DEVOTION ▼ ——

Rest Easy

When was the last time you felt truly rested? Maybe it was after your last vacation, an especially good night's sleep, or an afternoon nap. Since soul rest includes more than just resting our bodies, maybe you feel rested after preparing a special meal, during the closing credits of a great movie, or while watching the sun set.

We all long for true, deep-down, soul-satisfying rest, but seldom seem to get it. What if the secret isn't the activity—or lack of it—but the anchor? When we relax and let go of all our worries, our faith anchors us to the goodness and sovereignty of God. He's in charge, not us.

The secret to real rest is anchoring yourself to a foundation that never moves. Your life changes constantly, but God's love for you never changes. Who he is, his character, never changes. He is the same last week as he is today. The same today as he is ten years from now.

You can rest easy.

—— DAILY INTERACTION ▼ ——

 CONNECT: Share your favorite ways to relax with others at JesusDaily.com.

*He who dwells in the shelter of the Most High
will rest in the shadow of the Almighty.*

PSALM 91:1

▼ DEVOTION

Rest Your Soul

It's great to sleep in and catch up on our rest. Most of the time, we answer to our alarms (or snooze buttons) as we wake up and begin to get ready for the day. At the end of the day, we may have a little time before bed to relax, but rarely does this provide the kind of rest our soul needs in order to be refreshed.

Rarely do we take the time to enjoy a real day of Sabbath rest. Even Sundays can seem jam-packed with church services, family activities, and preparing for the upcoming week. But as God establishes in Genesis, when he created our world and everything in it, he took a day off. On the seventh day, he rested. Scripture doesn't say that he only created a couple of little things that day, or that he caught up on all those things he had been meaning to create. No, he *rested*.

Today, cancel an appointment, reschedule a meeting, or break your routine and simply rest your soul before God.

DAILY INTERACTION ▼

 CONNECT: Go unplugged for at least one hour during the day.

March 25

The LORD is my shepherd, I shall not be in want.
PSALM 23:1

 got jesus?

What Money Can't Buy

Some days you feel as though you will never have enough, never get caught up let alone get ahead. Whether it's money or time, possessions or opportunities, our contentment often seems conditional on having more. Especially when we look around and see what others have, it's natural to feel as though we don't have all that they have.

When you're tempted to compare yourself to someone who seems to be living the life you desire, though, remember one thing. When your desires for your life align with God's, you'll never feel envious or jealous. Instead, just the opposite—content, joyful, fulfilled!

Our primary need each day is to know him, grow closer to him, and know his peace. Focused on this truth, following our Good Shepherd, we become content in a way that money cannot buy.

CONNECT: Look at different artists' renderings of Jesus as the Good Shepherd; choose one to use as your wallpaper today.

> *He makes me lie down in green pastures, he leads me beside quiet waters, he restores my soul.*
>
> PSALM 23:2–3

▼ DEVOTION

Soul Restoration

Many people never slow down until they're forced to do so. They get sick, have an accident, or lose their job. Suddenly, they have no choice but to reduce their speed and change their normal fast-paced routine. Most of the time, this process yields positive results, even if the individuals initially resisted their required rest periods.

Sometimes our lives become so overwhelming that God intervenes and brings his supernatural peace to our minds. We can't explain it. Our to-do list remains just as long, the demands on our time just as daunting. But somehow we sense that it's all going to be okay. Whether we get everything done doesn't seem to matter so much any more. Simply being present and trusting God's goodness becomes our priority.

It's nice when we can venture outside, lie back under a shade tree or umbrella, and watch the surface of a nearby lake or river. But most of the time, we probably can't. Nonetheless, the same sense of tranquility can be ours when we allow God's peace to envelop us.

DAILY INTERACTION ▼

 CONNECT: Forego the time you usually spend online after work and cross another item off your list that needs doing.

got jesus?

*He guides me in the paths of righteousness
for his name's sake.*
PSALM 23:3

A Trustworthy Guide

Because of who God is, we can trust him and follow him. It's not just that he's all-knowing and all-powerful; it's that he loves us and wants what is best for us. He's not only a trustworthy guide, but also a compassionate one committed to helping us reach our divine destination.

The route he takes will be one that's consistent with his character and his Word. He won't take shortcuts that put you at risk or ask you to walk where he has not been. He won't ask you to sin or compromise truth along the way. You may not always be comfortable or travel at the pace you would choose, but there's something reassuring about not having to control everything.

God knows where he's leading you so let him. His way is the right way.

CONNECT: Study a map of the local parks and hiking trails near your home. Choose one and invite a friend to meet you there later this week.

"Repent, then, and turn to God, so that your sins may be wiped out, that times of refreshing may come from the Lord."

ACTS 3:19

▼ DEVOTION

Be Patient

Sometimes we wrestle with decisions, thinking through pros and cons and all the angles we can imagine. We may pray about our options but then go with the one that feels right to us. After the fact, when circumstances don't go the way we expected, we realize we did not wait on the Lord. Yes, we asked for his guidance, but then we charged ahead and did what we wanted—not necessarily what he wanted.

If we learn from these missteps, we often become more patient the next time we seek God's direction for our lives. Sometimes events are urgent and we have to act quickly. But most of the time, we would benefit from praying diligently and waiting patiently to see what our Father reveals in his time.

It's not easy, and we naturally become impatient. But if we want to follow our Father's plan for our lives and not go our own way, we must learn to wait.

DAILY INTERACTION ▼

CONNECT: Make an appointment to video call with a good long-distance friend. How long will the two of you have to wait before being together in person again?

got jesus?

> *This is what the Sovereign LORD, the Holy One of Israel, says: "In repentance and rest is your salvation, in quietness and trust is your strength."*
>
> ISAIAH 30:15

———— DEVOTION ▼ ————

Stay on Track

When most people think of getting a little "R and R," they mean "rest and relaxation." But maybe getting some "rest and repentance" would be even more refreshing. When we know we're going the right direction, it makes all the difference in the way we enjoy the journey.

Repentance simply means turning away from our own course of direction and aligning ourselves with God's path. Like a traveler realizing he was off track, we make a correction to our life's journey whenever we ask God to forgive us for wandering away. His grace restores us and we find ourselves back on the path of life and fruitful purpose.

What direction are you taking today? Turn away from your own instincts and return on the trail toward home. Your Father always welcomes you back.

———— DAILY INTERACTION ▼ ————

 CONNECT: Email, text, or chat with a friend and ask them to hold you accountable for following God's direction this week.

*Let us fix our eyes on Jesus, the author and perfecter of our faith,
who for the joy set before him endured the cross, scorning its
shame, and sat down at the right hand of the throne of God.*

HEBREWS 12:2

▼ DEVOTION

Eyes Fixed on Jesus

If you wear glasses or contacts or have ever had your eyes checked, you probably had to look through lots of different lenses as the doctor tested your eyes. There's usually a lot of going back and forth between combinations of different kinds of lenses—ones that magnify, others that clarify, some that correct the distortions from our impaired vision.

"Is the chart clearer with number 1 or number 2?" the optometrist asks. "Can you see better with option A or option B?" Seconds tick by. "That's A . . . or B?"

As we age, our eyes typically degenerate and need help for us to see as clearly and sharply as we once did. Similarly, the only way our vision remains clear throughout the course of our lives is when we focus on Jesus. Our circumstances change, our feelings go up and down, people in our lives come and go. But Christ remains constant, providing us with a perfect and clear example of serving the Father out of loving obedience.

DAILY INTERACTION ▼

CONNECT: Sort through recent photos you've taken and select one that reminds you of Christ's example to post on your personal page.

got jesus?

We fix our eyes not on what is seen, but on what is unseen.
For what is seen is temporary, but what is unseen is eternal.
2 Corinthians 4:18

—————————————— DEVOTION ▼ ——————

Toward the Light

Have you ever been swimming in the dark? Maybe in the ocean or a pool on a moonless night? It can be scary and then some. You feel disoriented, unsure of your direction, apprehensive about what you might run into. Without being able to see the shore, the horizon, the edge of the pool, or any landmarks, you lose your bearings and can't even be sure you're swimming in a straight direction.

Some days feel as though we're swimming in the dark. We can't see what's ahead and unexpectedly bump into the agendas of others and become forced to change course without knowing where we're going. We become frightened by the unknown in the face of disappointments and unmet expectations.

Don't be afraid of what you can't see. Just keep looking at Jesus and taking one stroke after another, swimming toward the light.

—————————————— DAILY INTERACTION ▼ ——————

 CONNECT: Post a picture of yourself or someone else swimming and ask others how they feel when swimming in the dark.

APRIL

All have sinned and fall short of the glory of God, and are justified freely by his grace through the redemption that came by Christ Jesus.

Romans 3:23–24

 April 1

*Wisdom, like an inheritance, is a good thing
and benefits those who see the sun.*
ECCLESIASTES 7:11

Seek His Wisdom

As children of the King, our inheritance in Christ holds vast riches. Certainly, the priceless gift of our salvation tops the list, but the wisdom that comes from following Jesus is just as precious. When we follow him, we lose sight of the many foolish pursuits we once chased after. On a day when fools seem to be celebrated as comical and silly, it's good to remember the value of this invaluable resource.

As we seek God's wisdom, we benefit like a sapling growing beneath the sunshine. Wisdom has a larger perspective and trusts God's sovereignty beyond what you can see, hear, and touch. Wisdom provides insight and understanding, compassion and caring. Wisdom emerges from the refining process when you go through the fire. The shallow, superficial things you once worried about are no longer important. You recognize what matters. That's wisdom.

Resist the folly of the world and trust in the wisdom of the Lord.

DAILY INTERACTION ▼

 CONNECT: Instead of pulling a practical joke on someone today, share a piece of wisdom God has recently revealed to you.

> *The God of all grace, who called you to his eternal glory in Christ, after you have suffered a little while, will himself restore you and make you strong, firm and steadfast.*
>
> 1 PETER 5:10

▼ DEVOTION

Through the Storm

Winter snow and ice storms may stretch into the spring, offering one last blast of bitter cold. A late burst of freezing temps can kill fragile blossoms and snap icy branches with bitter winds. Some trees will buckle under the weight of heavy spring snow and lean toward the ground, burdened by the unexpected, unseasonable storm. They will require assistance in their restoration, someone to brush the remaining snow away and sometimes to stake them upright.

You, too, may experience a late, unexpected storm. Things seem to be going well in your life and then suddenly, you hit a wall, overwhelmed by your responsibilities, weighted by countless burdens, unsure of how you'll keep going.

This is when God, our perfect and loving Gardener, will sustain and restore you. His grace is more than sufficient to keep you alive and fruitful. Don't be frightened when spring snows come.

DAILY INTERACTION ▼

 CONNECT: Send an e-card to someone who might need encouragement as they experience a trial or hardship.

> *Restore us, O God; make your face shine upon us,*
> *that we may be saved.*
>
> PSALM 80:3

"Follow" Him

Almost everyone online wants you to "follow" them and "like" them. Yet not all sources and sites are created equal. Online you run across all kinds of different information with various levels of credibility. Whether they're blogs focused on celebrity gossip, news sites from established networks, or personal pages sharing subjective opinions, online sources are not all created equal.

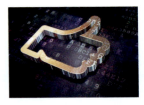

Like last hour's headlines, their news may feel dated and in need of being refreshed. Others may seem so over-the-top in their opinions that we're outraged, offended, or upset. Sometimes we want to post a "like," but resist because we don't really know if the person or site is really who or what it appears.

God is who he says he is. His "profile" and "status page" can be found in the timeless truth of his Word, the Bible. In a world of instant updates, friendly snapchats, and tempting tweets, it's good to remember we can like and follow him forever.

 CONNECT: Visit the Jesus Daily page and share something you like with a fellow believer.

> *Whenever anyone turns to the Lord, the veil is taken away. Now the Lord is the Spirit, and where the Spirit of the Lord is, there is freedom.*
>
> 2 CORINTHIANS 3:16–17

▼ DEVOTION

True Freedom

Have you ever been in a closed space for so long that you began to feel a little claustrophobic? Whether it was a windowless closet, a window seat on a crowded flight, or a filled-to-bursting subway train, these confinements leave us feeling cramped, crumpled, and contained. We feel hemmed in and trapped, knowing we will soon be free to leave our temporary prison, but nonetheless as anxious as a caged animal.

When you finally emerge from one of these experiences, there's an unbelievable feeling of freedom and exhilaration when you're finally able to walk outside, stretch your body, and see the beauty of wide open spaces.

Some days seem to leave us feeling just as trapped and claustrophobic. But we don't have to live this way. God has set us free, and the freedom we experience in his Spirit can lift and liberate us no matter the size of the space where we find ourselves.

DAILY INTERACTION ▼

 CONNECT: Connect with someone online who is not able to enjoy the same freedom to worship God that you enjoy. Commit to praying for this person.

Create in me a pure heart, O God,
and renew a steadfast spirit within me.
PSALM 51:10

———— DEVOTION ▼ ————

Spotless White

It can be hard to get back on our feet when we stumble and sin. We feel guilty, maybe ashamed, and don't like ourselves very much. We hate that we seem to struggle in the same areas over and over again. Disappointed with our failures, we become more vulnerable to further temptations, which only leave us feeling worse.

Thank God that we don't have to remain trapped in this undertow of emotions!

When we invite Jesus into our lives and ask God to forgive our sins, the scarlet scars of our mistakes fade into spotless white. Like a muddy brown field blanketed by snow, we find ourselves just as pure and bright. We can't always undo the consequences of our selfish choices, but we can absolutely count on God's grace to wash us clean. We don't have to try and change ourselves—we're already becoming more like Jesus, a new creation.

———— **DAILY** INTERACTION ▼ ————

 CONNECT: Search for or return to a site or blog that focuses on ways to overcome a recurrent temptation and sinful pattern.

> *Be made new in the attitude of your minds.*
> EPHESIANS 4:23

▼ DEVOTION

Be Made New

You can't deny the power that someone else's genuinely positive attitude can have on you. It can be a coworker, family member, friend from church, or even a stranger, but if they exude joy and confidence in the Lord, it's contagious.

Nonetheless, it can be frustrating when we're struggling through a hard day. If only we had a switch to flip that would change our attitude instantly. While it's not usually that quick and simple, we can still train our minds to filter our thoughts on God's truth. When we focus on God's character and the power of his Word, we directly influence our attitude and subsequently our feelings.

Just as it takes twenty minutes for our brains to receive the message from our stomachs that we're full, it may take a little while between the digestion of truth and our sense of satisfaction. But it will come if we keep up a steady diet of prayer, Bible study, and service to others.

DAILY INTERACTION ▼

 CONNECT: Doodle, draw, paint, or sketch the image or picture you think of when you consider the truth of God's Word, then post your artwork on the Jesus Daily page.

 April 7

> *"See, I am doing a new thing! Now it springs up; do you not perceive it? I am making a way in the desert and streams in the wasteland."*
>
> Isaiah 43:19

Streams in the Wasteland

Sometimes we go through a trial and wait for God to send water into our dry wasteland. While patience is important, we can often "prime the pump" through our praise, thanksgiving, and worship. As we reflect on our many blessings and celebrate what God has already done for us, our dry souls draw water from the well of his past mercies.

Often just remembering what God has done for you naturally leads to thanksgiving, praise, and worship. When you recognize the many gifts he's bestowed on you, as well as the many obstacles he's allowed you to overcome, your heart overflows with gratitude.

Suddenly, we can see the way God has transformed the arid soil of our hearts into a garden producing his fruits of the Spirit.

 CONNECT: Go to JesusDaily.com and share an audio file or link to a song that always inspires you to worship.

> *O God, you are my God, earnestly I seek you;*
> *my soul thirsts for you, my body longs for you,*
> *in a dry and weary land where there is no water.*
>
> PSALM 63:1

▼ DEVOTION

Let It Rain

The hot dry seasons can be unbearable in many parts of the world. The sun blazes down on parched ground, the temperature soars to new highs, and only the dry dust moves across the landscape. No shade, nothing green, no signs of life. The air becomes so hot that it's hard to breathe. Day after day the arid winds blow and the drought continues.

Then one afternoon a handful of clouds streaks across the sky. The next day more collect in front of the sun, providing temporary relief. After several more days, the sky shines dull and there's a sense of the land holding its breath, aware of moisture in the air.

One day the clouds open and drops of water begin to bounce like giant marbles across the dry, cracked ground. And then it continues falling and soon sheets of rain drench the thirsty land. The rainy season has begun, and there will be new life.

When we confess our sins to God, he refreshes us like rain after a drought.

DAILY INTERACTION ▼

 CONNECT: Check the weather forecast and look forward to the next time you can watch a spring shower bring new life around you.

> *"Whoever serves me must follow me;*
> *and where I am, my servant also will be.*
> *My Father will honor the one who serves me."*
>
> JOHN 12:26

DEVOTION ▼

Servanthood

Communication is essential for any relationship to grow, especially if both parties desire intimacy. God certainly demonstrates how much he loves us by sending his Son to die on the cross for us. He has made it possible for us to have this special kind of close-knit, Father-child relationship. The more we spend time with him, the better we get to know him. The better we get to know him, the more we trust him. And the more we trust him, the stronger we become transformed in the image of Jesus.

When we follow Jesus, we know that we are pleasing our Father. We become more like the model of servanthood that we see in Christ's life, death, and resurrection. We sacrifice our own wants and desires for the good of others.

Today, look for ways in which you can model the servant leadership of Jesus.

DAILY INTERACTION ▼

 CONNECT: Offer your professional services, free of charge, to a friend who could benefit from your expertise.

> *Be devoted to one another in brotherly love.*
> *Honor one another above yourselves.*
>
> ROMANS 12:10

▼ DEVOTION

Take the Next Step

Make note of the people you encounter today. You probably interact with some only in your respective roles: boss and employee, sales associate and customer, teacher and student. But beyond the many roles you fill, you should be able to have at least a few people who know all of you, not just your job description or contribution to the team.

Is there someone who's earned your trust? Someone with whom you can take the next step to be real?

Just as God is made up of Father, Son, and Spirit, we're designed in his image to need community. When Adam was alone in the Garden of Eden, God said it wasn't good for him to be alone, so God created Eve. Even Jesus, the Son of God, chose twelve men to be his disciples, his network of relationships with whom he could share the ups and downs of life.

Today, look for opportunities to become closer to other brothers and sisters in Christ.

DAILY INTERACTION ▼

CONNECT: Friend someone you admire online, whether you know them personally or not. Tell them what you admire most about them.

> *[Jesus said,] "A new command I give you: Love one another. As I have loved you, so you must love one another. By this all men will know that you are my disciples, if you love one another."*
>
> JOHN 13:34–35

DEVOTION ▼

Christlike Love

Sometimes it's easy to identify the group, club, company, or team to which an individual belongs. Whether it's a corporate dress code, a business logo, a particular uniform, or team colors, some details can reveal a lot about our affiliations. Most groups have their own jargon, insider perspective, jokes, and gestures. From the fraternity and sorority to the country club, the boosters' club to the baseball team, we like to show off our memberships.

If we're willing to do this for social groups, businesses, and sports, how much more we should be willing to be identified as followers of Jesus. While we may wear a cross or have something visibly identifying us as a Christian, most people won't notice those unless we back them up with our behavior.

The way we love one another tells the world around us who Jesus is and what he's all about, not just our clothes, stickers, books, and jewelry.

DAILY INTERACTION ▼

 CONNECT: Share your love for Jesus today with one of your Facebook friends.

*All have sinned and fall short of the glory of God,
and are justified freely by his grace through
the redemption that came by Christ Jesus.*

ROMANS 3:23–24

▼ DEVOTION

Be a Light

Often we want others to notice our acts of service and good deeds. This desire might reflect our prideful egos or the way we're overly concerned with what others think. No one is perfect, and we shouldn't try to present an image of perfection to those around us. In fact, if we want them to see God's grace in us, we will have to let them see our shortcomings.

Such transparency and strength illustrate a godly life more than any attention-getting "good deed" might reveal. Certainly, we want to be the light of Christ in the world's darkness, but this doesn't mean we have to set the place on fire! Sometimes the glow of one flame is enough to illuminate the darkest night.

Sharing our struggles with others also keeps us humble and dependent on the Lord. We don't try to take credit for his work, but instead use those moments when others notice as a natural way to share our faith. When others encounter us as down to earth even as we look to heaven, they will want to know our Father above.

DAILY INTERACTION ▼

 CONNECT: Share your current struggle with a trusted friend online and ask for their prayers.

*Put your hope in the L*ORD*, for with the L*ORD *is unfailing love and with him is full redemption.*
PSALM 130:7

— DEVOTION ▾ —

Open Your Heart

We all have days when we feel so lonely and unlovable that we can't bear looking inside ourselves. We don't like what we see inside and wonder how God could forgive us again, help us again, and continue to love us. Whether it's due to an acute crisis or chronic struggles, these times take a toll.

These are the days when we must accept the present of God's love despite the way we feel. There are steps that we can take, but God will come to us in ways we do not understand and whisper to us, "I love you. You are mine. I enjoy you. Nothing will take you away from me. You do not have to earn my love."

Receive His words. Look for his gifts. Open your heart to him. Express your feelings to him and let him comfort you with his unfailing love.

— DAILY INTERACTION ▾ —

 CONNECT: Post a love note to Jesus at JesusDaily.com, or if that feels too personal, send it to a trusted e-friend.

> *It was not with perishable things such as silver or gold that you were redeemed ..., but with the precious blood of Christ, a lamb without blemish or defect.*
>
> 1 PETER 1:18–19

▼ DEVOTION

No Expiration Date

Almost every item in our culture seems to have an expiration date. Most foods usually have a "fresh until" or "best if used by" date on their packages. Phones, TVs, computers, apps, and other e-gadgets become obsolete to the latest version, usually within months of each new release. Fashion trends come and go.

One permanent fixture in our lives, however, remains—our Savior's sacrifice on the cross, the source of our salvation. It has no expiration date! Death has been defeated and the timeless, eternal, foundational fact of God's grace lives forevermore.

We can rest assured that the basis for our faith is bedrock and will not change. Trends may come and go. Popular culture will alter its tastes with the latest products and performers. But Jesus remains the same yesterday, today, and tomorrow.

DAILY INTERACTION ▼

CONNECT: Make a list of tangible items that we usually think of as timeless and unchanging, such as the Grand Canyon. Consider the way your Solid Rock outdoes them all.

> *The fruit of righteousness will be peace; the effect of righteousness will be quietness and confidence forever.*
> ISAIAH 32:17

———— DEVOTION ▾ ————

The Fruit of Righteousness

Around this time of year, many people find themselves paying tax money to the government. While they may receive a refund if they've already paid in enough tax, others will be required to send a percentage of their wages to support their local and national governing bodies. Based on what you've produced, you determine the amount you have to pay.

While death and taxes have been famously described as the only certainties in life, as Christians we know that God's promises are the only sure things. Many of the truths found in his Word reveal a cause-effect, action-reaction kind of observation. With righteousness, we're told that the outcome or fruit produced includes peace, confidence, and calmness.

These qualities may not be as immediately tangible as tax forms, dollars, and cents, but they are much more valuable than any amount we can imagine.

———— **DAILY** INTERACTION ▾ ————

 CONNECT: Share your favorite fruit with someone and connect it to a fruit of the Spirit you desire in your life.

> *I urge you, brothers, in view of God's mercy, to offer your bodies as living sacrifices, holy and pleasing to God— this is your spiritual act of worship.*
>
> ROMANS 12:1

▼ DEVOTION

Nourish Your Body

Day after day we make choices about what we will eat and drink, what we watch on television, and which books we will read. We consciously decide where we will go on vacation or where we'll go to church. We often think these things don't really matter that much, not in the long run. But all of these decisions can affect our spirit and our body—how we feel, what we think, who we are.

Hopefully, our choices make us feel closer to God, but sometimes they draw us away. If we aren't careful and deliberate about all the variables influencing our minds, hearts, and bodies, we open ourselves up for temptation and snares from our enemy.

Today, nourish and protect your body as a gift from God, caring for it as a good steward.

DAILY INTERACTION ▼

 CONNECT: Check in with a friend or online acquaintance and ask them what they do to take care of their bodies. Discuss how you can hold each other accountable.

> *Let everything that has breath praise the Lord.*
> Psalm 150:6

—————————————————— DEVOTION ▾ ——————

The Gift of Laughter

When we think about praising God, we often consider praying and singing as our primary ways, which they probably are. However, we praise our Father when we stop to admire the beauty of his creation or revel in the goodness of his gifts. One of the most overlooked ways we can worship is having wholesome fun and sharing a laugh with one another.

Like our tears, laughter binds us together in contagious ways. We appreciate and admire people who don't take themselves too seriously, who can laugh at themselves or see the humor in everyday life. God shares in our laughter as well. Just as a baby's giggle or child's laughter warms the heart of her parents, we know that God delights in our ability to experience the soul liberation that occurs when we laugh.

Today, look for the lighter side of the situations you encounter. Thank God for your ability to laugh. Praise him for this wonderful gift.

———————— **DAILY** INTERACTION ▾ ————————————————————

 CONNECT: Trade family friendly jokes with friends on your Facebook page.

By his power God raised the Lord from the dead,
and he will raise us also.
1 CORINTHIANS 6:14

▼ DEVOTION

Resurrection Life

Occasionally, especially as we get older, we begin to wonder what our legacy will be. What will we have accomplished with our life that will endure after we've left this earth? Are we truly living out of our God-given purpose, or are we settling for less?

We tend to let our circumstances dictate how we feel, which in turn influences how we act. When we attach this kind of power to events beyond our control, we set ourselves up for dissatisfaction, disappointment, and discouragement. With this bleak mindset, soon it seems as though nothing matters, that regardless of what we do, it doesn't really change anything.

This is not living in the abundant life of the resurrected Christ. Circumstances remain beyond our control, and our souls will ache with the painful weight of disappointment sometimes. But when our hope is in Christ, we can see beyond our momentary discomfort. We can trust God with our past, present, and future, including our legacy.

DAILY INTERACTION ▼

 CONNECT: Read through the obituaries of some well-known Christians in history. What do they all have in common?

> *[Jesus said,] "Your Father knows*
> *what you need before you ask him."*
>
> MATTHEW 6:8

DEVOTION ▼

What You Need

Often we find ourselves praying our requests over and over again, not because God didn't hear us the first time or can't make up his mind, but because the timing isn't right to reveal his answer. He knows that when we're in need, when we have nowhere to turn or know that we can't achieve our goal by ourselves, we keep our hope fixed on him. He's able to purify our desires and help us see what's truly important and not just the possessions, events, and people whom we often ask him to bring into our lives.

Jesus tells us that even a wicked earthly father would never give his child a snake when he asked for a fish or a stone when the child asked for bread. So if our parental instincts are compassionate and generous, our heavenly Father's are beyond our imagination. God wants the best for his children. We may not get what we ask for, but we always get what's in our best interests.

Your Father loves you and will give you what you need.

DAILY INTERACTION ▼

 CONNECT: Post a prayer request on the Jesus Daily page. Remember to update your request once God answers it.

I am not ashamed of the gospel, because it is the power of God for the salvation of everyone who believes.

ROMANS 1:16

▼ DEVOTION

Never Ashamed

Sometimes no matter how hard we try, we just don't fit into our surroundings. Whether in a crowd of people very different than we are or exploring a new culture on vacation, we simply can't hide our differences. We may feel like the proverbial sore thumb, sticking out as a newcomer, a transfer, or a tourist, apologizing for our extra questions or lack of familiarity with procedure or etiquette.

However, we never have to apologize or feel ashamed for being a follower of Jesus. Sometimes we may cringe when we see other people who claim to know God condemning others, lying about circumstances, or acting hypocritically. Yes, this may create a false impression of believers in other people's minds. All the more reason, we must reflect the goodness, grace, and gentleness of Christ.

Today, make it clear to those around you that you love Jesus—not by what you say but by what you do.

DAILY INTERACTION ▼

 CONNECT: Volunteer to serve, offer to pray, and/or give generously to a cause you know Jesus would support.

 April 21

Not that I have already obtained all this, or have already been made perfect, but I press on to take hold of that for which Christ Jesus took hold of me.

PHILIPPIANS 3:12

Just As You Are

We have more choices, options, decisions, and opportunities than ever before in the course of human history. From what we want on our burgers to the composition of our homes, from how we travel to how we take care of the planet, we're encouraged to choose the "best" options—usually the ones that are most popular or appear to be perfect.

As a result, we often put pressure on ourselves that God simply doesn't. He doesn't expect us to be perfect. We're not machines. We're living, breathing, human beings made in the image of our divine Creator.

He doesn't require us to have a perfect life and didn't create us for a problem-free existence. Each day will hold enough trouble of its own. And God provides all we need to move through these circumstances. They may not be resolved and our hours will rarely conform to our ideal schedule. This is what it means to live in the present moment—to recognize that you can't control everything and rely on God for whatever you're facing today.

We will always have options, but there's only one that's essential: to follow Christ each day.

 CONNECT: Share ideas and verses with others who struggle with perfectionism. Offer to pray for one another as you learn to embrace grace.

*Be joyful in hope, patient in affliction,
faithful in prayer.*

Romans 12:12

Childlike

The creative views of children often remind us to enjoy the process of living even when it's far from perfect. With a finger-painted rainbow, a crayon-drawn portrait, or a mixed-media collage from an electronic tablet, children revel in reflecting their view of the world around them and sharing it with us.

We must live just as artfully, joyful to make the contribution that God has uniquely equipped us to make in this life. Too often we become blindsided by our problems and lose sight of the mosaic of God's majesty all around us.

When you choose to focus on Christ, you regain perspective about what's important, meaningful, and life-giving. You realize that your temporary inconvenience or slight discomfort is not the priority. Knowing God, growing closer to Christ, and serving others with the love of your Father—those are the real priorities of your day.

 CONNECT: Play a video game with a friend, family member, or someone who could benefit from being a kid again.

 April 23

If the Spirit of him who raised Jesus from the dead is living in you, he who raised Christ from the dead will also give life to your mortal bodies through his Spirit, who lives in you.
ROMANS 8:11

From Death to Life

Some days, we can't imagine how we're going to make it through all the demands we face in our schedule. Our families need us, our bosses and coworkers depend on us, and yet we have nothing left to give. We want to rely on God's strength so we pray, and somehow our Father gets us through.

The next day comes and we have an opportunity to begin again. If we've been blessed with ample rest from a good night's sleep, we can experience our job, school, and home through new eyes. Our problems don't seem as big and overwhelming. Our spirits feel refreshed and fully reliant on God. Our minds are sharp and once again can focus with clarity.

Our heavenly Father has restored us from death to life. He will continue to bring us new life so that we can accomplish what has been set before us, no matter how daunting.

 CONNECT: Request prayer for the areas in which you're feeling most overwhelmed. Commit to pray for someone else's needs as well.

> *[Jesus said,] "I have come that they may have life, and have it to the full."*
>
> JOHN 10:10

▼ DEVOTION

A Full Heart

Our lives are filled with more of everything—responsibilities, choices, options, obligations—and yet rarely do we feel full and satisfied. Our days are crammed full of stuff, but our hearts aren't full of joy and peace. The abundant life seems a distant ideal, something we long for but can't experience.

But we can.

Our primary need each day is to know Christ, grow closer to him, and know his peace. You don't have to block out hours of your day to spend in prayer and Bible study. It's great if you can, but your schedule is probably going to remain overflowing with obligations. Invite God's presence into those days the same way you would seek him if you went away to a beautiful setting for a retreat. His peace can transform the way we go through our day, reminding us that we have more than enough of whatever it requires.

DAILY INTERACTION ▼

 CONNECT: Post a favorite verse about praising God at JesusDaily.com and ask others to forward it if they like it.

Now is the time of God's favor,
now is the day of salvation.
2 CORINTHIANS 6:2

His Favor

Salvation occurs as a choice, our acceptance of the holy invitation that God has given to us through his Son. But our acceptance only begins the process of spiritual transformation that will take our whole lifetime. We don't have to know what to do or how to do it. And we sure don't have to do it perfectly.

We simply have to spend time with our Father and follow the model of his Son, Jesus. With Christ as our example, we can release our selfish pursuits and sinful choices and complete our Lord's will: loving and serving others as we proclaim the gospel in what we say and what we do.

Today, know that God's favor shines on you and that you have been saved. Enjoy the security that comes with being known and loved by the One who created you.

 CONNECT: Find an image of Jesus on the cross that inspires you and post it on the Jesus Daily page.

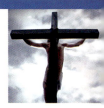

> *"Praise be to the name of God forever and ever; wisdom and power are his. He changes times and seasons..."*
>
> DANIEL 2:20–21

▼ DEVOTION

Spring Cleaning

Spring cleaning affords us the opportunity to clear out the cobwebs of winter and sort through the items we may have accumulated while indoors for so long. We can open our windows, sweep out the dust of the past few months, and welcome the warmer weather and gentle breezes of spring.

Clearing the clutter out of our lives, however, requires more than sorting through our old clothes and cleaning our closets, although those tasks certainly help. When we get rid of what's no longer useful, especially items that drain us of time and energy, we're pruning our lives to make room for new growth.

Sometimes God prunes our branches for us, even removing items that we may enjoy that aren't strengthening our faith. He makes room for each new season.

— DAILY INTERACTION ▼

CONNECT: Start a list of the things you love most about spring. Post it and ask others to contribute their favorites, too.

 April 27

*Set your hope fully on the grace to be given
you when Jesus Christ is revealed.*
1 PETER 1:13

Commit Time

About this time of year, you may find yourself looking ahead to the summer months. Your schedule looks as though it will get lighter, and vacation is right around the corner. School will be out soon, and more people will be enjoying time outdoors. You begin to make plans on ways to enjoy more leisure time, relaxing and spending more time with people you enjoy.

Maybe a better commitment of your time is committing to spend it alone with your Father. Time together and communication go a long way in any relationship, and yours with God is the same way. You not only make your requests known to him, but you also learn to quiet your heart and listen. His Spirit within us whispers and guides us in directions we might never choose ourselves. But we can rest in the daily steps we take on our journey when we know who we are following.

 CONNECT: Ask friends online their plans for this summer. See if you can make plans to fellowship together in the weeks to come.

*How great is the love the Father has lavished on us,
that we should be called children of God!
And that is what we are!*

1 John 3:1

▼ **DEVOTION**

Lavish Love

Lavish is one of those words that make us think of elegance and luxury, something that's intended to pamper us and reflect our true worth. Things like spa days, surprise vacations, and designer gifts may come to mind. We assume that wealthy people lavish these kinds of perks on their family and loved ones.

God may not bless us with material possessions or the luxury items we see in fancy advertisements, but he lavishes us with his love every day. With air to breathe, food for our bodies, and water to drink, we're reminded that what we often take for granted is still a gift. The people in our lives, the place we live, the work we do—all evidence of the blessings our Father bestows on us because he loves us.

Today, remember that you are God's precious child, a son or daughter of the King.

DAILY INTERACTION ▼

 CONNECT: Lavish someone you appreciate with compliments about the Christlike qualities you admire in their life.

 April 29

Just as you received Christ Jesus as Lord, continue to live in him, rooted and built up in him, strengthened in the faith as you were taught, and overflowing with thankfulness.
COLOSSIANS 2:6–7

DEVOTION ▼

The Risen Christ

Seeds have taken root and sprouted. Flowers have budded into first blooms. Trees have greened themselves into new life once again. Grass grows higher and higher, fueled by spring showers and longer days.

New life is all around us at this time of year. But it's also within us. At Easter, we celebrate the resurrection of our Savior.

This celebration means the most when we incorporate it into every day of our lives, not just Christmas, Easter, and a few Sundays. To keep the resurrection power of the risen Christ alive in you each day, focus on these three things:  1) the gift of salvation paid through Jesus' death on the cross, 2) his grace and mercy when you sin, and 3) the many blessings in your life of fruitful abundance. Like the combination of soil, sun, and water, focusing on these three never fails to produce blooms of joy and gratitude in your soul.

DAILY INTERACTION ▼

 CONNECT: Post pics of your recent gardening activities at JesusDaily.com, offering positive comments about other pics posted there.

[Jesus said,] "When you stand praying, if you hold anything against anyone, forgive him, so that your Father in heaven may forgive your sins."

MARK 11:25

▼ DEVOTION

Practice Forgiveness

If you've experienced the grace of God—if you truly know the depths of his forgiveness of your sins—you will naturally forgive others as well. You probably know this truth already, which doesn't make it any easier to practice. When our spouse, children, parents, boss, or others wound us through their sinfulness, we may not even realize how deep the wounds go. We hurt and become focused on the pain, often overlooking the ways that we have hurt others.

This is why we must constantly forgive and seek forgiveness for the ways we hurt others.

In offering us a model for how to pray, Jesus told us to ask our Father to "forgive us our trespasses [or sins] as we forgive those who trespass against us." We tend to think of trespassing as walking through protected property that does not belong to us. But trespassing encompasses all the ways we intrude into someone else's well-being, violating the boundaries and standards God has established.

Forgiveness works both ways, vertically and horizontally.

DAILY INTERACTION ▼

 CONNECT: Message someone who has hurt you recently and schedule a time to meet so that you can discuss the issue and forgive them.

Today 10:43 AM

I've been trying to call you.
Are you OK?

 | Send

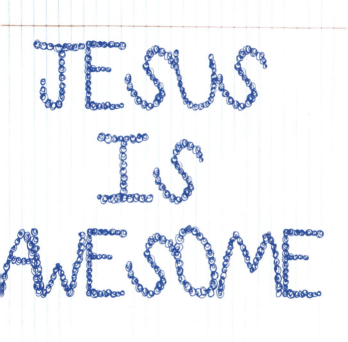

JESUS IS AWESOME

MAY

I call to God, and the LORD saves me.
Evening, morning and noon I cry out
in distress, and he hears my voice.

Psalm 55:16-17

JESUS IS AWESOME

> *I sought the LORD, and he answered me;*
> *he delivered me from all my fears.*
>
> PSALM 34:4

— DEVOTION ▼ —

Fears Disappear

Fear has a way of sneaking up on us. It often begins when some small detail gets derailed or something we counted on goes awry. Then, like dominoes toppling, one thing after another seems to lead to bigger and larger problems. The snowflake that we tried to ignore appears to have become an avalanche while we weren't looking.

Maybe you're worried about something looming in the future. Or you might be feeling sad as you grieve the loss of something or someone important to you. It could be your finances and the way there never seems to be enough money. You might be reeling from a friend's betrayal or fighting an addiction all on your own.

No matter how large or small your concern, your Father wants to comfort you and calm your heart. He knows about emotions—after all, he created us and made us in his own image. But he doesn't want our feelings to control us or lead us into temptation. He will deliver you from your fears, no matter how great or small.

— **DAILY** INTERACTION ▼ —

CONNECT: Text or call a friend and share one of your fears that is looming on the horizon. Ask this person to pray for you to be strong in the Lord.

[Jesus said,] "But when he, the Spirit of truth, comes, he will guide you into all truth. He will not speak on his own; he will speak only what he hears, and he will tell you what is yet to come."

JOHN 16:13

JESUS IS AWESOME

▼ DEVOTION

He Sees the Future

If we could predict the future, we assume that we would have a carefree life. We could forecast the stock market, know which team wins the ball game, dress perfectly for tomorrow's weather, and avoid problems before they cross our path.

But the truth is this: if we could see everything the future holds the way God sees it, most of us would be paralyzed with fear. We would glimpse unexpected events, unpredictable changes, and terrifying trials that we could not imagine overcoming. In the face of such monumental obstacles, we forget the infinite power of our sovereign Lord and King.

Our Father has everything in control. He has left his Spirit with us to reassure us and to guide us through the perilous times ahead. Your future holds nothing that God has not already seen and overcome. We can rest in the security of his power.

DAILY INTERACTION ▼

CONNECT: Send an e-card of encouragement to a family member who needs reassurance of God's strength for a problem they're facing.

Whether you turn to the right or to the left,
your ears will hear a voice behind you, saying,
"This is the way; walk in it."
Isaiah 30:21

DEVOTION ▼

He Knows Your Voice

New parents are often amazed at the way their hearing suddenly becomes so acutely attuned to their newborn's cries. Whether whimpering in their sleep or crying in the church nursery, a baby's attention-getting cry is distinct from any other sound a mother or father may hear. Even among other crying children or in a noisy surrounding, a parent zeros in on their little one's distinct sound.

Similarly, babies and children know the voices of their mother and father. Many expectant parents will even read and sing to their baby in utero, so the newborn will already be familiar with the voices of mom and dad. Sometimes when in distress, a child only needs to recognize the voice of assurance coming from their caretakers.

We, too, as children of God, need to hear our Father's voice and be reassured of his love, guidance, and protection. How wonderful that we can know that he hears us as well—distinct and unique from all his other sons and daughters!

DAILY INTERACTION ▼

CONNECT: Change your phone's ringtone to something that reminds you of your Father's love when you hear it.

JESUS
IS
AWESOME

> *"The LORD will guide you always; he will satisfy your needs in a sun-scorched land and will strengthen your frame. You will be like a well-watered garden, like a spring whose waters never fail."*
>
> ISAIAH 58:11

▼ DEVOTION

He Waters Our Soul

One of the many reasons we love spring is because of the many flowers bursting into bloom around us. Yellow daffodils, red tulips, bluebells, and lilacs decorate the lush green fields and lawns that had been brown and frozen only weeks before. Our heart seems to rejoice as we thank God for the startling beauty of his creation, the way his natural paintbrush colors the landscape.

In biblical times, most gardens had to be cultivated and watered regularly in order for flowers to bloom. The arid Middle Eastern climate in Israel did not always facilitate the natural blossoms we enjoy. Sometimes it must have seemed like a miracle when the sandy, sun-scorched soil soaked up the rain and yielded wildflowers.

This is the kind of miracle God delights in performing in our hearts. We become thirsty and dry, but he waters our souls with his Word. Like tender buds leaning toward the sun, we follow him and blossom into new life.

DAILY INTERACTION ▼

 CONNECT: Research one of your favorite kinds of flowers or blooming plants and post a picture of it at JesusDaily.com.

> [Jesus said,] "I tell you the truth, unless you change
> and become like little children, you will never enter
> the kingdom of heaven."
>
> MATTHEW 18:3

DEVOTION ▼

Like a Child

Sometimes there's a fine line between being childlike and childish. When we're childlike, we are willing to trust, to believe, and to hope with a sincerity and innocence that life's blows often try to beat out of us. We remain in the present moment, looking for glimpses of our Father wherever we go. When we're childlike, we engage life with a sense of wonder and possibility, keenly aware of the beauty and blessings around us.

By contrast, when we're childish, we simply wait passively, feeling entitled to get what we want because our lives seem so hard. When we're childish, we act like spoiled brats, pouting when God doesn't do what we want when we want it. We lapse into being victims of life instead of victors of the glorious riches we have in Christ.

Today, become like a little child without *being* childish.

DAILY INTERACTION ▼

 CONNECT: Explore one of the many wonderful ministries aimed at the needs of children and commit to praying for the work they're doing.

> *He guides me in paths of righteousness*
> *for his name's sake.*
>
> PSALM 23:3

▼ DEVOTION

Study His Names

In virtually every culture throughout history, names carry enormous significance. Often they embody a family's story from generation to generation. Sometimes they identify the lineage and legacy of the individuals who share a common name. Names also reveal personal attributes and character traits, which may in turn reflect different kinds of businesses or professions.

Throughout the Old Testament, we find dozens of different names for God: Jehovah, the Great I AM, the Lord Almighty, Immanuel, El Shaddai, and many more. Each one expresses a different facet of God's glorious character—his mercy, his generosity, his protection, his patience, his omniscience, his sovereignty.

If you want to get to know God at a deeper, more intimate level, studying his names can be a wonderful facilitator.

DAILY INTERACTION ▼

 CONNECT: Conduct a little poll on your personal page or on the Jesus Daily page, asking others for their favorite names of God.

> *If I rise on the wings of the dawn, if I settle on the far side of the sea, even there your hand will guide me, your right hand will hold me fast.*
> PSALM 139:9–10

Always with You

For many people around the world, air travel has now become as common as traveling by bus. Whether flying across country for work, traveling to an exotic vacation, or delivering a product or service to another country overseas, we no longer think of flight as a luxury. It's simply an accepted mode of travel in our tech-advanced world.

Similarly, the "world wide web," which sounds a bit old-fashioned these days, shrank the globe into an electronic community at our fingertips. Not only can we search sites originating anywhere in the world, we can email, chat, and video conference in real time. What once sounded like science fiction has become second nature.

Nonetheless, it's good to know that God is always with us. In the air or on the ground, online or offline, he never leaves our side.

 CONNECT: Video conference with someone you miss who lives a long distance away from you.

Good and upright is the LORD: therefore he instructs sinners in his ways. He guides the humble in what is right and teaches them his way.

PSALM 25:8–9

▼ DEVOTION

A Life That Pleases Him

Most products, technological or not, try to be "user friendly." Companies know that most people don't want to wade through pages of directions or dozens of "how-to" instructions. We want to jump in and "intuitively" know how to use the latest version of software, app, exercise equipment, or kitchen appliance.

However, sometimes it's not that easy. We're forced to slow down, read the owner's manual, and progress through the various steps according to the manufacturer's guidelines. Once we do, it's a relief to understand what we need to do in order to enjoy our new purchase or gift.

Living by faith is much the same way. We sometimes want to do things our own way without studying God's Word and obeying his instructions for what's truly in our best interests. But relying on what feels good to us rather than what God says is right doesn't work.

DAILY INTERACTION ▼

 CONNECT: Share an area where you struggle to obey God's instructions for your life with a trusted friend or confidant online. Request prayer to help you obey.

> *The God of Israel gives power and strength to his people.*
> PSALM 68:35

The Source of All Power

In many parts of the world, electricity provides a standard of living that's easily taken for granted. Lamps, heaters and air conditioners, and other conveniences rely on electric power to generate illumination, warm and cool air, and time-saving, effort-reducing assistance for our homes, businesses, schools, and churches.

When a power outage occurs for any length of time, we're forced to return to the basics of surviving. Suddenly, how we remain at a comfortable temperature is not so easy. Ways to preserve our fresh food become a priority. Tasks that take seconds or minutes seem to require minutes and hours.

When things are going smoothly in our lives, we might be tempted to take God's strength and power for granted. However, when our own abilities fail us, we once again get back to basics. We realize that the Lord is the source of all our power. Anything we accomplish is only because of him.

 CONNECT: Unplug for at least an hour today, using the time offline to pray, meditate, or rest in the strength of the Lord.

JESUS
IS
AWESOME

> *His divine power has given us everything we need*
> *for life and godliness through our knowledge of him*
> *who called us by his own glory and goodness.*
>
> 2 PETER 1:3

▼ DEVOTION

Ultimate Authority

A person with real power and authority never needs to bully anyone. They rest in the confidence of knowing what they can do if necessary to accomplish their responsibilities. These people are often natural leaders who inspire confidence in the people around them. They respect others and earn their followers' respect, rather than demanding it because of title, rank, or position.

God holds ultimate authority and will always be more powerful than anyone or anything we can imagine. Yet he wields his power and holiness with compassion and mercy, patiently pursuing us when we stray and guiding us in his ways. God is not a bully or dictator. He's a loving Father.

Welcome the opportunities to obey God today as ways to recognize and honor his glorious authority and grace-filled power.

DAILY INTERACTION ▼

CONNECT: Email a leader or person in authority whom you admire and tell them why you appreciate them.

May 11

> *The voice of the LORD is powerful.*
> PSALM 29:4

Listen Closely

With the frequency with which we use earbuds and headphones, it's no wonder that doctors often warn us about the consequences of listening at high volumes. Maybe we love a particular song or vocalist so much that we want the music as loud as possible. Maybe we want to hear each word of our audio book clearly above the ambient noise around us.

At times, most of us probably wish we could turn up the volume on God's voice, hearing his response to us loud and clear. Most of the time, however, we have to slow down, still our hearts before him, and listen closely. Our Father rarely shouts in our ears; instead he whispers in our hearts through the presence of his Spirit.

Even when it's only a whisper, the voice of the Lord remains powerful. We don't need to put on earphones to hear it. We simply have to listen.

 CONNECT: Post an audio file with a sound that you love— a child's laugh, a dog snoring, or rain on a tin roof, just to name some possibilities.

"My grace is sufficient for you, for my power is made perfect in weakness."

2 Corinthians 12:9

JESUS IS AWESOME

▼ DEVOTION

He Is Our Strength

Most people are not comfortable with weakness. Our society praises the strong and powerful, whether they're Olympic athletes, corporate tycoons, or government leaders. We admire individuals who are physically strong, emotionally strong, and fiscally strong. And we usually feel pressure to become stronger in all areas as a result.

While it's good to exercise, maintain self-discipline, and practice responsible stewardship, we must also recognize our limitations. No matter how hard we work out or work our way up the corporate ladder, we all have weaknesses. And we're only human—not superhuman and certainly not as strong as God. Sometimes we have a hard time remembering and respecting our limitations.

God wants us to rely on him as the source of our strength—not our own ability. Today, rest in the knowledge that you don't have to make everything happen in order to be strong.

DAILY INTERACTION ▼

 CONNECT: Share with others a verse from God's Word that gives you strength today.

JESUS
IS
AWESOME

> "I am the LORD, the God of all mankind.
> Is anything too hard for me?"
> JEREMIAH 32:27

———————————————————— DEVOTION ▼ ———

Be Ready, Be Willing

Baking a perfect cake. Earning an advanced degree. Saving enough to retire. Rebuilding a car engine. Speaking in public. Turning somersaults. Completing a marathon.

You might consider some or all of these endeavors as being "too hard" for you to accomplish. Or if not these goals, then others likely cause you to back away as being impossible for you to achieve. While we've all been blessed with certain abilities, talents, and gifts, we also have weaknesses, flaws, and deficits. We're not perfect, and we don't have to be great at everything. Discerning the areas where our strengths lie and where we can have the greatest impact is part of maturity.

However, we must also realize that when God asks us to do something, he will empower and equip us to do it. Whether we think we have what it takes to accomplish the goal doesn't matter. If the Lord wants to use us, nothing is impossible! We only have to be willing.

——— **DAILY** INTERACTION ▼ ———

 CONNECT: Forward a post from JesusDaily.com to five friends who need to be reminded of the Lord's strength.

> *"He gives strength to the weary and
> increases the power of the weak."*
>
> Isaiah 40:29

▼ DEVOTION

Do the Impossible

Whether we're rooting for an unranked team against one that's a champion powerhouse or hoping the everyday Joe wins the love of the beautiful woman in the movie, we love underdogs. So does God.

He often chooses people who are weaker, smaller, less talented, poorly equipped, and outnumbered to advance his kingdom. From David facing Goliath to Moses parting the Red Sea, from his Son being born in a manger to uneducated fishermen being chosen as his disciples, God delights in using the least likely candidates to become the most powerful conduits of his grace.

And he still empowers us the same way today. We don't think we can accomplish it, but God knows that if we allow him, he can do the impossible through us. No matter how great the odds seem stacked against you, your Father can use you.

DAILY INTERACTION ▼

 CONNECT: Offer to pray for a friend who's currently facing a challenge that feels too big for them.

God did not give us a spirit of timidity,
but a spirit of power…
2 TIMOTHY 1:7

———— DEVOTION ▼ ————

Confident and Bold

Sometimes there's a fine line between good manners and bold behavior. Our culture often conditions us to be polite, deferential, reserved, and conciliatory to those around us. On the other hand, we learn quickly that we'll get run over if our priority is having others think that we're "nice."

Jesus told us that we are to be as innocent as doves and as shrewd as serpents. As Christians, we often practice the former but struggle to practice the latter. But even as we're told to turn the other cheek, it's clear that we're not supposed to be passive doormats. We can only go the extra mile and turn the other cheek if our strength allows us to maintain our confidence and faith.

When we rely on God's strength as our power source, we don't have to be shy about it. We can be confident, bold, and secure in knowing that we can indeed do all things through Christ.

———— **DAILY** INTERACTION ▼ ————

 CONNECT: Chat or start a threaded discussion with others about what it looks like to strike this balance between manners and means.

> *I am not ashamed of the gospel, because it is the power of God for the salvation of everyone who believes.*
>
> ROMANS 1:16

▼ DEVOTION

No More Hiding

Spilling tomato sauce on a white blouse. Leaving your wallet at home when it's your turn to pay. Saying something negative before thinking about its impact. Taking a sick day from work and running into your boss at the mall.

We've all done things that make us feel embarrassed, awkward, or outright ashamed. From little accidents that happen to everyone to situations that snowball out of control from a bad decision we've made, most of us know that feeling of wanting to hide our mistakes.

Adam and Eve experienced the same feeling after disobeying God in the Garden. They grabbed fig leaves to cover their nakedness as they ran to hide. They knew they had blown it and couldn't bear to face their Father.

Thanks to the gift of salvation through Christ, we have nothing to be ashamed of ever again. Today, you don't have to hide.

DAILY INTERACTION ▼

 CONNECT: Post a selfie or silly pic that you're usually too embarrassed for others to see. Let them know why you have nothing to hide!

JESUS IS AWESOME

> *"If my people, who are called by my name, will humble themselves and pray and seek my face and turn from their wicked ways, then I will hear from heaven and forgive their sin…"*
>
> 2 CHRONICLES 7:14

DEVOTION ▼

Pursue Him Wholeheartedly

Sometimes we ignore a scratch or minor cut until it becomes infected and demands our attention. What started as a small wound can suddenly become a life-threatening injury. If we take a few moments to clean and bandage the small cut, we save ourselves time, trouble, and further treatment down the road when it's more serious.

Living a life of repentance requires the same kind of attention to the small sins each day. If we ignore them and don't confess them as soon as we're aware of them, we risk our sins festering into larger problems, addictions, and idols. We will never be perfect and sin-free this side of heaven; however, we can pursue God wholeheartedly and remain diligent to confess our sins each day.

Don't allow a small sin to become a big problem. Today, ask for God's forgiveness, cleansing grace, and healing love.

DAILY INTERACTION ▼

CONNECT: Check in with an accountability partner, someone who knows your areas of struggle and prays for you.

JESUS
IS
AWESOME

> *[Jesus said,] "When you stand praying, if you hold anything against anyone, forgive him, so that your Father in heaven may forgive you your sins."*
>
> MARK 11:25

▼ DEVOTION

Real Grace

It's tempting to blame others when life doesn't work the way we want it to. Whether it's our parents, kids, spouse, siblings, or other family members, we often hold them responsible for holding us back. Sometimes we may pin blame on our supervisor, coworkers, or employees. Many times, these other people in our lives may have offended, injured, or hurt us in some way—that's how they ended up in the bull's-eye of our blame circle.

But Jesus reminds us over and over again that there's a direct correlation between how we handle the offenses of others and how we handle God's grace. If we're not willing to forgive others—let alone quit blaming them for our responses—we're not able to embrace the grace of God. It's not that he withholds it from us based on our unwillingness to forgive; it wouldn't be grace if that were the case.

It's simply that when we experience the fullness of God's forgiveness in our lives, we're eager to forgive others. Real grace is always contagious.

DAILY INTERACTION ▼

CONNECT: Post a favorite verse about God's mercy and grace on the Jesus Daily page. Choose at least three verses posted by others to like.

JESUS IS AWESOME

> *"You will call upon me and come and pray to me, and I will listen to you. You will seek me and find me when you seek me with all your heart."*
> JEREMIAH 29:12–13

DEVOTION ▼

Call upon Him

Ever have one of those days where you seem to keep losing things—your keys, your phone, your wallet or purse, your peace of mind? It's terribly frustrating and inconvenient when we have misplaced something important  to us. We have to retrace our steps and search for the missing item in the obvious places, but more importantly, we must look in the unexpected spot where it will undoubtedly turn up.

Sometimes we may feel as though we've lost our faith or that somehow God is no longer close by us. Like a rudderless ship on a storm-tossed sea, we may feel lost, powerless, untethered from our security.

All you have to do is call out to your Father. He is never far away. He is right here with you right now. When we seek him with all our heart, we discover that he was there all along.

DAILY INTERACTION ▼

👆 **CONNECT:** Post a picture on your personal page or Jesus Daily page that illustrates what it feels like to be lost.

JESUS
IS
AWESOME

> *The Spirit helps us in our weakness. We do not know what we ought to pray for, but the Spirit himself intercedes for us with groans that words cannot express.*
>
> ROMANS 8:26

▼ DEVOTION

The Spirit Knows

Speaking in public remains near the top of popular opinion polls of people's greatest fears. Year after year, the majority of people rank giving a speech or making a presentation as frightening as death, illness, and violence. This includes praying in public.

Praying with other people is certainly an intimate act as you share your hearts before God together. However, even when you're alone and trying to pray, sometimes it's hard to know what to say or how to say it.

Thankfully, we have the Holy Spirit within our hearts, speaking and interceding on our behalf before our Father. Better than any language translator or messenger service, the Spirit can express what we know but can't put into words. We don't have to give a speech or say one word out loud. The Spirit knows.

DAILY INTERACTION ▼

CONNECT: Using a basic cipher method found online, send a coded message to a friend. Think about how this represents the way the Spirit deciphers our hearts before God.

JESUS IS AWESOME

> *"Before they call I will answer;*
> *while they are speaking I will hear."*
> ISAIAH 65:24

DEVOTION ▼

Even Before You Call

"I was just thinking of you," the person on the other end of our phone conversation says. Or, "I was just about to hit SEND when I got your email." Maybe you've even been texting with someone and your texts seem to cross in cyberspace, each answering the other's question before it was asked.

While science fiction presents telepathy and mental powers of mind reading and future telling as normal, it's not. Unless, that is, you're God. He always knows what's on our minds, in our hearts, and ahead of us. We don't have to worry that he won't hear us when we call out to him—he already knows what we need before we do.

You can relax today, knowing that there's nothing you'll face that God has not already known and equipped you to handle.

DAILY INTERACTION ▼

CONNECT: Send an email to a friend, anticipating what they need to hear from God's Word to remind them of his truth.

...in everything, by prayer and petition, with thanksgiving, present your requests to God. And the peace of God, which transcends all understanding, will guard your hearts and minds in Christ Jesus.

PHILIPPIANS 4:6–7

JESUS IS AWESOME

▼ DEVOTION

His Peace

Often we think of peace as a calm, tranquil surface on a body of water. Waves crash, the tide rolls in, and ripples echo across the water most days. But when we experience God's divine peace, we are suddenly still. The surface sparkles like glass, reflecting the dappled sunlight and clouds above.

During the course of our day, we sometimes feel as though we're on a raft hurtling down class-five white-water rapids, about to plunge over a Niagara-sized waterfall. Deadlines get moved up, bosses play favorites, kids get sick, bills pile up. Tempers snap, obstacles pop up, and impossible demands are made. We don't know how we can remain peaceful in the midst of such a tsunami of forces overwhelming us.

But we can. The peace of the Lord is never about the absence of conflict, stress, or problems. The peace of the Lord is about trusting him to guide you through the rapids. His peace not only transcends our understanding, but it guards both our hearts and our minds.

DAILY INTERACTION ▼

CONNECT: Compare video clips online of Niagara Falls to a calm lake. Pass them on to someone who needs to be reminded that God can provide peace in every situation.

> *I call to God, and the LORD saves me. Evening, morning and noon I cry out in distress, and he hears my voice.*
> PSALM 55:16-17

——————————————————————————— DEVOTION ▼ ———

Stop and Pray

During the course of a busy day, we may not have time for lunch or a trip to the bathroom, let alone a prayer time with God. However, once we wind down and the busyness stops, we begin to worry all over again. We anticipate resuming the hectic pace the following day, knowing we must gear up for what's ahead.

This kind of worry creates constant anxiety, which makes it hard to rest and recuperate when we have downtime. Especially when we lie awake in the middle of the night, we play out all kinds of scenarios and fret about what might, could, or should happen.

This is when we must cry out to our Father. And maybe the answer is not waiting until we're sleepless and anxious, but somehow finding a way to slow down and pray to God throughout the day, not just when we can't shut our minds down. Just a few seconds of crying out to our Abba Father every hour or so can make an enormous difference in our lives. When we remember he's in control, we can take a deep breath and relax.

——— DAILY INTERACTION ▼ ———

 CONNECT: Unplug from personal time online and use it to take a nap, meditate on God's Word, pray, or just still your heart before him.

We are God's workmanship, created in Christ Jesus to do good works, which God prepared in advance for us to do.
EPHESIANS 2:10

JESUS IS AWESOME

▼ DEVOTION

His Work in You

The Industrial Revolution transformed the way we create, sell, purchase, and utilize products that once required enormous amounts of time, human effort, and attention to detail. With machines, assembly lines, and now automated computerized mechanisms, we can mass-produce virtually every tangible product—from measuring spoons to cars—for a mass market.

But faith cannot be mass-produced as a one-size-fits-all commodity. Our relationship with Christ is personal, specific, and unique. While it's not subjective and simply based on our feelings, our faith journey is one that is ours and ours alone. We learn from others, we share miles along the way, but we also know that ultimately, God is both our travel guide and fuel source.

The good work he's doing in you probably won't look the same way it looks in someone else, and certainly not at the same pace. Today you can enjoy the ride, knowing that even when the road gets bumpy, God is doing his good work in your life.

DAILY INTERACTION ▼

CONNECT: Plan a "virtual road trip" with a group of friends. Schedule a time when you can all video conference or chat online, sharing what God is doing in your lives.

JESUS IS AWESOME

The LORD will fulfill his purpose for me; your love, O LORD, endures forever—do not abandon the works of your hands.

PSALM 138:8

DEVOTION ▼

Never-ending Love

In many cities, you can find a number of buildings that have been abandoned. Broken windows, graffiti messages, and vacant echoes all testify to the sense of failure, loss, and abandonment. The prior owner could not care for the property or chose not to maintain it, for whatever reason, and now the dilapidated structure decays day by day.

Of course, buildings aren't the only things that suffer from abandonment. Homes, careers, and relationships may not show the same visible symptoms of decline as a tenement in the inner city, but the emotional scars remain just as fresh.

God not only heals and restores those wounds, but he has promised never to abandon us. He will not allow us to remain alone, suffering from neglect, decaying from lack of loving attention. He is our Father, and he loves us more than we can ever realize. We will never be orphaned—*never*—not with a Dad who loves us so much.

DAILY INTERACTION ▼

CONNECT: Visit JesusDaily.com and remind someone who's struggling that they are not alone.

> *Make it your ambition to lead a quiet life, to mind
> your own business and to work with your hands.*
>
> 1 Thessalonians 4:11

▼ DEVOTION

A Quiet Life

When we think of someone being ambitious, we tend to imagine a competitive, driven individual who let's nothing get in their way to accomplish their goals and achieve the success they so obviously desire. From having your fifteen minutes in the spotlight to being a leader in your field, ambitious people like to be out in front of the pack, the star of the show.

Rarely if ever do we think about someone's ambition being "to lead a quiet life." And yet, as we follow the example set by Jesus, we know that fulfillment in this life is not about glorifying ourselves or inflating our egos. It's not about how much money we make or how many goals we set and attain. It's about how we love.

When we're devoted to loving and serving our Father and his kingdom, our ambition is centered on his goals, not our own. We may still be in the spotlight, the leader's role, or a place of prominence, but the difference is that we're not defined by it. As stewards of God's blessings, and not entitled, self-made success stories, we achieve something glorious for eternity, not temporary for our own benefit.

DAILY INTERACTION ▼

 CONNECT: Share your life goals with someone online and offer to pray for each other.

📅 **May 27**

*Better a dry crust with peace and quiet
than a house full of feasting, with strife.*
PROVERBS 17:1

DEVOTION ▼

What's Missing?

Historians tell us that we live in one of the most affluent times in all of history. Living in such abundance, many people still aren't satisfied. We have enough food, clothes, homes, and cars, but not enough peace, joy, security, and love. Ironically, though, we still seem to look for fulfillment in the pursuit of more money, status-worthy possessions, and more prestigious titles.

For most people, this only produces more stress, anxiety, and burdens of responsibility. Which in turn reinforces what's missing—true satisfaction, the peace that comes from serving something larger than yourself, and the grace of the Lord.

Perhaps what you long for cannot be found in another gadget, app, designer label, or purchase. Maybe you need fewer possessions and more peace. Today, search your heart for what's missing in your life.

DAILY INTERACTION ▼

 CONNECT: Post at least one usable item to give away on a site where people shop for secondhand items.

> *"The LORD will fight for you;*
> *you need only to be still."*
>
> EXODUS 14:14

He Fights for You

We often admire people who don't give up easily and are willing to stand up and fight for what they believe. We appreciate their tenacity, strength, and resilience as they oppose other people and groups who take them on. At some point or another, everyone must stand up for themselves and what they believe.

However, too often we fight when we don't need to do so. Instead of trying to make things happen for ourselves, we can relax and allow God to open the door ahead of us. We don't have to battle everyone we encounter, assuming the worst and overcoming everything we face.

Sometime we have to realize the power that comes from being still. We have to quit fighting and trying to make things happen on our own and allow God to fight for us and make things happen. We're not alone, and we don't have to face life by ourselves.

Today, let your Father win the battle for you.

 CONNECT: Encourage someone to stop fighting their battle and let God overcome their obstacles instead.

I have stilled and quieted my soul; like a weaned child with its mother, like a weaned child is my soul within me.
PSALM 131:2

DEVOTION ▼

Maturing in the Faith

Many people refuse to become who God made them to be because they won't grow up. They would rather remain limited in their development than risk failing and growing stronger. Even when we're willing to grow and mature, we may still fear change. It's scary to move forward into the unknown, blazing a trail into unfamiliar territory.

Although change is scary, remaining a nursing child forever is even more frightening. We would be appalled to see a twelve-year-old still nursing. We would be disgusted to see an adult throwing a temper tantrum like a two-year-old. In the same way, we must be willing to grow, mature, and be weaned from the childish things of the past.

Our Father wants us to become adults, not remain babies. While we are indeed his children, dependent on him for all we have, we also have a responsibility to mature and serve him in the fullness of our gifts.

DAILY INTERACTION ▼

 CONNECT: Ask someone you trust and respect for some honest feedback on your life. Discuss areas where they see you failing to live up to your full potential.

> *Surely, O LORD, you bless the righteous;*
> *you surround them with your favor as with a shield.*
>
> PSALM 5:12

▼ DEVOTION

Receive His Words

As a father loves taking his kids to the park to play, God just enjoys spending time with us. He's seen our work and activity for him, and he appreciates it, but he wants to give something to us that no one else can—time alone with him. Restoration. In the quiet moments, he comes to us and, in ways we do not understand, he pours himself into us and we are refreshed.

There are many ways we encounter such refreshment. We can focus on his love poured out for us on the cross. We can sit quietly at his feet or imagine ourselves in his lap as he tells us how precious we are to him. We can remember that he has forgiven all of our sins and doesn't hold any of it against us or even remember them. We can focus on these truths and many more in his Word. He gives us many gifts and has placed them strategically in our paths to remind us of his love.

When we need it most, God will often come to us in ways we do not understand and whisper, "I love you. You are mine. I enjoy you. Nothing will take you away from me. You do not have to earn my love."

Today, receive his words, look for his gifts, and open your heart to him.

DAILY INTERACTION ▼

 CONNECT: Post a verse that expresses God's love for you in a special, personal way. Ask others to share their own special favorites.

> *Pleasant words are a honeycomb, sweet to the soul*
> *and healing to the bones.*
> PROVERBS 16:24

———————————————————————————— DEVOTION ▼ ——————

Gracious Words

As children, we enjoyed our favorite candy as a special treat. Whether it was gummy bears or chocolate bars, peanut butter cups or licorice twists, we delighted in the burst of sweetness—and the spike of sugar in our system—until the next special occasion.

As adults, we still look forward to special treats. From gourmet toffee to fresh berry pies, it's hard to pass up a delicious dessert. We may have more sophisticated palates now, but the sweet taste remains the same.

Gracious words have the same impact as that first bite of our favorite treat. Flavorful, juicy, and sweet, they have the power to heal grudges, solve problems, and encourage another weary soul.

What you say matters. Today, use your words carefully, sharing their sweet flavor wherever you go.

—————— **DAILY** INTERACTION ▼ ——————————————————————

 CONNECT: Post a description of your favorite sweet treat or dessert at JesusDaily.com and ask others to share their own.

JUNE

He who is kind to the poor lends to the LORD,
and he will reward him for what he has done.

Proverbs 19:17

📅 June 1

> *So then, just as you received Christ Jesus as Lord, continue to live in him, rooted and built up in him, strengthened in the faith as you were taught, and overflowing with thankfulness.*
>
> COLOSSIANS 2:6–7

Soul Care

When a garden has been well planned, well tended, and maintained, it becomes a work of art. And it obviously requires work. Young trees have to be staked so they grow strong and tall, undeterred by the forces of wind and rain. Hedges must be trimmed and shaped rather than allowed to grow at odd angles. Flower beds require weeding to make sure that only the desired blooms receive the nourishment the soil has to offer. Gardeners know their tasks produce health, beauty, and fruit in the plants and trees they're devoted to nurturing.

Our Christian faith requires the same kind of attention. We need nourishment from God's Word, the light of his presence, and the Living Water of Christ's love. We also need pruning from time to time, straightening and correcting. We must weed out temptations and harmful influences that would pull us away from our first love.

As every gardener knows, their craft requires daily practices. Today, make sure that you're tending your soul with all that it needs to flourish and bloom.

CONNECT: Send an e-card with a pic of your favorite flower or plant to someone who needs encouragement. Or order a floral arrangement for delivery to them.

> *And whatever you do, whether in word or deed,*
> *do it all in the name of the Lord Jesus,*
> *giving thanks to God the Father through him.*
>
> COLOSSIANS 3:17

▼ DEVOTION

In Word or Deed

Does what you do during the course of your day match the words you speak during that same day? Does what you say align with what you're actually doing? As followers of Jesus, we all want to "walk the talk" and not just give lip service to our faith. But, to put a fine point on it, this is easier said than done!

Words can flow easily, almost effortlessly at times. We tell people what they want to hear and get on with our day. Problem solved, issue sorted, and case closed. And yet, do our words reflect the grace of God and the truth of his Word? And does our behavior match our message?

It's easy to say one thing and do another. The real evidence of our commitment to following Jesus emerges in the synchronicity between our speech and our actions. Today, let your Christlike actions speak louder than anything you say.

DAILY INTERACTION ▼

 CONNECT: With your discretionary time, stay offline today. Instead, perform an act of service for someone in need.

> *Let your conversation be always full of grace, seasoned with salt, so that you may know how to answer everyone.*
> COLOSSIANS 4:6

—————————————————————————————— DEVOTION ▼ ——————

Spicy Words

While the right words at the right time can be as sweet as honey, they must also include a little spice. Without seasoning, most foods would remain bland and flavorless. Salt brings out the flavor in virtually everything—meat, bread, soup, crackers, even sweets such as salted caramels.

Grace-filled conversations are the same way. They're not only sweet tasting but flavorful and challenging, with just enough of an edge to inspire, encourage, and motivate. When we speak the truth of God's love and mercy, we're seasoning and bringing out the life-changing flavor of the gospel.

When our speech is both sweet and salty, we offer a message to those around us that's irresistible.

—————— **DAILY** INTERACTION ▼ ——————————————————

 CONNECT: Visit JesusDaily.com and offer a flavorful message of hope and truth to a fellow Christian.

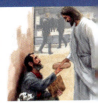

Do everything without complaining or arguing,
so that you may become blameless and pure …

PHILIPPIANS 2:14–15

▼ DEVOTION

Serve Gladly

We've all done things that had to be done while making sure the people around us knew how we felt about it. Whether a menial chore at home or drudging work at the office, we do it, but we also want everyone else to notice us, feel sorry for us, or admire us. Maybe we talk the whole time we're doing it, calling attention to ourselves and the great sacrifice we're making.

These moments do not glorify God or reflect his generous, loving character. When we grumble, complain, whine, and bicker, we're allowing opportunities for strife, competition, comparison, and bitterness to creep in. We're focusing on our own comfort and selfish desires more than serving others with a Christlike spirit.

Today, let everything you do be done as if doing it for the Lord. Whether answering an email, filing a report, placing an order, caring for children, or leading a team, do it the way Jesus would do it, humbly and confidently.

DAILY INTERACTION ▼

CONNECT: Go on a message board or respond to a post and rather than criticize or complain, find something to praise or someone to encourage.

Restore to me the joy of your salvation and grant me a willing spirit, to sustain me.

PSALM 51:12

DEVOTION ▼

Drink the Living Water

In warm weather, we have to make sure we stay hydrated. We perspire more than we realize in the hot temperatures, and the heat takes a toll on our bodies. We expend more energy doing basic, everyday functions such as walking, running, and working. We need water to stay alive, and sometimes we need more water just to maintain a healthy body.

We need a regular dose of God's grace just as our bodies need water to survive. When we confess our sins, the Lord tells us that he's merciful and quick to forgive, removing our transgressions from us as far as east is from west. We experience the refreshment of spirit that comes from knowing we've been made clean and pure, not by any of our own efforts but totally by the grace of our Father.

Today, make sure your soul stays hydrated with the grace of God. Tell him what's troubling you and ask for his forgiveness for your sins. Drink in the Living Water of his mercy and kindness.

DAILY INTERACTION ▼

 CONNECT: Provide a drink of Living Water to someone online today, sharing with them a verse, an insight, or an answered prayer from this week.

> *Cleanse me with hyssop, and I will be clean; wash me, and*
> *I will be whiter than snow. Let me hear joy and gladness…*
> *Hide your face from my sins and blot out all my iniquity.*
>
> PSALM 51:7–9

▼ DEVOTION

Let It Snow

Unless you live in high mountains or the southern hemisphere, you're probably not accustomed to seeing snow in June. However, when we confess our sins before the Lord and ask for his forgiveness, we can know the clean, white freshness of snowfall within our hearts all year round.

When we harbor sin in our lives, we begin to feel weary, dirty, and burdened by the weight of our own selfishness. Left to our own devices, we can try to make amends, read self-improvement books, and justify our mistakes. But only God can forgive us and make us new again. Only he can wash us clean and make us feel as beautiful as a muddy field blanketed by snow looks.

Spend some time confessing your sins before the Lord, asking him to let it snow in your heart.

DAILY INTERACTION ▼

 CONNECT: Message someone who needs a little "snow" in their lives and encourage them to seek the Lord's forgiveness for their sins.

 June 7

The sacrifices of God are a broken spirit; a broken and contrite heart, O God, you will not despise.

PSALM 51:17

A Fresh Start

Appliances stop working, phones die, cars get totaled, and furniture needs new upholstery and paint. Often it's easier and more cost-efficient to discard something broken and purchase it new rather than invest the time and money into repairing the old. Why bother with the inconvenience of fixing a broken coffeemaker when you can toss it in the trash and buy a new one for the price of a few pounds of coffee?

People, however, cannot be thrown away and discarded. While others may judge us or we them, it's often our own condemnation, fueled by the enemy's accusations, that blocks our restoration. Sometimes we despise our brokenness and hate feeling so weak and defeated. We wish we had the power to control our lives and make things work the way we want them to work. We wish we could abandon our old self and have a fresh start.

With God, this is exactly what we get. He has promised to never abandon or forsake us. He is committed to forgiving our sins, healing our wounds, and blessing us with an abundant life.

 CONNECT: Offer to repair something that someone else has broken, whether it is a kitchen appliance or a promise.

> *For physical training is of some value, but godliness has value for all things, holding promise for both the present life and the life to come.*
>
> 1 Timothy 4:8

Spiritual Exercises

You can't scroll through a browser home page without seeing at least one or two articles on diet, exercise, healthy living, and longevity. People want to feel better by losing weight, performing cardio and weight training exercises, and getting enough rest. These endeavors all increase our quality of life, but on average they also extend our years on earth. Most of us want to live longer, to enjoy our health as long as possible into old age well beyond retirement.

While these pursuits promote good physical health, our spiritual exercises not only improve our life now but in the eternal hereafter. We're not simply praying, studying God's Word, worshipping, and serving others out of obedience, but because of the change that's taking place in us as we grow deeper in love with God. Through our spiritual training, our faith becomes stronger and our impact greater for our Father's kingdom. We become more like Christ, giving all we can give to those around us.

Today, make your spiritual exercise be just as rigorous as any physical exercise.

 CONNECT: Share a favorite verse from the Psalms today that expresses what you're feeling in your relationship with God.

Don't let anyone look down on you because you are young, but set an example for the believers in speech, in conduct, in love, in faith and in purity.
1 Timothy 4:12

DEVOTION ▾

Set an Example

Whether it's a new job, a new role, or a new team, we all like to be recognized for our contribution to our organization's success. We want to be welcomed, accepted, and appreciated for our ability to improve productivity, boost morale, and solve problems.

In a new position, however, it's often challenging to prove yourself. You don't want to talk too much and appear as if you don't value listening. But you don't want to come across as quiet and reserved, or worse, aloof. You want to demonstrate your abilities without appearing to be arrogant or overconfident.

Most leaders agree that the best way to show your value to your coworkers, friends, and peers is to lead by example. Communication is important and cannot be ignored. But what you do speaks louder than what you say. Others will be watching to see if the two match, but more importantly, they'll be learning what motivates you.

Today, show others how you are empowered by God to strive for excellence in all that you do.

DAILY INTERACTION ▾

 CONNECT: Send an email of encouragement to a younger friend, student, or new Christian, offering to help them in any way you can.

But godliness with contentment is great gain. For we brought nothing into the world, and we can take nothing out of it. But if we have food and clothing, we will be content with that.

1 TIMOTHY 6:6–8

▼ DEVOTION

An Attitude of Gratitude

Most of us need far less than we have to survive. We're blessed to have homes, food, heating and cooling, electricity, and clothing. And even though our culture often encourages us to accumulate material possessions and wealth, the reality remains the same for all of us. When we die and our mortal bodies expire, we cannot take anything with us—not one dollar, donut, or designer handbag. We entered the world without any possessions, and we will leave it the same way.

With this awareness before us, we can once again be reminded to take nothing for granted. Everything we have is a gift of God. He asks us to be stewards, not owners, and to enjoy his blessings without being consumed by them. When we maintain this openhanded attitude of gratitude, we take nothing for granted.

Today, notice the many blessings that you typically take for granted—things such as clean water, fresh food, a warm bed, and people who love you.

DAILY INTERACTION ▼

CONNECT: Go to JesusDaily.com and post a running list of items for which you're especially grateful today and invite others to add to it.

For the love of money is a root of all kinds of evil. Some people, eager for money, have wandered from the faith and pierced themselves with many griefs.

1 Timothy 6:10

DEVOTION ▼

The Love of Money

When a weed takes root in your garden, it drains nutrients in the soil away from other plants, such as flowers or vegetables. Many weeds often bind themselves around the roots of other plants to anchor themselves into the soil deeper. They not only choke off the other plants, but they also secure themselves into the ground. Eventually, they replace the flower and its natural systems of survival with their own roots, shoots, and tendrils.

The love and pursuit of money can be an enormous weed in our spiritual garden. With thorns that entrap you and greed that grows like dandelions, desire for wealth can block your vision, disrupt your path, and kill your heart. There's nothing you can save, buy, or spend that you can take with you for eternity. Only the fruit of the Spirit that you cultivate now will last.

Spend time today tending your spiritual garden, eliminating the weed of greed.

DAILY INTERACTION ▼

 CONNECT: Make a donation to your church, a charity, or a ministry today, something more than just your usual tithe.

> *A heart at peace gives life to the body,*
> *but envy rots the bones.*
> PROVERBS 14:30

▼ DEVOTION

No Comparison

Movies, TV shows, and advertisements all encourage us to compare ourselves to the actors, celebrities, and models we see. Needless to say, without stylists, designer clothes, and Photoshop, we come up short. We feel dissatisfied with our lives and wonder what's missing. Inevitably, we make a new purchase or at least face the temptation to buy something that will help us feel better about ourselves.

Similarly, whenever we surf Facebook or personal pages, we're tempted to compare. Everyone looks so happy and successful in their pictures as they travel to exotic places, meet other successful people, and generally enjoy an amazing life. Their families appear happy and healthy, eager to be together and enjoy one another's company.

Our lives can't compare, nor should they. These are fantasies—either projected by people trying to make money off our envy and insecurities or by our own imagination.

God provides everything you need. Today, don't lose sight of what you have by focusing on what you don't.

DAILY INTERACTION ▼

 CONNECT: Write an email to someone whom you envy, telling them what you envy about them. It may be wise to not send it.

And God is able to make all grace abound to you, so that in all things at all times, having all that you need, you will abound in every good work.
2 CORINTHIANS 9:8

DEVOTION ▾

Fully Equipped

It's difficult to sew a garment, build a cabinet, or repair an engine without the proper tools. From tailor's shears to a jigsaw, from a socket wrench to a sewing machine, the right tools save time and energy and provide workers with maximum efficiency.

While we may not always feel as prepared as we would like to tackle a problem or minister to others, God always equips us with what we need. Sometimes this may require us to be resourceful, creative, and innovative, which in itself is part of his plan. But we never have to feel insecure or fearful of doing what he asks because we don't have the right tools.

You're equipped with all you need to fulfill God's purposes today.

DAILY INTERACTION ▾

 CONNECT: Post a brief description of your favorite online tool or resource and why you like it.

> *Teach me to do your will, for you are my God;*
> *may your good Spirit lead me on level ground.*
>
> PSALM 143:10

▼ DEVOTION

A Level Path

Climbing hills is hard work. If you've ever attempted a steep incline while hiking, let alone climbed a mountain, you know how challenging it can be. Your calves ache, your legs hurt, your hips become tired from leaning your body forward to maintain balance. Going downhill is easier in the sense that gravity can assist you; however, the toll on your body, especially your knees, is even greater.

Level ground, of course, provides us with an even and balanced surface upon which to walk or run. We don't have to work harder to climb up or down. We don't have to exert extra energy to overcome obstacles in our path.

God's way is on level ground. He leads us by the route that will take us on the journey for which we've been equipped. There will still be some bumps in the road and the occasional detour, but we won't have to climb over mountains either. Whether we're facing a mountain or molehill, the Lord has gone before us and made a way through it.

DAILY INTERACTION ▼

 CONNECT: Chat or video conference with a friend and plan a walk, run, or short hike together later this month.

 June 15

If you have any encouragement from being united with Christ, if any comfort from his love … make my joy complete by being like-minded, having the same love, being one in spirit and purpose.

PHILIPPIANS 2:1–2

Community

So often tragedy is what unifies us these days. With violence in our schools and public places, with natural disasters wreaking havoc, and with terrible crimes claiming lives, we come together to mourn, grieve, and regroup. Sometimes we band together to take action and prevent the calamity from happening again. Other times we simply unite in order to serve, restore, and rebuild.

While unity born of tragedy helps us survive and recover, we don't have to wait until there's a shared loss to come together as community. We can show the love of Christ to one another without any reason other than exercising our joyful, obedient heart.

When we are one in spirit and unified in shared beliefs, we become stronger than any one individual. God is among us and promises to bless us with his presence. We can meet one another's needs and experience the transformation that comes from both giving and receiving.

 CONNECT: Find a group online that shares your faith in Christ and serves others in some significant way.

"Come, follow me," Jesus said, "and I will make you fishers of men." At once they left their nets and followed him.

MATTHEW 4:19–20

▼ DEVOTION

Good Fishing

You don't have to send a money order for a product advertised on late-night cable TV to know that some items you buy aren't the same as what was promised in the commercial. What looked solid, sturdy, technologically advanced, and efficient in the ad seems flimsy, cheap, and time-consuming in actuality.

It's a classic example of what's often called "bait and switch." One thing is promised but something else of lesser value is substituted and delivered. And late-night infomercials are not the only ones to use such a tactic. Politicians, corporate leaders, and retail websites have also been known to use this less-than-ethical practice of dangling a carrot but delivering a stone.

God never uses the "bait and switch" technique in his relationship with us. In fact, it's just the opposite. When we accept the gift of salvation and accept Christ into our hearts, we get more than we ever imagined—an abundant life of purpose and joy in this life and eternal life with God in heaven later.

— DAILY INTERACTION ▼

 CONNECT: Write an email to someone who does not know the Lord. Share the gospel with them in a way that makes God's grace clear and relevant.

> *And now, dear children, continue in him,*
> *so that when he appears we may be confident*
> *and unashamed before him at his coming.*
>
> 1 John 2:28

A Faith That Fits

When clothes shrink, they no longer fit us properly. Maybe we washed a delicate fabric in warm water or maybe the garment just wasn't made very well. Regardless, when something becomes smaller in size, it's hard to wear, ill-fitting, and uncomfortable.

When our faith shrinks, it also feels too small for the challenges we're facing in life. Our doubts poke through the fabric and tear at the seams of what we believe and hold dear. Our losses and disappointments create tight bands that squeeze our commitment to God like a too-small waistband.

The only way we can survive the trials and triumphs of life is with a faith that fits. Such a tailor-made garment requires daily attention. We must invest in our relationship with our Father if we expect to persevere through hard times and trust him. It's difficult to trust someone you don't know.

Don't let your faith shrink. Invest in it today by spending time in prayer and Bible study with the Lord.

 CONNECT: Look for an online Bible study or commentary to supplement the verse above or another passage of Scripture you've been studying.

> *... whatever is true, whatever is noble, whatever is right, whatever is pure, whatever is lovely, whatever is admirable—if anything is excellent and praiseworthy—think about such things.*
>
> PHILIPPIANS 4:8

▼ DEVOTION

Good Things

With so many graphic, violent images in our lives today, it's no wonder that we often feel anxious and afraid. From video games to cop shows, from advertisements to news stories, we are bombarded with physical pain, human suffering, and disturbing images.

Now more than ever, we must practice the only remedy for our souls: the truth of God's Word, the beauty of his creation, and time alone with him. Once an image is in our minds, we cannot remove it. We can try and forget it, but it's still inside us. The only way we can overcome our fear, concern, and shock is to submit it to the Lord.

Today, dwell on the good things that God is doing around you. Meditate on his Word and the powerful, positive transformation he is working in your life. Celebrate the wonderful ways he is providing for people in need, healing the sick, and comforting the lonely.

DAILY INTERACTION ▼

 CONNECT: Visit JesusDaily.com and ask others to share some of the exciting, wonderful things God is currently doing in their lives.

> *"You have heard that it was said, 'Love your neighbor and hate your enemy.' But I tell you: Love your enemies and pray for those who persecute you."*
>
> MATTHEW 5:43–44

DEVOTION ▼

Love Your Enemies

Often we have a hard time thinking of people in our lives who are our enemies. Perhaps this is due in part to the fact that we tend to think of enemies as villains, criminals, and evil people who are intent on harming us. Darth Vader, Voldemort, and orcs are easy to hate on the page or onscreen. Rarely are our real-life villains so clear-cut and identifiable.

In fact, we must realize that our enemies may simply be people who are hostile or unfriendly toward us. These everyday enemies may simply be caught up in their own selfish agendas, personal competitions, and petty vendettas. In this sense, the rude waiter, manipulative coworker, and gossipy neighbor may be our enemy as well. These people need to experience God's love as much as any hardened criminal.

Today, show the love of Christ to someone who does not treat you with kindness.

DAILY INTERACTION ▼

 CONNECT: Message someone who demonstrates the heart of Jesus toward others and tell them how much you can see Jesus through what they do.

> *For through him we both have access*
> *to the Father by one Spirit.*
> EPHESIANS 2:18

▼ DEVOTION

All the Time

While technology now permits us to call, email, text, and video conference with one another around the world and even in space, we may not be able to contact everyone we wish to contact. World leaders, celebrities, actors, and corporate CEOs usually have filters in place to ensure that not just anyone can access them directly. If not, their fans, followers, friends as well as opportunists would constantly bombard them with messages.

The only One who truly deserves such a level of authority and privilege has done just the opposite. God makes himself available and accessible to everyone, everywhere and anytime, 24/7/365. We don't need to go through his staff members, personal assistant, or levels of bureaucracy to talk with him directly.

God allows us to speak with him directly. We do not have to make an appointment or call ahead. He's eager and waiting to talk with us, anytime and all the time.

DAILY INTERACTION ▼

CONNECT: Choose a prominent person you admire or follow and try to email or call them. Consider what you will say or ask them in case you should get through!

 June 21

"But you will receive power when the Holy Spirit comes on you; and you will be my witnesses in Jerusalem, and in all Judea and Samaria, and to the ends of the earth."
ACTS 1:8

Share Your Story

Eyewitnesses to crimes, natural disasters, and spectacular events have more credibility than anyone else when reporting on what they've seen. Others may have factual data, secondhand speculation, and descriptive commentary. But witnesses provide firsthand, direct, and personal accounts of what they've encountered.

When we share our faith with other people, we do so as witnesses who have firsthand experience in what we're talking about. While we include factual information and biblical truth, it's clear that our motivation comes from the change we ourselves have experienced.

When you use a new product for the first time and love it, you can't wait to tell others to try it, too. How much more excited and deliberate we should be in wanting to share the most significant life-changing news we have—the grace of God through the gift of Christ!

 CONNECT: Connect with another believer and share what you've seen God do most recently in each of your lives.

Love is patient, love is kind…
1 Corinthians 13:4

▼ DEVOTION

Patience and Kindness

Someone makes a gift for you—perhaps a painting, sweater, or chair—and spends weeks and months sketching, knitting, and building it. Their familiarity with you ensures that you can use their gift, but their personal investment in it ensures that you will love it. They have put time, energy, heart and soul into creating something. They didn't just spend money on this special gift; they invested themselves into every detail.

This is the kind of love we see Christ demonstrating—magnified many times over, of course. He knew that patience without kindness doesn't have much invested. And kindness without patience may not be able to give at the right times. However, when patience and kindness come together, love is demonstrated.

Today, infuse your patience with kindness for those around you. Demonstrate the kind of mature love that we see in the life of Christ, the kind Paul describes in 1 Corinthians 13.

DAILY INTERACTION ▼

 CONNECT: Post an illustration or picture that depicts patience and kindness working together.

For you died, and your life is now hidden with Christ in God.
COLOSSIANS 3:3

— DEVOTION ▼ —

Trials into Trophies

When we accept Christ into our lives and follow him, our sins are forgiven and our past is buried. However, we often continue living as if our past struggles still have power over us. Like some monster in a story or movie, our mistakes come back to life and seem to refuse to stay buried. So we keep trying to suppress them, deny them, and keep them underground—only to find ourselves struggling with them a short time later.

Instead of considering our past mistakes and sinful choices as something hideous that we must kill and bury, perhaps we would do better to rethink how we look at things. What if you viewed your past offenses as seeds of redemption, bulbs to be planted in the soil of grace and watered by the love of the Father? You don't have to keep burying seeds and bulbs; you do it once and then wait for them to push through the soil and bring new life. The flowers, buds, and branches that result look nothing like the seeds and bulbs from which they sprang.

God is doing something beautiful from your past. You don't have to run from your old mistakes. You only have to turn them over to the Lord and let him transform them.

— DAILY INTERACTION ▼ —

 CONNECT: Email and encourage someone who's struggling by sharing a way God has redeemed something from your past.

> *"I have swept away your offenses like a cloud,*
> *your sins like the morning mist.*
> *Return to me, for I have redeemed you."*
>
> Isaiah 44:22

▼ DEVOTION

Redeemed

Regardless of where you live, you've probably experienced some dramatic changes in weather. Residents of many places often joke that they experience all four seasons in a given day. "If you don't like the weather," they often say, "just wait an hour and see if you like it then." From clear to cloudy, from warm to cool, from sunshine to rainy, the atmosphere seems in constant flux, keeping us guessing about what to expect in the elements.

While weather patterns frequently and rapidly change, God's mercy and forgiveness are permanent. When he sweeps your sins away like a cloud or mist, we can know that it's forever, not just until the next cold front moves through.

We don't have to carry our sins, guilt, shame, and regret around with us. Like chalk drawings on a sidewalk, they dissolve when the cleansing rain washes them away. God is always willing to forgive and restore us. No matter what season, rain or shine.

DAILY INTERACTION ▼

 CONNECT: Connect with a friend in another part of the world and compare your weather with theirs. Share with them how grateful you are that God's love never changes.

> *Therefore, there is now no condemnation for those who are in Christ Jesus.*
> ROMANS 8:1

———— DEVOTION ▼ ————

Forgive Yourself

Condemned buildings and houses usually sit vacant, decaying and falling into further disrepair, waiting until they can be destroyed or demolished. Such sites are eyesores, blemished shadows of their former glory when they were new, strong, firm, and freshly painted.

Too often we treat ourselves like a building that's been condemned instead of like a home that has been renovated and restored. God forgives us, loves us, and brings new life. What's old has passed away; he is doing a new thing in us. But often we create an enormous challenge for ourselves simply because we're not willing to forgive ourselves even though God has.

Our standard is surely not higher than God's, is it? No, his standard is holiness. And through the gift of his Son, Jesus, our Father provided the ultimate firm foundation for our faith.

———— DAILY INTERACTION ▼ ————

CONNECT: Go to JesusDaily.com and check in with a trusted friend or accountability partner regarding an area of struggle in your life.

He who is kind to the poor lends to the Lord,
and he will reward him for what he has done.

PROVERBS 19:17

▼ DEVOTION

Pass It On

God constantly provides for our needs. And he allows us to participate in this process by helping one another, sharing what we've been given with those around us. When we allow our lives to be conduits of blessings and not storage containers, we constantly experience more blessings to replace the ones we're giving away and passing on to other people. Any container, no matter how big, has limitations. Eventually, it gets full and cannot hold anymore.

A conduit, passageway, or channel, however, transports what it carries. It was never intended to hold and store its contents. Whether electricity, water, or internet data, conduits transfer their material and remain active, dynamic, and highly functional. Containers, on the other hand, can become stagnant, inert, and inoperable.

It's not that we share what we have with others to get something else. It's that the process of giving blesses us as much as receiving it in the first place. Conduits run in both directions. Containers don't.

DAILY INTERACTION ▼

 CONNECT: Introduce someone new to the Jesus Daily page. Share with them why you enjoy it so much and how God has used it to bless you.

📅 June 27

[Jesus said,] "Do not let your hearts be troubled.
Trust in God; trust also in me."
JOHN 14:1

— DEVOTION ▼ —

Choose to Trust

Sometimes we forget how much control we have over the state of our hearts. Jesus told us not to let our hearts be troubled. He didn't say not to feel what you feel or to ignore your problems. He said to trust him. It's not as though we can flip a switch and make our hearts carefree and unburdened, but we can decide not to dwell on our problems and worries. We can decide to trust him and take the next step, whatever that may be.

When we dwell on our worries, we accomplish nothing other than preventing our hearts from experiencing God's peace. If we choose to trust him, our feelings will follow the path of our thoughts. We can't flip a switch and make our troubles go away or change our emotions. But we can control how we react and the choices we make in response to our circumstances.

Today, when you're tempted to worry, make a choice to trust God with whatever is causing your concern.

— DAILY INTERACTION ▼ —

 CONNECT: Post a request for others to share their go-to verses when they're struggling with anxiety.

Our light and momentary troubles are achieving for us an eternal glory that far outweighs them all.

2 CORINTHIANS 4:17

▼ DEVOTION

The Birthing Process

Mothers undergo enormous physical discomfort for around nine months in order to bring a baby into this world. At times, their suffering escalates to excruciating pain that feels unbearable. They can't sleep comfortably, can't eat normally, and can't move at the same pace they once did. And as their baby grows inside them and develops, the mother's pain and inconvenience only increases up until labor and delivery.

Often we can't see what God is birthing in our lives. We only know that we're struggling with new challenges and unexpected obstacles. Changes occur that we don't know how to accept. So we have to grow into them and trust God each step along the way.

We may be uncomfortable and inconvenienced by our circumstances, but we must never forget that God is creating something that we cannot always see.

DAILY INTERACTION ▼

 CONNECT: Assure someone who's facing heartache that their suffering has meaning.

The Lord knows how to rescue godly men from trials.
2 PETER 2:9

Life's Whys

Often when we're facing a trial in our lives, we ask, "Why? Why did this happen to me? Why now? What's the purpose of this?" Sometimes we get so caught up in focusing on why something happened that we lose sight of how to push through it.

We may never know exactly why certain things happen in this life. Nonetheless, we have to trust God—even when it makes no sense whatsoever. We struggle with our faith sometimes because we like to think we're reasonable, intelligent, logical people. We're well informed, educated, and technologically—and scientifically—advanced. We're used to finding answers and having them follow a kind of pattern or logic.

However, in matters of faith, we're often forced to suspend our insistence on understanding and instead embrace our trust in the Lord. That may feel fragile or even flimsy at times, and other people will not always understand, but when we have a relationship with God, we know his character, his heart, and his goodness. He loves us. He hurts with us. And he rescues us. Even if it's not the way we want him to.

CONNECT: Call or video conference with a family member who lives far away and needs to be reminded of the bond you share.

There will be a time for every activity,
a time for every deed.

ECCLESIASTES 3:17

▼ DEVOTION

Surprises

I t's amazing how differently most days go than what we expected. We set appointments and schedule meetings, pencil in calls on our calendars, and follow routines, itineraries, and agendas. But life, other people, and God remain surprisingly unpredictable. While his character, power, and mercy remain the same now and forever, the way our Father interacts with us often requires him to surprise us.

We think we know how to manage our time and what to expect with each day, each week, each month and season of our lives. But the truth is that only God knows the best time for everything and everyone. We can plan all we want as long as we rely on God's timing to intercede.

We would save ourselves a lot of frustration if we didn't try to control the time we're given each day. Today, allow God to guide you according to his schedule and not your own.

— **DAILY** INTERACTION ▼

 CONNECT: Swap stories with a fellow believer at JesusDaily. com about the way you've seen God's timing in the recent past.

July

Consider the blameless, observe the upright;
there is a future for the man of peace.

Psalm 37:37

For a thousand years in your sight are like a day that has just gone by, or like a watch in the night.
PSALM 90:4

DEVOTION ▾

In His Time

Do you ever feel as though you don't *get* time? Some weeks are over before you know it, and other weeks seem to contain two or three Wednesdays. You can remember your fifth birthday party with the pony rides in vivid detail, but last Christmas seems so long ago. Time may be a measurement, but it will never give us a complete picture of our lives.

God sees all time at once. He knows every moment as Now. There is no such thing as being late in God's timeline. Everything is happening exactly when it should, at the perfect time. He sees the "big picture"—past, present, and future all at once. We will never understand this, but can we trust this? God gives us opportunities to trust him every day, to believe that he has everything under control and nothing happens by accident. He uses everything in our lives, even time, to let us know that He has a plan for us. He gives us everything in its time.

The next time you are stuck in traffic and it's making you late, trust God enough to say, "This is perfect."

DAILY INTERACTION ▾

 CONNECT: Keep a record in your journal of the times when God gives you exactly what you need in his perfect timing.

> *[Jesus said,] "Watch out! Be on your guard against all kinds of greed; a man's life does not consist in the abundance of his possessions."*
>
> Luke 12:15

▼ DEVOTION

Be on Your Guard

We've all heard the joke about the hearse with the U-Haul trailer behind it. The punch line, "You can't take it with you," is a message that when you're gone, it doesn't matter about the wealth you've attained in your life. What will the measurement of your life be? How can we "watch out" for the greed that can easily overrun our lives?

Each of us has a message that God has given us for our lives. This message is His gift to the world through us. It is how he uses us to impact others. When we start to think of what we want, what we can get for ourselves, what we can keep for our own, that message is lost. Jesus says, "Watch out!" Apparently it is easy to get sidetracked if we don't remain aware. Awareness is noticing, knowing, and understanding what is happening around you (and in you!). When we notice greed, we know we've moved away from the message.

DAILY INTERACTION ▼

 CONNECT: Explore online some of the great prayers of Christians such as St. Francis, Julian of Norwich, Jonathan Edwards, etc. Use these to help discover your own message.

> *[Jesus said,]* "Do not store up for yourselves treasures on earth…But store up for yourselves treasures in heaven…"
> MATTHEW 6:19–20

─── DEVOTION ▼ ───

Invest in Eternity

Pirates store treasure in treasure boxes. Bankers put money in vaults. Museums display valuable collections in glass cases under a guard's watchful eyes. Will any of these precious items last? The Bible speaks of "moth and rust" destroying them, but even if they  remain, do we take anything with us when we leave this earth? What are the treasures that can be stored in heaven?

We're often conditioned to save and savor possessions, status trophies, and souvenirs of our accomplishments. Regardless of where and how we store all that we accumulate, we're still not taking anything with us when our mortal bodies expire. When we show compassion, forgiveness, mercy, and loving-kindness to others, we invest in eternity, producing a heavenly dividend for ourselves and God's kingdom.

─── DAILY INTERACTION ▼ ───

 CONNECT: Make a plan with a friend online to help each other declutter when you're both next available.

Delight yourself in the LORD and he will give you the desires of your heart.
PSALM 37:4

▼ DEVOTION

Declaration of Dependence

The United States celebrates Independence Day today. The statesmen who drafted the Declaration of Independence, the document proclaiming freedom from the British, emphasized the importance of "life, liberty, and the pursuit of happiness" for each citizen. These ideals remain foundational today for the U.S. as well as many other democratic nations around the world.

However, often our "pursuit of happiness" is not very fulfilling. We chase after things we hope will make us happy only to discover that the emptiness inside us remains. We are created for relationship with our Creator, and nothing—whether material possessions, professional achievement, or political power—can ever fill our deepest longings but him.

Today, as you celebrate your nation's independence and give thanks for those who have sacrificed their lives for your freedom, remember to celebrate your dependence on your Father's loving care.

DAILY INTERACTION ▼

 CONNECT: Share at least a couple items from your "Declaration of Dependence" list at JesusDaily.com.

> *You need to persevere so that when you have done*
> *the will of God, you will receive what he has promised.*
> HEBREWS 10:36

DEVOTION ▼

Cross the Finish Line

Think of some of the great athletes whom you see in the Olympics. Many of them have heartwarming or heartbreaking stories of overcoming obstacles to be excellent in their sport. Their friends and families might have believed in them, or they may have abandoned them in their attempts to be a winner. Some of them have a lot of natural talent. Some of them have had to work twice as hard to get where they are. Most of them lost race after race before they started winning. Each person is unique, but they all have one thing in common. They have persevered with gritty determination, and they have not given up. They are champions.

Not all of us can be Olympic athletes. We have other journeys and goals. Most of us don't know what waits for us at the finish line. It gets hard to keep going, to work hard, to fail and get back up, but God asks us to keep on. Our goal is to please God and do His will—every day. God does not ask us to win every race. He only asks us to cross the finish line. Anyone can give up, but God's rewards, his pleasure, are for those who finish. We are champions, too.

DAILY INTERACTION ▼

CONNECT: Take time to journal online about a hard time in your life. What helped you keep going on?

> *To the man who pleases him, God gives
> wisdom, knowledge and happiness.*
> ECCLESIASTES 2:26

▼ DEVOTION

Journey with Jesus

When we are learning how to swim, it is understandable that we might be somewhat afraid and even resistant to get in the pool. But after a bit of time and a lot of lessons, we have no problem floating, and we master strokes that carry us through the water. It feels good to swim. We can't wait to get to the pool. We dream of competing and immerse ourselves in practice and endurance. Our ability soon seems above and beyond anything we thought we'd achieve when we started out in the tadpole class.

So it is when we start our journey with Jesus. We don't know him very well. We begin to spend time with him, and he speaks to us. We sense that he knows us. We feel his love more and more. We learn how to worship. We draw closer and closer to him. He is all we want. We desire him above all. He has become both our delight and our desire.

How does this happen? When we delight in the Lord, we spend time with him, as with a friend. We speak to him and he speaks to us. Our love grows and our hearts want more and more of him. He gives us great pleasure and happiness. He becomes our desire.

DAILY INTERACTION ▼

 CONNECT: Organize a group hike, run, bike ride, or picnic by posting an invitation online for your friends and family.

 July 7

> *Consider the blameless, observe the upright;*
> *there is a future for the man of peace.*
> PSALM 37:37

Today

Most of us spend a considerable amount of time planning future events. Some are big undertakings and require lots of details, such as a wedding, corporate retreat, or family reunion. Others are simply appointments, routine meetings, and events we want to attend. Often we invest a lot of time, energy, and money into our future endeavors but overlook the opportunity we have right now.

The actions you take today sow the seeds of your future. Your daily habits will create a cumulative impact on what you do tomorrow, next week, and next year. If you practice peace, righteousness, and kindness, you know the future will yield peace, joy, and a closer relationship with your Father.

When you're planning for the future, don't forget to invest in eternity today.

 CONNECT: Start a discussion with other believers on Jesus Daily or your own page and ask, "How do you remain focused on what God wants you to do today?"

> *. . . the mind controlled by the Spirit*
> *is life and peace.*
> ROMANS 8:6

▼ DEVOTION

Mind Control

Who usually controls your mind?

When we consider our minds being controlled, it sounds rather ominous, like space aliens or nano-chips implanted by spies as part of a government conspiracy. This kind of "mind control" may turn up frequently in science fiction stories and big screen spy thrillers. However, there is a real sense that what we focus our thinking on will determine what, and who, controls the landscape of our minds.

When we focus on our fears, responsibilities, obligations, and problems, we allow our minds to be controlled by anxiety and worry. When we allow God's Holy Spirit to control our minds, we experience life and peace, not worry and doubt. God has everything under control, and we must trust him fully—with our body, soul, and mind.

Today, consider the way your thoughts shape your expectations and color your perspective.

—— DAILY INTERACTION ▼

 CONNECT: Connect with someone on JesusDaily.com and hold each other accountable to memorize a favorite passage of Scripture.

> *[Jesus said,] "Blessed rather are those who hear the word of God and obey it."*
> LUKE 11:28

Obey His Word

Most parents spend a lot of time telling their kids what to do—chores, homework, act a certain way, take responsibility, apply for jobs and colleges. And often parents feel as though they repeat themselves over and over again, mostly because their children don't always act on what they hear. In an ideal world, we would only have to tell our kids to do something one time and they would then immediately obey us and do it.

God may feel this way about the way we listen to him. It's one thing for us to study our Bibles, hear teaching and preaching from the Scriptures, and memorize verses. But it's another thing for us to absorb the truth of God's Word into our hearts and to act on this truth. Our Father wants us to obey him by following the example set by his Son, Jesus.

If we love our Father and want to please him, we will do more than just hear what he says. We will obey what he asks us to do for him.

 CONNECT: Ask others to help you serve a need in your community or church—perhaps serving food to the homeless or organizing transportation for the elderly.

> *But if anyone obeys his word, God's love is truly made complete in him.*
>
> 1 JOHN 2:5

Father Knows Best

It's 2 a.m. and you're sitting at a red light that hasn't changed in over two minutes. The roads are completely deserted, and you can see for almost a mile in every direction. Do you keep sitting there, waiting for the light to turn green? Or do you go ahead and run through the stoplight, since the reason it's there (to control the flow of traffic at a busy intersection) is invalidated by the late hour and the faulty timer on the stoplight?

How would your choice be influenced by knowing you would not be caught?

Much of the reason we obey rules in everyday life stems from the logic or rationale behind them. When we understand the reason for a rule—such as the obvious necessity for a stoplight to regulate a busy traffic intersection—it's easy to comply. In our relationship with God, however, we can trust that his commands are always just and holy. Our Father knows what's best for us, whether we can see or understand the basis for it or not.

 CONNECT: In a chat room or other online venue, discuss the ways that man's laws and God's laws are different.

For it is not those who hear the law who are righteous in God's sight, but it is those who obey the law who will be declared righteous.

ROMANS 2:13

———————————————————————— DEVOTION ▼ ——————

A Perfect Life

Most people like to believe that their country's laws are just and fair. The law's validity applies to everyone and requires obedience from rich and poor, professionals and laborers, educated and uneducated alike. However, even in the most democratic countries, the legal system often has loopholes, grey areas, and corrupt officials. While the laws apply to everyone equally in theory, the reality is that innocent people sometimes suffer in the system while guilty ones go free.

With God's law, however, we know that it applies to everyone and that no one escapes the Lord's justice. All human beings are sinful and condemned under the perfect and holy requirements of God's law. However, our Father loved us so much that he sent Jesus to receive the punishment for our sins and pay the price that we could not bear. Through Christ's death on the cross and resurrection, we are all guilty and yet we all can be free if we accept the gift of salvation.

Today, obey God's law as a loving response to his grace, mercy, and forgiveness. He doesn't expect you to be perfect and fulfill the letter of the law—that's why Jesus came. God only wants you to love him enough to obey him.

———————————— DAILY INTERACTION ▼ ——————

 CONNECT: Ask someone to forgive you for something you've done to hurt them this week; forgive someone who has done something to hurt you.

> *By the word of the LORD were the heavens made,*
> *their starry host by the breath of his mouth.*
>
> PSALM 33:6

▼ DEVOTION

By His Breath

When you look up at the dark sky on a clear night, you can usually see hundreds—no, thousands—of stars twinkling back at you. Like flickering campfires across a darkened hillside, the celestial majesty of God's creation inspires sheer awe. It's impossible to fathom the distance between you and the stars, let alone the sheer power and beauty of each one.

And yet the psalmist tells us that God only had to speak and his very breath brought the celestial lights into being. In other words, creating the billions and billions of stars required no more effort on God's part than simply speaking and breathing. It takes mankind centuries to devise and develop rockets and spacecraft to take us into space, while it only takes God a moment to breathe the galaxies into existence!

We have no idea just how powerful, creative, and sovereign our God really is. Today, each time you look at the sky, remember who created everything here on earth as well as up above.

DAILY INTERACTION ▼

 CONNECT: Post a picture of your stargazing or find a pic of a starry night sky. Ask others to share their own pictures and favorite constellations.

The heavens declare the glory of God;
the skies proclaim the work of his hands.

PSALM 19:1

DEVOTION ▼

Wonders All Around

Remember as a child lying in the grass, how you would look up and watch the clouds scroll across the sky? Sometimes the sky was blue and the clouds barely seemed to move, just a little at a time, taking on shapes like circus animals and giant objects. Other times, a gray sky filtered frantic storm clouds past you, waiting to unload rain and thunder and lightning.

Today a cloudy sky can take us back to childhood as it beckons us to identify shapes and faces amidst the cumulous and nimbus formations. Whether gray rain clouds or giant cotton balls of fluffy white, the clouds also carry another message within their folds. As the stars at night, the clouds reveal the glorious and beautiful handiwork of our Creator.

Like so many of the natural elements around us, most days we take the skies and clouds for granted. And yet, like an artist's signature to a masterpiece, they urge us to remember the Source of so much beauty.

DAILY INTERACTION ▼

CONNECT: Share a pic from your cloud gazing and ask others what they see in the shapes. Post it with the verse above or another that reflects the glory of God.

> *God...reconciled us to himself through Christ*
> *and gave us the ministry of reconciliation.*
>
> 2 CORINTHIANS 5:18

▼ DEVOTION

Reconciled and Reconciling

You don't have to be a counselor or Nobel Peace Prize winner to be in the business of reconciliation. If you're a follower of Jesus, you're automatically a person who reconciles. And in our world today, there are plenty of individuals, groups, tribes, and nations at odds with one another. Even just in our daily lives, we don't have to look far to find individuals who clearly take a combative stance against most everyone they encounter. You may feel this way yourself sometimes.

But God is in the business of forgiving, reconciling, and healing. Having been at odds with us because of our sinfulness, our Father knew that the only way to reconcile with us permanently was to pay the debt once and for all. And that's what Christ did for us—he is the ultimate mediator, bridging heaven and earth, fulfilling a penalty we could never pay.

As followers of Jesus, we must seek to reconcile those around us. People who are at odds, who can't agree, who seek to resolve conflict through violent aggression need to know that God's peace can reign supreme.

DAILY INTERACTION ▼

 CONNECT: Post a picture on the Jesus Daily page of what reconciliation looks like to you. It can be one of your own or one you find. Ask others to share theirs, too.

I rise before dawn and cry for help;
I have put my hope in your word.
PSALM 119:147

Hope in Him

Sometimes we awake in the middle of the night and can't go back to sleep. Our mind spins with appointments, responsibilities, and obligations for the following day. We worry about money and bills, about loved ones and problems looming on the horizon. Soon sleep seems impossible, so we go ahead and get up to read, trying to calm our frantic minds before the day starts. Our weariness goes with us through the day, and soon we return home only to repeat the process another night.

When we are troubled and can't sleep, we must cry out to God. When we awake early because our minds and hearts are troubled, we must put our hope in what our Father has promised. He is with us and will never leave us or forsake us. He is in control and devoted to our growth for his good purposes.

Today, you can rest easy knowing that your hope is from God and not your own efforts.

 CONNECT: Visit JesusDaily.com and ask others how they handle sleepless nights and agree to pray for one another for a good rest tonight.

Let me understand the teaching of your precepts;
then I will meditate on your wonders.

PSALM 119:27

▼ DEVOTION

First Trust

Are you the kind of person who likes to think about a problem a long time before tackling it? Or do you tend to jump in and act first and think later? Regardless of the way we usually respond to something we don't understand, we can learn but also be transformed by the teaching in God's Word.

Sometimes we like to ponder a problem or process circumstances in order to understand them. While this can be insightful, God wants us to trust him whether we fully grasp the answers or not. Often we try to meditate in order to understand, and certainly we do gain new insight when we immerse ourselves in God's Word through meditation. However, if we try to comprehend and apply first and then reflect, we're letting God know that we're willing to be obedient—that's what we understand above all else—rather than just contemplative.

Today, practice what it means to understand God's truth before you meditate on the wonder of it.

DAILY INTERACTION ▼

CONNECT: Post a Bible verse that has special meaning in your life for its wisdom in resolving a past conflict or difficult situation.

📅 July 17

We love because he first loved us.
1 John 4:19

He Simply Loves Us

Many couples believe that one partner often needs the other more. And if they're fortunate, they both know they need each other and that there will be different seasons when each will need to lean on the other.

With God, however, it's always true: we're able to love because he loved us first. It's not just a matter that we need him and are created to be in relationship with him. It's simply a natural reaction if we experience his love for us. He doesn't need us in the sense that we often think of the concept of "need." But we are his creation, his sons and daughters, and God simply loves us. He desires a relationship with us—so much so that he made the ultimate sacrifice, his only Son.

You will always need God, and he's always willing to be there for us. Our very ability to have a relationship with him originates with love for us!

 CONNECT: Send a long-distance loved one an e-card sharing how much you need and appreciate them in your life.

Above all, love each other deeply, because love covers over a multitude of sins.

1 PETER 4:8

▼ DEVOTION

Love Covers

When criminals murder, steal, and harm others, it's difficult to understand how their families and others continue to love them. But even the most hardened criminal or heinous offender is someone's son or daughter, perhaps someone's spouse, sibling, or parent. The people who love them somehow see beyond the crimes committed to the individual they love underneath.

While most of us don't think of ourselves as criminals, we are just as sinful in our nature. Yet through the power of Christ's sacrificial death on the cross, God sees beyond our weaknesses and shortcomings and regards us as his beloved children. His love encompasses us in a way that is not conditional upon what we've done. Similarly, we can't earn his love by good behavior.

We've all sinned and deserve to be punished. But our Father's love transcends even the worst things we've done. We are free to become new people, transformed by his Spirit.

DAILY INTERACTION ▼

CONNECT: Visit a blog or website that reflects beliefs that you do not share. Earnestly spend time in prayer for others you might be tempted to criticize or judge.

📅 **July 19**

Love the LORD your God with all your heart
and with all your soul and with all your strength.

DEUTERONOMY 6:5

With All Your Heart

When we eat in a fancy restaurant, we usually expect several courses to our meal: appetizer, entrée, and dessert at the very least. When we attend a play or concert, we know that it will include a beginning, middle, and end in order for the performance to be complete. And when we meet someone we love, someone who clearly loves us just for who we are, we want them to know us completely. We want to be seen and understood fully.

With God, the same is true. He wants us to love him with all dimensions of our being, not just when we go to church or say an occasional prayer. Our relationship with him is the most important one we will ever have. So we must be committed to giving him everything we've got—our full attention, dedication, and devotion.

Today, consider how you can love God more fully by what you think, say, and do.

CONNECT: Research online someone you admire who exemplifies a wholehearted love for the Lord. How did they use their heart, soul, and strength to serve God?

*The fear of the L*ORD *adds length to life …*
PROVERBS 10:27

▼ DEVOTION

Reverence and Awe

When we think of fear, it's usually not a positive response. We think of danger, of bills we can't pay, and problems we can't solve. However, at its essence, fear carries a healthy respect and recognition that something is different and more powerful than we are. Fear recognizes that there's a fundamental separation between yourself and your perception of what's about to happen, what could happen, or what might happen again.

When we fear the Lord, we must understand that it's not the kind of fear you feel when a burglar breaks in or when an unfair judge sentences you to a crime you didn't commit. Instead, it's a healthy reverence, appreciation, and sense of awe of how magnificent, holy, and glorious God is. Our fear, in the biblical sense, indicates that we respect the difference between our humanity and his divinity, our limited views and his limitless views.

We don't usually think of fearing someone we love, at least not in a healthy relationship. However, with God our fear is part of the love we feel. He's so much bigger, better, stronger, and greater than we are and yet he still chooses us.

DAILY INTERACTION ▼

CONNECT: Research something you're afraid of—such as snakes, spiders, or heights—and share it on your personal page. Ask your friends to share their fears as well.

July 21

DEVOTION ▼

The Fountain of Life

During the summer months, we notice and appreciate the impact of rain on lawns, flower gardens, and farmers' fields. When there's no rain, especially over an extended period of weeks or months, a drought develops and soon reveals its impact on the natural beauty we're used to seeing. Instead of green we see brown and tan, crops shrivel, and flowers wither. Water is essential to life.

Jesus told us that he offers us Living Water, the kind that quenches our thirst for meaning, purpose, and spiritual connection in our lives. His Father is the wellspring for this Living Water, the fountain of life that brings life and light to all it touches. We need this nourishment in order to live, grow, and thrive.

When we experience a spiritual drought, it's usually because we have not looked to the source of our refreshment. Today, spend some time reviving your heart in the fountain of life.

DAILY INTERACTION ▼

 CONNECT: Post a recipe for one of your favorite summer dishes, perhaps a fruit pie, a vegetable casserole, or herbed salad. Let others taste and see that the Lord is good!

> *...knowledge of the Holy One is understanding.*
> PROVERBS 9:10

▼ DEVOTION

Remember His Goodness

Sometimes we know a lot about a topic, substance, or issue without understanding its complexities or true nature. With God, however, when we spend time in his Word gaining knowledge of his character, his deeds, and his loving pursuit of us, we come to understand his motives. We gain a greater depth of comprehension, both through insight and experience, about God's character. And through this process we're consistently reminded of his passionate pursuit of us.

In biblical times, God's people would often erect a sacrificial altar or other monument (often called an *Ebenezer*) to commemorate something significant that God did for them. Whether it was rescuing them from the Egyptians, empowering them to defeat an opponent, or dramatically providing for their needs, the Israelites knew that reminders do two important things: 1) ignite worship by helping them to remember God's goodness; and 2) jog their memory when facing doubts and fears.

We, too, need to remember what God has done for us in order to grow in both our knowledge and understanding of him.

DAILY INTERACTION ▼

CONNECT: Email or text a friend with whom you have experienced a time of serving God together. Remind them of how God blessed you both and how he will continue.

> *…the prudent are crowned with knowledge.*
> PROVERBS 14:18

DEVOTION ▼

Be Prudent

You don't hear words such as *prudent* very often anymore. It's old-fashioned sounding and may remind us of its derogatory cousin, the word *prude*. But being prudent has nothing to do with being a prude. *Prudent* means wise, shrewd, and aware of the big picture. *Prude* means someone who is easily shocked by standards different than their own who then judges others.

Both words, perhaps, draw on a person noticing the difference between where they are and what they see around them. However, the wisdom and knowledge that comes from being prudent does not give us a license to judge others. People who are prudent are not easily shocked and understand that the wisdom of the Lord includes grace and compassion.

Today, be prudent without becoming a prude.

DAILY INTERACTION ▼

 CONNECT: Post a question and ask others to define the difference between *prudent* and *prude*.

*But grow in the grace and knowledge of
our Lord and Savior Jesus Christ.*

2 PETER 3:18

▼ DEVOTION

Grow in Grace

At the beginning of the spring, it seemed as though nature held its collective breath waiting for the consistency of sunshine, rain, and warm temperatures. Then all at once trees, fields, and yards deepened into emerald shades of green. Wildflowers dotted the hillsides and cornfields sprang up. Soon corn stalks towered over six feet trying to keep up with sunflowers.

Living creatures grow, and nowhere is this clearer than in the middle of summer. The natural world erupts with color, life, and vibrancy, yielding delicious produce and beautiful blossoms. When we walk with the Lord and remain nourished by his Word, by fellowship with other believers, and by our service to those around us, we also grow and flourish.

God wants his children to mature in their faith, trusting him more and more each day.

DAILY INTERACTION ▼

 CONNECT: Post a picture of your favorite summer landscape and ask others to share theirs. Let each one remind you of what it means to grow in your faith.

> *[Jesus said,] "Do not be afraid, little flock, for your Father has been pleased to give you the kingdom."*
>
> LUKE 12:32

—————————————— DEVOTION ▾ ——————————————

Be Not Afraid

We're told to "fear the Lord" but also not to "be afraid," which reminds us that there's a crucial difference in meaning between these words that we often consider synonymous. As we've seen, the "fear of the Lord" simply acknowledges respect and reverence for the holiness and majesty of God. When Christ tells us not to be afraid, it's much more in the conventional sense, the anxious uncertainty and dread about what could or might happen.

Jesus reminds us that since God has given us his kingdom, we have nothing to fear. Our Father is not only sovereign and in control, but he allows us to participate in advancing his kingdom. When we know we're part of something bigger, something that's clearly part of God's purposeful design, we can relinquish our fears. We don't have to worry about the future because it's already secure in God's hands.

Today, think about the way your actions as a follower of Christ can alleviate your present fears.

—————————————— DAILY INTERACTION ▾ ——————————————

 CONNECT: Choose a prayer request at JesusDaily.com and let the person know you're lifting them up to the Father. Encourage them not to be afraid.

> *The LORD has established his throne in heaven,*
> *and his kingdom rules over all.*
>
> PSALM 103:19

▼ DEVOTION

The King of Heaven

As children, most of us enjoyed stories where princesses and princes found true love and the monsters were always defeated. Such fairy tales often end with order, goodness, and joy restored to the characters and the kingdom. While "happily ever after" rarely seems to happen in real life, there's something in us that instinctively longs for peace, harmony, and contentment.

This longing is part of our desire for the ultimate King to reign and to restore our lives. We want our Father to dispel sin, suffering, and darkness once and for all. We want an eternal "happily ever after."

What we may forget in the midst of our longing is that we get to participate in this process. As royal heirs by adoption through Christ, we have already been guaranteed eternity in heaven as well as an abundant life of purposeful service in this life. No matter how difficult our circumstances may be, the happy ending has already been written.

DAILY INTERACTION ▼

CONNECT: Ask someone about their favorite fairy tale or Bible story and how it reminds them of God's sovereignty and goodness.

———— DEVOTION ▾ ————

An Attitude of Kindness

Retaliation and revenge are no longer words used mostly to describe warring countries and rival gangs. Whether in the workplace or the schoolyard, we often hear of the way people attack one another and then create an ongoing conflict in their words and actions. It happens in lines at fast-food counters, across tables in boardrooms, and in shopper-frantic parking lots.

All the more reason that we as followers of Jesus are called to treat others with patience, kindness, and compassion. While many people become more intent on getting what they want at any price, we must demonstrate a different set of priorities that have nothing to do with getting ahead, and everything to do with what we leave behind.

An act of kindness is a good start, but an attitude of kindness influences everything we think, say, and do.

———— DAILY INTERACTION ▾ ————

CONNECT: Thank someone with a quick text, email, or e-card for the way they consistently display an attitude of kindness toward you.

> *Many seek an audience with a ruler, but it is*
> *from the LORD that man gets justice.*
> PROVERBS 29:26

▼ **DEVOTION**

Justice and Mercy

Courtroom dramas and stories of legal suspense continue to fascinate people, whether in movies, TV shows, popular fiction, or tabloid accounts. Perhaps our intrigue lies in the way various laws are interpreted, executed, and upheld. And issues of guilt, innocence, context, fairness, and justice always remain in the mix.

No matter what happens to characters in a story or even people in real life, the essence of justice can only be found in the character of God. If righteousness is the ultimate standard of perfection by which we measure justice, our only pure basis of comparison comes from the perfect holiness of the Lord.

We can never attain such a spotless status, but we don't have to try. We can't earn our favor with God because it's freely given when we confess our sins and accept Christ as our Savior. We know that the only one who could grant us mercy under the law is the only one who fulfills it.

DAILY INTERACTION ▼

 CONNECT: Go to JesusDaily.com and share a prayer request for justice in a particular area of concern.

For the LORD is a God of justice.
Blessed are all who wait for him!
ISAIAH 30:18

— DEVOTION ▾ —

Shalom

The concept of justice is closely linked to the Hebrew word *shalom*, which we often think of as "peace." However, *shalom* means much more than just peace; it's a concept, an attitude, a lifestyle that's committed to blessing, grace, and forgiveness. It's about reconciliation and restoration. It's the turning point where mourning gives way to dancing, where tears of sorrow become tears of joy.

In our world today, we often struggle to see and experience justice and shalom. We can point out all kinds of injustice and hatred, greed and strife, but it's hard to see where people are honoring God and obeying him through their efforts to serve humbly and to respect others peaceably.

Is there an injustice in your life, or even in the world today, that upsets you? As you continue to pray for the Lord's will to be done in regard to this area, begin the process by embracing the peace he wants to give you.

— DAILY INTERACTION ▾ —

 CONNECT: Remain offline in your free or personal time today, using the space instead to pray for people who are suffering injustice around the world.

> *Light is shed upon the righteous*
> *and joy on the upright in heart.*
>
> PSALM 97:11

▼ DEVOTION

Shine

Summer nights seem made for twinkling lights, whether from stars, flashlights, campfires, or fireflies. Somehow in the darkness, those small flickering lights seem to shine brighter and to appear more noticeable.

As followers of Jesus, our actions should sparkle with the same brilliance against the darkness that often surrounds us. When we walk closely with the Lord and trust him for each step along the way, it's clear to people around us that  we have a light to share. We're not just groping around in the darkness of life trying to find our own way. We have a Light who illuminates our paths. We experience a joy that comes from loving and serving him.

Allow yourself to shine today, to reflect the joy of the Lord that you have deep in your soul, knowing he loves you and that he has saved you.

DAILY INTERACTION ▼

 CONNECT: Connect with a friend or loved on online and tell them how much you appreciate the way they represent Christ, bringing light to everyone they meet.

> *Those who sow in tears will reap with songs of joy.*
> PSALM 126:5

——— DEVOTION ▼ ———

Songs of Joy

When you plant a rose bush, you expect to see roses. When you scatter grass seeds, you watch for that bare spot in your lawn to become lush and green. When you plant watermelon seeds, you anticipate having a simple, delicious dessert for your summer picnics. When we cry tears of grief, however, we rarely expect them to be transformed into "songs of joy."

In fact, it's often hard to see the way our heartaches get transformed into blessings until long after they occur. But perhaps if we think of our tears as seeds of future joy, a radical transformation that only God can bring about, maybe we will experience some comfort. While we're sad in the present, we know we don't have to remain stuck in the midst of our grief. God delivers us and delights in healing us and restoring us to new life. What appears to devastate us today might be what turns out to deliver us in the future.

As the Master Gardener, God is able to produce spiritual fruit in our lives from even the smallest, hardest seeds.

——— DAILY INTERACTION ▼ ———

 CONNECT: Find a way to meet a practical need for someone going through a painful trial—mow their lawn, buy their groceries, do their laundry, babysit, whatever they need.

AUGUST

*"I have loved you with an everlasting love;
I have drawn you with unfailing loving-kindness."*

Jeremiah 31:3

 August 1

> *"Call to me and I will answer you and tell you great and unsearchable things you do not know."*
> JEREMIAH 33:3

His Word Is True

We all know people who say one thing but mean another. Sometimes we don't trust what we hear, especially when we know there may be an unspoken, underlying message. So we end up feeling as though we have to crack the code and read between the lines, deciphering what the other person actually means to communicate.

God is never like this. He means what he says and says what he means. We know that his Word is true and that he keeps his promises. When we communicate with God through prayer, we know that he hears us and answers us. In fact, we're told that the Holy Spirit intercedes for us with our Father when we don't know what to say. We don't have to worry about getting the words right or be afraid of saying the wrong thing.

God loves communicating with his children. We can trust that we're speaking the same language.

 CONNECT: Schedule a video conference with someone you haven't communicated with in a while. Let them know how much you want to catch up.

He has made everything beautiful in its time.
ECCLESIASTES 3:11

▼ DEVOTION

Transformation

We often speak of athletes, celebrities, and leaders as reaching a peak in their career, a point of achievement that will be the capstone for the hard work they've invested in their careers. With these individuals, there's often a beauty to what they do and how they do it. Often these people have taken their natural talents, honed skills, and stubborn determination to the place where no one can do what they're doing in quite the same way. And the result is like seeing an artist create a masterpiece.

If we appreciate these stars' abilities and accomplishments in their respective fields, how much more should we marvel at what God has created and continues to do. The natural world consistently displays the wonders of his divine imagination and extraordinary beauty. Even better, there's the amazing transformation that God continues to reveal in your life as you become more and more like his Son, Jesus.

DAILY INTERACTION ▼

CONNECT: Post a picture of a painting, photo, sketch, sculpture, or other artifact that inspires you and reminds you of the immense creativity and beauty of God.

> *…I urge you to live a life worthy of the calling you have received.*
> Ephesians 4:1

Your Unique Purpose

Once you've committed to a relationship with God by accepting Christ into your heart, your calling becomes clear: to use your unique gifts and talents for your Father's kingdom. There is no higher calling than to feel the contentment that comes from fulfilling the purpose for which you were created.

We're often dissatisfied with life because we lose sight of our focus. We get pushed and pulled into other people's expectations and agendas, or we chase after goals of our own that we think will fulfill us. However, you're only going to be truly content when you're living within the purpose for which your Father created you. If you're discovering this purpose, ask him to reveal it more clearly to you.

God has placed a call on you and your life and has equipped you for your unique purpose. Your life has meaning because it counts for eternity!

 CONNECT: Connect with someone who serves as a role model for you in living out your purpose. If possible, ask if they will mentor you or at least pray for your path.

So God created man in his own image, in the image of God he created him; male and female he created them.

GENESIS 1:27

▼ DEVOTION

God's Design for You

One of the unique and beautiful ways God reveals himself is through his creation. And how wonderful for us that he created both men and women in his own image. While very different in many ways, we each reflect the strength, determination, tenderness, and compassion in the Lord's own character. Just as he reflects all these traits and many more, we, too, can display both power and mercy, both grit and grace. Whether as a man or a woman, we can know that our identity is inherently from our Creator.

Our society often tries to dictate what makes a "real man" or a "real woman," but these traits aren't always accurate, let alone biblical and godly. Today, accept that God has made you as the kind of man or woman you are deliberately. You are his precious daughter or son, created in his image to reveal himself to those around you. Stop trying to live up to others' standards of masculinity or femininity and rest in the knowledge of God's design for you.

DAILY INTERACTION ▼

 CONNECT: Issue an invitation to a handful of other same-gender friends for a time of fellowship soon.

August 5

> *Remember me for this also, O my God, and show mercy to me according to your great love.*
> NEHEMIAH 13:22

He Never Fails

Most parents know that even when their child does something they don't like, they still love them and want what's best for them. Jesus told us that if we, as imperfect human parents, want to give good things to our kids, how much more does our Father in heaven want to lavish us with his love.

Even after becoming Christians, we sometimes succumb to temptation and fail. We know we've disobeyed God and disappointed him as well as ourselves. We ask for his forgiveness and know we've received it, but we still feel guilty and condemn ourselves for our weakness. Our enemy usually seizes these opportunities to cause us to pour contempt on ourselves and doubt our faith and God's ability to love us.

But God never fails to love us no matter what we do. His grace and mercy not only prevail, but he wants us to know our true worth and not the enemy's lies. Sometimes when we fall, we have to regain our balance before taking the next step.

 CONNECT: Visit JesusDaily.com and ask for ongoing prayer to sustain you as you move forward and grow in your faith.

> *Perseverance must finish its work so that you may*
> *be mature and complete, not lacking anything.*
>
> JAMES 1:4

▼ DEVOTION

All You Need

You can find plenty of books, seminars, sermons, and opinions on what it takes to experience happiness in our world today. And yet, very few people seem to be truly joyful most days. Perhaps part of the reason is that we live in a consumer culture always telling us that we don't have enough—enough clothes, shoes, cars, toys, vacations, you name it.

Our culture only compounds the problem, especially commercials and ads that try to persuade us that another purchase will bring us satisfaction, at least temporarily. And yet the process of persevering in our faith requires us to realize that we have everything we need. We may feel as though we're missing something or we may want something else based on faulty thinking, but God is faithful to provide and equip us for our present journey.

You don't need to live in a way that's conditional on attaining more in the future. Your Father has already provided an abundance of blessings for all you need today.

DAILY INTERACTION ▼

 CONNECT: Ask others to share what they're especially grateful for having in their lives today. Share a prayer of thanksgiving together.

 August 7

> *Wait for the LORD; be strong and
> take heart and wait for the LORD.*
> PSALM 27:14

Wait on His Timing

Whether we're waiting for a table at our favorite restaurant, for traffic to move on the highway, for our appointment at the doctor's office, or in line for tickets to a concert, we all have to wait. And not many of us like it, let alone are good at practicing patience.

However, much of the Christian life involves waiting on God's timing rather than insisting that events happen on our timetable. We like the predictability and certainty that comes when appointments are kept on time, traffic runs smoothly, and lines move quickly. But most days, we encounter at least one area that's beyond our ability to control or change. Patience is the only way through the obstacle.

Whenever you're discouraged and disheartened by having to wait, remember that God has a bigger perspective and a different sense of urgency than our own. Today, we can wait patiently in the knowledge that he's in control.

 CONNECT: Share something you're currently waiting to happen and ask other Christians to pray that you would have patience.

> *O LORD, be gracious to us; we long for you. Be our strength every morning, our salvation in time of distress.*
>
> ISAIAH 33:2

▼ DEVOTION

Our Source of Strength

Each day we make it through as best we can—we get up, go to work or school, come home, do necessary chores, eat, relax a little, and go to bed. Sometimes it can become so routine that we wonder if we're ever going to get out of the rut. And then some unexpected trial or problem arises that sends our usual routine for a loop. We realize how smoothly things had been going before this new crisis broke.

Then we wonder if life will ever get back to normal, whatever that may be. While our routines may not be the same again, we can trust that God remains the source of our strength, our salvation, and our peace. Just as storm clouds move through and unleash thunder, lightning, and rain, events may catch us off guard and leave us frightened and anxious. However, each day we can know that no matter what storms life may bring, our Father has already gone ahead of us.

The storms of life will pass and sunshine returns. God is with us!

DAILY INTERACTION ▼

 CONNECT: Search pictures online that capture the full power of a storm. Post a pic along with a verse that reminds others of God's power even in the midst of adversity.

> *When I called, you answered me;*
> *you made me bold and stouthearted.*
> PSALM 138:3

—— DEVOTION ▼ ——

He's Always There

With our modern technology, it's rare that we can't reach someone with whom we want to connect. If they don't pick up our call, we text them. If we don't hear back, we look for them on Facebook, in a favorite chat room, or we shoot them an email. We've become so conditioned to reaching the other people in our lives that when we can't connect with someone, we grow frustrated.

Sometimes we may feel as though God isn't answering our attempts to communicate either. But even if we don't hear from him the way we want, when we want, we can know that he's still there, listening and caring. He does answer us and he does embolden us with his power, strength, and grace.

Our Father never ignores our calls or fails to answer our requests. He is always available to us, no technology needed.

—— DAILY INTERACTION ▼ ——

 CONNECT: Clean out your email inbox today, responding to as many messages as possible.

A happy heart makes the face cheerful…
PROVERBS 15:13

▼ DEVOTION

A Happy Heart

The taste of a delicious grilled steak. The mural of colors projected by a gorgeous summer sunset. The sound of a child's laughter. The smell of freshly cut grass. The embrace of someone who loves us. We all have moments of delight that make our hearts happy. Often our senses are involved and perhaps a pleasant memory associated with whatever we're enjoying.

When our hearts overflow with joy, peace, and hope, our contentment shows in our words, expressions, and actions. Others notice that we have something deep within us that fuels our satisfaction and may even ask us about the source.

Even when circumstances spin out of control or cause problems we haven't anticipated, we can hold on to our joy and keep the smile on our face. Our certainty in Christ remains rock solid no matter how demands swirl around us. We have time to stop and smell the roses as well as to cut a few and take a bouquet to someone else!

DAILY INTERACTION ▼

 CONNECT: Post a pic of yourself enjoying your action above and ask others to share what has brought them joy lately.

> *Find rest, O my soul, in God alone;*
> *my hope comes from him.*
>
> PSALM 62:5

Rest in Him

Do you have trouble sleeping when you're worried about something? Many people do and can't rest easy until they've found a way to let go of their anxiety. When we don't feel responsible for solving and fixing problems, we can release our worries, knowing that God's got everything under control. When we place our hope in him, we can find the deep kind of rest that not only recharges the body, but renews our minds and refreshes our souls.

A weary body and restless spirit make it difficult for us to face the day ahead. But the peace of God and the refreshment that comes from trusting him will always see us through.

Today, let yourself rest in the security of God's embrace.

 CONNECT: Unplug for as long as possible today—the whole day if your work and schedule will allow you. Try to clear out the mental cobwebs cluttering your mind.

"For my thoughts are not your thoughts, neither are your ways my ways," declares the LORD.

ISAIAH 55:8

▼ DEVOTION

His Way

Part of what we appreciate about other people—as well as what often frustrates us—is our differences. When a problem emerges in a group, each individual member might solve it in his or her own unique way. One person might address the problem head-on, while another might wait as long as possible to see what develops. One individual would break the problem into small components that take time to address, while another looks for the quickest solution to the biggest issue.

Most of us think that we know how certain problems in our lives should be fixed. We think, *If only . . .* or *Why can't they see what has to be done?* We come up with all kinds of ways that events could proceed so that we get what we want, when we want it. This rarely happens, however.

While God wants us to be actively engaged with life, he also wants us to depend on him. Our way of doing things—perhaps especially when it comes to problem solving—is not the same as his way. His perspective cuts across time, geography, history, culture, and all the other barriers that can cloud our perspective. Our Father truly knows best.

DAILY INTERACTION ▼

CONNECT: Visit JesusDaily.com and encourage someone to solve a problem in their life head-on. Offer to assist them as best you can.

> *"Here I am! I stand at the door and knock.*
> *If anyone hears my voice and opens the door,*
> *I will come in and eat with him, and he with me."*
> REVELATION 3:20

—————————————————————— DEVOTION ▾ ——

Share Your Life

It's no wonder that sharing a meal together is one of the very oldest ways that people have come together to fellowship. When we enjoy food and drink in the company of others, we naturally connect through the reminder of our humanity. No matter how different we may be, we all need sustenance. Jesus certainly took many opportunities to dine with his followers, from feeding the 5,000 to the Last Supper. After his resurrection, he even prepared breakfast on the beach for his disciples who had been out fishing all night.

When we invite Christ into our heart, we open the door into an intimate relationship with our Savior. He's not some aloof, distant, detached person who rules from afar. No, he enters into our lives with the comfortable, intimate familiarity of sharing a meal with a friend.

—— **DAILY** INTERACTION ▾ ——————————————————————

 CONNECT: Plan a group potluck with several of your friends, members of church, or extended family. Ask God to bless the preparations for your fellowship.

> *But I trust in you, O Lord; I say, "You are my God."*
> *My times are in your hands; deliver me from*
> *my enemies and from those who pursue me.*
>
> PSALM 31:14–15

▼ DEVOTION

He Has Your Back

Mountain climbers always travel in groups of at least two so that they can help each other scale the peak before them. The relationship between climbing partners is naturally one of incredible trust, commitment, and communication. Similarly, soldiers in battle must depend on one another in ways that entrust their safety and very lives to one another's care. They not only have a responsibility to keep going toward their goal for themselves; they must work as part of a team or partnership.

God is committed to this kind of partnership with us and then some. He wants us to rely on him in all areas of our lives. He always has our back! While we may face adversity for a season or our enemies may triumph temporarily, the Lord will always deliver us. Like a mother bear protecting her cubs, God loves us with an unfailing devotion.

DAILY INTERACTION ▼

 CONNECT: Offer to help someone who's attempting to overcome a challenge that requires more than their own efforts. Enlist other friends who can also contribute.

> *...we have not stopped praying for you and asking God to fill you with the knowledge of his will through all spiritual wisdom and understanding.*
>
> COLOSSIANS 1:9

—— DEVOTION ▼ ——

Enjoy Your Family

Asking others for prayer is not always easy. While we're more than willing to pray for the people in our lives, it feels vulnerable and needy to request that they do the same for us. And yet God's Word clearly instructs us to pray as individuals as well as with others. Sharing burdens with others and experiencing God's answers and provisions bond us as a spiritual community in ways that praying alone does not.

When we hear of an answered prayer from someone for whom we've been praying, we rejoice with them and remain aware of God's presence throughout the world. When we can share our needs with others, we feel lighter and even comforted, grateful not to be alone with our burden any longer.

God created us as social beings who are to be in relationships with one another. And as we relate to him as our Father, he wants us to enjoy the fellowship of our brothers and sisters in Christ. Today, enjoy being part of the family of God.

—— DAILY INTERACTION ▼ ——

CONNECT: Choose a need for prayer posted at JesusDaily.com and let the person know you'll be praying for them throughout today.

> *"I have loved you with an everlasting love;*
> *I have drawn you with unfailing loving-kindness."*
>
> JEREMIAH 31:3

▾ DEVOTION

Gift Givers

Sometimes the smallest acts of kindness can produce enormous rewards. When someone holds the door for us, surprises us with a cup of coffee, or says "thank you" for our help, we feel respected, appreciated, and valued. Often these little gifts of courtesy and compassion have a larger impact than anything anyone can give us.

When we give these same kinds of gifts to others, we may have no idea of how we're impacting their day. But the little kindnesses add up and remind each of us—both giving and receiving—of the source of all true gift giving, our Lord.

His kindness is indeed unfailing and always present in everything he does. Even if we can't see or understand what he's doing— remember, his ways are not our ways—we can still know that his kindness remains a key ingredient.

Today, let your attitude of kindness reflect your Father's kindness to you.

DAILY INTERACTION ▾

 CONNECT: Write and thank someone whose kindness has blessed you recently. Let them know that you see God's kindness through their actions.

📅 August 17

> *"The LORD is slow to anger, abounding in love and forgiving sin and rebellion."*
> NUMBERS 14:18

DEVOTION ▼

His Love Remains

We each handle anger differently. Some people snap back immediately when something sets them off and make their anger part of their default defensive setting. Others may go weeks or even months before they reach their boiling point. Some people express their anger through words while others take—or avoid taking—action to communicate their displeasure.

With God, we're told he is slow to anger. And even when we disappoint him through our disobedience, his love for us leads to his forgiveness when we confess our sins to him. He doesn't blow up like a hothead with a short fuse. We don't have to walk on eggshells out of fear that he will explode with rage.

Greater still, we know that even when God is angry, his love and compassion remain. He will not become so furious with us that he cannot forgive us. His nature is love and through the gift of his Son, Jesus, he's chosen to always forgive us so that we can be with him forever.

DAILY INTERACTION ▼

 CONNECT: Post a favorite verse about anger and ask others how they handle their tempers.

> *The LORD upholds all those who fall*
> *and lifts up all who are bowed down.*
>
> PSALM 145:14

▼ DEVOTION

Supernatural Strength

When you sprain your ankle or break your leg, you will likely rely on crutches, a walker, or a cane to help you stand and walk while your injury heals. It's usually slow going for many weeks and months as you recover and grow stronger. The additional support provided by your crutch or cane enables you to relieve stress on the injury while helping you balance and move forward.

Our faith provides this kind of support for us in our daily walk. Far from being a crutch, however, it gives us the security of a parent holding a child's hand while walking through the park. Our Father upholds us with a supernatural strength and power that enables us to keep going when we aren't able to stand on our own. He knows our limitations and catches us when we fall.

We may feel immobilized temporarily, but our spirit is never paralyzed. God lifts us to our feet and makes the ground firm beneath us. We only have to hold his hand and follow his lead.

DAILY INTERACTION ▼

CONNECT: Provide a shoulder for someone else to lean on. Offer to listen, pray, or provide assistance to someone who's fallen or struggling to get back on their feet.

*Let us hold unswervingly to the hope we profess,
for he who promised is faithful.*
HEBREWS 10:23

DEVOTION ▼

Be Unswerving

Summer is a great time for a road trip with an unplanned destination. Along with friends or family, you just get in your car and drive, stopping along the way to check out the back roads and byways that you normally drive by. You discover small town diners and take detours to see sites that you've always wondered about, such as a local museum, craft fair, or farmers' market.

Without a set destination, you're free to amble and swerve, turn and circle back that you normally wouldn't. This kind of leisure trip is enjoyable but, without a destination, may leave you uncertain about where you're going, let alone how to get there.

When we follow God, when our hope in Christ guides us, we can know that no matter how many detours appear, we're sure of our destination. While our path may seem to twist and turn, when we "hold unswervingly to the hope we profess," God is faithful.

DAILY INTERACTION ▼

 CONNECT: Ask others to share some favorite pics from their last vacation or getaway. Share your plans on where you're planning to go.

"The LORD does not look at the things man looks at. Man looks at the outward appearance, but the LORD looks at the heart."

1 SAMUEL 16:7

▼ DEVOTION

Our True Selves

What would the people around you see if they could look inside your heart today? Would they be surprised by what's there? Would *you* be surprised by what's there?

Most of us cultivate a public mask or face we show to the world. We hide our problems, disguise our disappointments, and try to appear pleasant and professional. When someone asks how we're doing, we say, "Just fine, thanks. And you?"

While it's not always appropriate to bare our souls to anyone who asks how we're doing, we must also realize that when we risk being authentic, we give others permission to do the same. Having integrity means being wholehearted and not fragmented or compartmentalized. We can let others glimpse our true selves the same way that God sees what's inside our heart.

DAILY INTERACTION ▼

 CONNECT: Go to JesusDaily.com and share something positive about your heart that you usually don't reveal.

 August 21

> *...make my joy complete by being like-minded,*
> *having the same love, being one in spirit and purpose.*
> PHILIPPIANS 2:2

One in Spirit

One of the joys of team sports is working together as individuals to achieve a shared goal. Although some players may play key roles and serve as leaders, each and every player becomes significant if the team is to win. In the Body of Christ, this must be our mindset as well. We each have different and unique gifts, skills, and capabilities, but all of us are equally important.

When we allow disagreements and differences to define us, we are not pleasing our Father. He wants us to love one another, forgive one another, and work together toward advancing his kingdom. As we collaborate and cooperate, we discover the joy and satisfaction that comes from participating in a cause so much bigger than ourselves.

Because of what God has done in our lives, we have more reason to celebrate than a team that just won the Super Bowl or the World Series! We should treat one another accordingly.

 CONNECT: Share your team spirit with others online and respect the sports teams that they support, even if you don't like those teams!

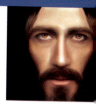

> *…let us draw near to God with a sincere heart in full assurance of faith, having our hearts sprinkled to cleanse us from a guilty conscience and having our bodies washed with pure water.*
>
> HEBREWS 10:22

▼ **DEVOTION**

Cleansed

After a long hot summer day, you not only feel tired and depleted, but you feel dirty and sweaty. Maybe this is why we love the beach so much; there's no better feeling on a sizzling day than hitting the water. Whether it's the ocean, a lake, a swimming pool, or a backyard pond, we love the sensation of immersing ourselves in the cool clear water.

When you've carried around a burden of shame, guilt, and remorse, experiencing the cleansing current of grace can feel even more refreshing. The weariness we feel from holding on to this burden melts and even our body feels lighter.

You don't have to carry around your sin or burden yourself with a guilty conscience. God is always willing to grant mercy and forgiveness to those who confess and earnestly seek him. He loves us so much and wants us to experience the clean, fresh sensation of a cool shower on a hot day.

DAILY INTERACTION ▼

 CONNECT: Post a photo of a favorite beach or body of water at JesusDaily.com and ask others to share theirs.

Yet I am always with you; you hold me by my right hand.
Psalm 73:23

DEVOTION ▼

Hold His Hand

Parents hold their children's hands, especially when the child is small. Lovers hold hands. Wounded or weary people may hold another's hand to steady themselves while standing or walking. A teammate might offer his hand to a fallen comrade to assist him to his feet as a sign of respect and good sportsmanship.

Holding someone's hand is a sign of affection, support, comfort, and confidence. God extends his hand to us this way on a daily basis, reminding us that we never have to walk alone. We are loved, we are strong, and we are protected. His hand holds ours and connects us to him as his beloved child. We have intimate access to the God of the universe—so much so that he holds our hand!

Today, celebrate being God's child and allow him to hold your hand.

DAILY INTERACTION ▼

CONNECT: Reach out to someone across the miles and let them know you care about them and are praying for them, a virtual way to hold their hand.

> *For the kingdom of God is not a matter of*
> *eating and drinking, but of righteousness,*
> *peace and joy in the Holy Spirit.*
>
> ROMANS 14:17

▼ DEVOTION

Be Vigilant

What we put in our bodies is certainly important—after all, our bodies are the temples of God's Spirit. Yet, we know that being obedient and pleasing to God requires more than just watching what we eat and drink, or watch and hear. We must also remain diligent about our minds and hearts, the thoughts and feelings that rise up in us and how we respond to them, especially with our actions.

With so much information clamoring for our attention, with so many pop-ups, ads, and seductive sales pitches aimed at us, we're constantly taking in more than we realize. More images, more ideas, more sensations—and yes, often more temptations—than we realize.

As our world becomes even more digitalized and media-saturated, you must take responsibility for what you see, hear, think, and feel. Don't let your default setting be one without filters. Seek to please God by all you allow into your mind, heart, and soul.

DAILY INTERACTION ▼

 CONNECT: Stop following a site, blog, or page that's causing you to stumble or that's not building you up in your faith.

> *Be imitators of God, therefore, as dearly loved children and live a life of love, just as Christ loved us and gave himself up for us as a fragrant offering and sacrifice to God.*
> EPHESIANS 5:1–2

———— DEVOTION ▼ ————

A Sweet Aroma

Scientists tell us that scents carry great power to stimulate our memories. While other sensory data may fade, the smell of honeysuckle, gasoline, or aftershave will usually trigger a memory or association for most people. People often become synonymous with certain scents, usually a favorite cologne or perfume they wear frequently. Cosmetic companies spend millions of dollars to create fragrant combinations that will appeal to people who wear their products.

Perhaps the greatest and sweetest fragrance ever known, however, belongs to Jesus. His scent is not literal as much as figurative. Before his death and resurrection, the temple priests performed sacrifices before God and usually burned incense or some kind of sweet-smelling substance to mask the scent of the sacrificed animal burning. When Christ, as the Lamb of God, gave himself as the final sacrifice for our sins, the smell of his humility, love, and suffering must have been richer than any French perfume and more pungent than the sharpest odor.

We are called to give off this same scent by all that we say and do in the name of the Lord.

———— DAILY INTERACTION ▼ ————

 CONNECT: Post one of your favorite smells and an appropriate image to represent it and ask others to share theirs.

> *"Whoever can be trusted with very little can also be trusted with much, and whoever is dishonest with very little will also be dishonest with much."*
>
> LUKE 16:10

▼ DEVOTION

Be Authentic

Who are you when no one is looking? How do you behave when no one around you knows your name or will likely ever see you again? When you travel, do you act differently than when you're at home? When you're on vacation, is there a different attitude toward other people than when you're going through a normal day?

We're often encouraged by other people and by our society at large to present one face in public and another behind closed doors. However, God desires us to live with purity, integrity, and honesty—the same whether we're at home, at work, at church, or on vacation. It's not only our own reputation that's at stake; it's the witness we bear to who Christ is in our lives. When others see us changing our behavior according to where we are, they assume that our faith is only a role, a temporary part of our crowded lives.

Today, be a worthy ambassador of Jesus, sharing your authentic faith with everyone around you, no matter the context.

DAILY INTERACTION ▼

CONNECT: Check in with a friend online who always loves and appreciates you for who you really are. Let down your guard and share with them what's on your heart.

> *...learn to do right! Seek justice, encourage the oppressed. Defend the cause of the fatherless, plead the case of the widow.*
>
> Isaiah 1:17

———— DEVOTION ▼ ————

Give Generously

It's hard to know who to trust these days. So many people take advantage of the kindness of others. They pretend to be in dire straits or lie about their situation only so others will feel pity and help them. Nonetheless, we are called to share what we have with those in need around us. We may suspect that the man who appears homeless is really just scamming us, but what if he's not? We must remain generous and compassionate even when we're uncertain of the motives or honesty of others.

People who would be willing to lie, steal, or cheat you need to experience the love of Christ just as much as someone who's injured, homeless, or hungry. The attitude and example you set honors the Lord, and it will have a definite impact on those around you.

Today, don't be afraid to give openly and generously to the people in need around you. Let them see how much God cares for them, regardless of their motives in seeking your help.

———— DAILY INTERACTION ▼ ————

 CONNECT: Tell others about a person, cause, or ministry that needs additional help and resources. Ask them prayerfully to consider what they can contribute.

Therefore, as we have opportunity, let us do good to all people, especially to those who belong to the family of believers.

GALATIANS 6:10

▼ DEVOTION

The Family of Believers

Jesus said that people would know that we're his followers by the love we show to others. This is especially true for how we as believers treat one another. While others might not expect us to show love and kindness to our enemies, they would certainly take notice if we didn't treat our brothers and sisters in Christ with respect and compassion. While we're called to be like Christ to all people, if we fail to do it with those who share our beliefs, we've truly failed indeed.

Too many people today have mistaken ideas about what it means to follow Jesus. They see believers arguing, condemning, cheating, and hurting others and understandably want no part of such a faith. However, this kind of sinful behavior among Christians grieves God just as much as those watching.

You have the opportunity to determine how those around you define the Christian faith. Your example speaks louder than you realize. Show others what it means to encounter the love of Jesus.

DAILY INTERACTION ▼

 CONNECT: Invite a friend or acquaintance who doesn't know the Lord to check out JesusDaily.com or another faith-based site that you enjoy.

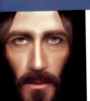

"Do not seek revenge or bear a grudge against one of your people, but love your neighbor as yourself."
LEVITICUS 19:18

DEVOTION ▼

Love Your Neighbor

Our neighbors are all around us, whether we live next door to them or even know their names. The young woman serving our coffee, the older gentleman sitting across from us on the bus, the teenager in our youth group at church. Basically, anyone with whom we come in contact is our neighbor. And we're told to treat them—no, to love them—the same way we love and regard ourselves.

A follower of Jesus asked him, "Lord, who's my neighbor?" And his answer probably surprised and maybe even disturbed them. Christ said that our neighbors are all around us, the people we encounter throughout our day. It might be easier if we could categorize the nice people next door as the only ones we need to treat with kindness, but that's not what God tells us.

Today, love every neighbor you encounter, not just those who live close by.

DAILY INTERACTION ▼

 CONNECT: Touch base with someone whom you used to know who has since moved away—a neighbor, coworker, or friend.

> *He heals the brokenhearted and*
> *binds up their wounds.*
>
> PSALM 147:3

▼ DEVOTION

He Heals Our Wounds

When we break a bone, the worst kind of injury occurs when the bone shatters into multiple pieces. With a clean break, the bone can be set and the healing process begins right away. However, with more than one break, the bone fragments and jagged pieces can make the recovery process long and painful.

Our hearts often feel the same way. Some losses seem like clean breaks. We know they're coming, brace ourselves for them, and move on. Others seem to chip away at our love for someone or our hope for the future. Each hurtful word or offensive action leaves us feeling just a little more raw and jagged. Eventually, we're not sure how to forgive them or heal the damage that has been done.

God knows how to heal even the deepest wounds and most painful assaults on our hearts. Like a master surgeon, he can bind our broken pieces and fill the holes inside us with his love, grace, and mercy. Bones heal, and so will our hearts.

DAILY INTERACTION ▼

CONNECT: Let someone know you're praying for their healing, confident that God will continue to restore their heart and life.

August 31

Do nothing out of selfish ambition or vain conceit, but in humility consider others better than yourselves.... look not only to your own interests, but also to the interests of others.

PHILIPPIANS 2:3–4

DEVOTION ▼

Put Others First

How would you respond today if someone asked you, "Are you a vain person?" Most of us would hope that we're not, and even if we knew the truth about ourselves, we would be reluctant to admit it. However, in our age of constant social media, we face more temptations to value ourselves too highly than ever before. From what we post on our status to the selfies we snap to share with others on a daily basis, we're encouraged to be the star in our very own reality series called life.

However, as Christians, we're called to put others first. To not be focused on our own appearance, identities, or needs and to instead look for opportunities to serve those around us. In a culture that encourages us to chase after our fifteen minutes of fame, it's not always easy, but with Christ as our role model, it's always possible.

Today, let someone else be the star of the show as you support and serve them.

DAILY INTERACTION ▼

 CONNECT: Forego posting a new status, pics, or updates on your own pages and instead comment on what you love on other people's pages.

JESUS HEALS

SEPTEMBER

But the Lord is faithful, and he will strengthen and protect you from the evil one.

2 Thessalonians 3:3

📅 **September 1**

"If anyone wants to be first, he must be the very last, and the servant of all."

MARK 9:35

The Servant of All

We place a lot of stock in numbers, wanting to finish first, wanting to know where we rank compared to our peers. Lists are compiled annually of the wealthiest, the most influential, and the most famous. Athletes are used to being ranked, and most businesses rely on numbers to determine their budgets, their goals, and their margins. Usually, people are only happy when they're moving up on the list.

However, there's one list that we should hope to be last on: those people who want to be first in the kingdom of God. Jesus tells us that if you want to demonstrate your passion, commitment, and dedication to the Lord, you must be the servant of all—last on the list. In a dog-eat-dog world where competing means knowing your numerical place, it's not easy to adopt a mindset of servanthood.

Today, let Jesus be your role model for how to be first by being last.

 CONNECT: Post your desire to serve others in one specific way or offer to help someone in need who has already posted a request.

"See, the former things have taken place, and new things I declare; before they spring into being I announce them to you."

Isaiah 42:9

▼ DEVOTION

Proclaim the Good News

Even though our society is not as formal as it once was, we still follow traditions around major events. For engagements, weddings, and the birth of children, many people still send out announcements to let the world know their happy news. Other formal announcements similarly report something that has already happened, relaying news that others need to know.

Our Father not only proclaims the good news of grace through Christ, but he foretold that news for hundreds of years before Jesus' birth. Similarly, he often prepares us for what's about to happen in our lives even if he doesn't outright announce it to us. He wants us looking ahead, placing our hope in him.

As we are transformed into the likeness of Christ, we have good news to announce, too. We know how to receive forgiveness of sins, enjoy an abundant life, and spend eternity in heaven. Such news is too good to keep to ourselves!

DAILY INTERACTION ▼

CONNECT: Visit JesusDaily.com and post an announcement of something big in your life that's coming up or that's just happened recently.

📅 **September 3**

> *So David triumphed over the Philistine with a sling and a stone; without a sword in his hand he struck down the Philistine and killed him.*
> 1 Samuel 17:50

Giant Slayers

Underdogs remain popular heroes for the very reason that they're outnumbered, underestimated, and overwhelmed. Many people don't expect them to win, and even if they support them, they can't imagine how they can overcome the odds and achieve victory. We want to root for the underdog, especially when he's battling injustice.

One of humanity's favorite underdogs remains the shepherd boy who went on to become king of Israel. David displayed his fearlessness and reliance on God as he squared off against the mighty Philistine giant Goliath, a bully intent on taunting the Israelites and mocking their God. After killing many of their men, the giant grew even louder and prouder of his brutish accomplishments.

David wasn't about to let this guy get away with this kind of behavior, not without a fight. So the young warrior drew on his experience as a shepherd defending his sheep from bears and lions. He used weapons familiar to his ability and comfort level. And he dropped Goliath face down in the dust.

We have the same power of faith, courage, and determination at our disposal. We are giant slayers.

CONNECT: Ask for support and accountability in an area of struggle. If you need professional or medical help, make an appointment.

JESUS HEALS

> *"You intended to harm me, but God intended it for good to accomplish what is now being done, the saving of many lives."*
>
> GENESIS 50:20

Life's Curve Balls

You've probably heard about or seen an Australian boomerang, an aboriginal hunting weapon that has become a popular souvenir and toy. The L-shaped piece of light wood, when thrown by a practiced expert, travels away from its thrower in an arc before returning to the same spot from which it was thrown.

Often what we give to others is what we end up getting for ourselves. When others intend to hurt us, God protects us and transforms our suffering into strength. The negative impact echoes back to those who wished us harm. While no one likes experiencing pain, disappointment, and betrayal, we can take comfort knowing that our wounds will not destroy us. Our Father uses everything in our lives to equip and strengthen us, transforming anything that others might throw at us.

Even when life throws us a curve ball, we know God's going to use it to score a victory in our lives.

 CONNECT: Post a prayer request on JesusDaily.com and commit to pray for others struggling with the same need.

September 5

The fear of the LORD teaches a man wisdom,
and humility comes before honor.
PROVERBS 15:33

DEVOTION ▼

All Wisdom

We often think of wisdom as being synonymous with age and maturity. However, many people grow older and become even more foolish. Having more years under your belt doesn't automatically guarantee that you've learned from your mistakes and grown in wisdom.

The people who grow in wisdom are the ones who trust in the Lord. Young people often mature quickly because they're willing to step out in faith and trust God with their futures. They learn from their mistakes, listen to the wisdom passed down from those ahead of them, and study the truth of God's Word.

When we look to God as our source for wisdom, and not human-made sources, we can know that we will remain humble and grounded. With God as our source, we will not take credit for what we've learned but will point others back to him. He is the wellspring of all wisdom.

DAILY INTERACTION ▼

CONNECT: Share a favorite Scripture verse about wisdom on your page and ask others to post theirs.

September 6

O Lord my God, you are very great;
you are clothed with splendor and majesty.

Psalm 104:1

▼ DEVOTION

His Fingerprints

As summer draws to a close, it's tempting to think that nature has peaked and revealed its most beautiful season. But then autumn begins and we realize that the dazzling display of color, beauty, and amazing transformations only continues. The leaves begin to blur and fade into new colors, from green to tan, gold, scarlet, orange, and brown. The sky takes on a richer shade of blue. The air becomes crisp and soon the first frost leaves a diamond-etched layer of ice coating everything outside.

God's beauty is always before us. Regardless of the season, his fingerprints leave indelible images for us to enjoy and to use as visual reminders of his glory, creativity, and power. We can revel in the sensual delights of autumn and use them as reminders to give thanks and praise for the wonders of the Creator's handiwork.

DAILY INTERACTION ▼

CONNECT: Post a pic of a favorite fall activity—raking leaves, tailgating at football games, or gathering a harvest, to name a few—and ask others to share theirs.

📅 September 7

"Stand at the crossroads and look; ask for the ancient paths, ask where the good way is, and walk in it, and you will find rest for your souls."
JEREMIAH 6:16

DEVOTION ▼

The Ancient Paths

Since we have GPS apps and map software on phones and tablets—or even installed in our vehicles—few people have to stop while driving and ask others for directions anymore. However, we still benefit from the knowledge and wisdom of other travelers. When we visit a new area of our country or travel overseas, we often consult guidebooks, reviews from other travelers, and recommendations from experts.

Our spiritual journey is the same. We can benefit so much from the hundreds of years of wisdom and experience that other Christians have left us as their legacy. When we read the writings of ancient pilgrims of the faith, we're able to look into the heart of another brother or sister in Christ. We can understand their struggles, appreciate their insight, and learn from their timeless faith in the Lord.

The wisdom of other Christians provides us with a bigger road map on our journey. We can see beyond what we've experienced and realize that we will be stretched and called to venture into unknown territory, places that have already been blazed by other believers who have gone ahead of us. We're never traveling alone.

DAILY INTERACTION ▼

CONNECT: Surf online and look for Christians from history who capture your interest. Find some of their writings and see how their wisdom applies to your life.

So whether you eat or drink or whatever you do,
do it all for the glory of God.
1 Corinthians 10:31

JESUS HEALS

▼ DEVOTION

Taste His Goodness

Gourmet cooking shows hosted by celebrity chefs. Kitchen utensils, tools, and implements for every imaginable culinary need. Countless recipes and cookbooks. Restaurants catering to virtually every culture and palette combination under the sun. We have so many great ways to enjoy food that we sometimes forget to credit the source. Each time we eat or drink we're given an opportunity to taste God's goodness and thank him for his bounty.

Whether you're enjoying apple cider and pumpkin bread or the last apples and corn of the season, it's hard not to savor the delicious flavors of autumn. There's a bounty of produce and preparations to be made for the winter ahead. Many people still make their own preserves, jellies, jams, and canned fruits and vegetables. They know there's nothing like the taste of homemade marmalade made from their grandmother's recipe.

Today, reflect on the food you eat with an extra measure of thanksgiving and an extra appreciation for those who grow, harvest, produce, cook, prepare, and serve your meals.

DAILY INTERACTION ▼

CONNECT: Send out invitations for an upcoming "recipe swap" potluck with close friends and family, with each person bringing a favorite dish and recipe to share.

JESUS HEALS

> *"Do not call anything impure that God has made clean."*
> ACTS 11:9

DEVOTION ▼

The People Changer

We're often encouraged to trust our first impressions and go with our gut when it comes to people. And even if we're willing to form our assessment of others over a long time, it's difficult to overcome negative behavior at the beginning of a relationship. But our impressions are not always accurate, and even if they are, we have to allow for the possibility that people can change. Or, to be more accurate, to allow for the fact that God changes people.

We often form impressions of people and judge them. Sometimes if our opinion is negative, we dismiss them and don't treat them kindly and compassionately. We think a leopard can't change his spots. Which may be true, unless he's washed by the blood of the Lamb.

People can change through the power of God's love and the grace of Christ. We have to accept them and treat them the same way we want them to accept and treat us, knowing that we're not who we used to be.

DAILY INTERACTION ▼

 CONNECT: Ask someone who knows you well to give you a reality check, an assessment of the growth that they've seen in your life in the past year.

> *Jesus answered, "Everyone who drinks this water*
> *will be thirsty again, but whoever drinks*
> *the water I give him will never thirst."*
>
> JOHN 4:13–14

JESUS HEALS

▼ DEVOTION

The Desert Within

Imagine that you've just finished a long run or completed a strenuous hike. Your body has perspired so much that you feel as though there's no moisture left in you. Your throat's so dry that it's hard to swallow, and there's a gritty taste in your mouth from all the dust you swallowed on your journey.

Now imagine that you reach for a tall glass of ice-cold water. The sensation of the chilled water going down your throat instantly refreshes you. As you continue drinking, you can almost feel the water coursing down into your body all the way to your toes. You keep drinking and feel as though you can't get enough of this precious liquid.

Our souls were made to find life-giving refreshment in God. He alone satisfies the deep, seemingly unquenchable thirst that often aches within us. In him we drink from the Living Water that brings new life and new joy to the desert within.

DAILY INTERACTION ▼

 CONNECT: Post a pic and testimonial online about your favorite drink and ask others to share theirs. How do these beverages remind us of our thirst for Living Water?

📅 September 11

"I have loved you with an everlasting love …"
JEREMIAH 31:3

Everlasting Love

When tragic events unfold, we usually don't know how to make sense of them. When people seem motivated by hatred, greed, and evil to the point they're willing to take other human lives, it's difficult to fathom. Why would God allow such suffering and devastation to take place at the hands of people clearly not interested in serving him? Surely, he could stop these people from harming others, so why doesn't he?

The simple answer is that he's given us choices about how we live our lives. Adam and Eve exercised this gift of free will by choosing to disobey God and go their own way. Ever since, we've been living in a world filled with the consequences of this sinful choice. Our selfishness grows like a cancer if left unchecked by the grace of God and the love of Christ.

This life will always be painful, but we have the cure for our sinful condition. God did not abandon us after our original parents blew it. He sent his only Son to save us from our sins and give us eternal life. His love is truly everlasting!

CONNECT: Let at least three loved ones know that you're praying for them and lifting them up to your Father. Remind them that they are not alone.

Do not be wise in your own eyes;
fear the LORD and shun evil.

PROVERBS 3:7

JESUS HEALS

▼ DEVOTION

The Truly Wise

As much as we want to grow wiser and more mature, we're often not the best judges of our own progress. In fact, the more we remain focused on our own growth, the more likely we are to become proud, arrogant, and self-righteous. Our humility fades as we begin to feel pretty good about ourselves and our spiritual development.

However, this is not the way that truly wise people behave and grow. Maybe you've heard the saying, "The more I know, the more I know that I don't know!" In many ways, this is the attitude of the spiritually mature. Their humility grounds them and keeps them from being a know-it-all prone to tell others how to grow closer to God. Instead, they learn from their experiences and are always willing to share it with others, but never in a way that's smug, superior, or condescending.

They know that we all learn from one another, both the new believer and the mature lifetime Christian. Those who are truly wise realize that God alone is the source of all wisdom.

DAILY INTERACTION ▼

 CONNECT: Consult someone you consider spiritually mature and wise regarding an upcoming decision you need to make.

📅 **September 13**

And do not forget to do good and to share with others, for with such sacrifices God is pleased.

HEBREWS 13:16

DEVOTION ▼

Do Good and Share

Many people naturally seem prone to save and be frugal. They hold on to what they earn and are reluctant to give it away. They may have a little or a lot, but their miserly attitude influences almost every decision. On the other hand, many others love giving what they have away. They know that it's truly more blessed to give than to receive, and they delight in being a blessing to others.

Regardless of our natural inclinations or personality, when we practice generosity, we find it's easier to give away what we have. When you don't cling to possessions, wealth, or power as the source of your security or identity, you realize that you don't need to hold on to them. You know that God is the source of all you have, and as a result, you're merely his steward, using what you've been given to advance his kingdom.

Whether it's a kid sharing his lunch with another in the school cafeteria or a little boy sharing his lunch with Jesus to bless and multiply for the 5,000, there's always a sense of the miraculous when we're willing to give others what we have.

DAILY INTERACTION ▼

 CONNECT: Visit a site where people with needs are matched with people who have items, services, and money to donate.

> *Therefore, as we have opportunity, let us do good to all people, especially to those who belong to the family of believers.*
>
> GALATIANS 6:10

▼ DEVOTION

Do Your Best

Often we think of doing good as always saying the right thing, being prepared for any response or action from others, and always having something to give to those around us. In short, "doing good" gradually becomes "being the best." But this is not what serving God and others requires. We don't have to be perfect. There's no competition and no "best" to achieve.

Doing good simply means living a life based on God's love, guidance, and generosity. It means just treating other people the same way you want to be treated. It's an attitude of compassion, understanding, and acceptance that reflects the grace you've been given.

You don't have to be perfect. There's no "right way" to do everything in your day. You're only required to offer wholehearted efforts fueled by your love of God and his creation. Doing your best, you can rest in Christ's perfect love.

DAILY INTERACTION ▼

CONNECT: Go to JesusDaily.com and ask others how they handle perfectionism in their lives, especially in their faith. Agree to pray for one another.

— DEVOTION ▼ —

More Than Good Enough

Many people think of themselves as "good people," individuals willing to treat others kindly and to do what they can to improve the world around them. Many people fear that they're not "good enough," and so they try to do extra service and show extra kindness to others. However, if we're totally honest, no one is really good—at least, not in the sense that God is good.

No matter how nice, kind, caring, and compassionate, even the best people are still sinful. In this lifetime, we'll never reach perfection even as we're transformed by the power of God's Holy Spirit dwelling within us. We simply have to remember that God is the source of our goodness. He provides the standard as well as the power for all we need to do.

Although we'll never be perfect here, we're already more than good enough because of what Christ has done for us. We can share this good news with others, fueled by our desire to see others experience God's forgiveness, grace, and love.

— **DAILY** INTERACTION ▼ —

 CONNECT: Post a picture that illustrates God's goodness on JesusDaily.com and see how many "likes" you get.

JESUS HEALS

> *Be joyful always; pray continually;*
> *give thanks in all circumstances, for this is*
> *God's will for you in Christ Jesus.*
>
> 1 Thessalonians 5:16–18

▼ DEVOTION

Count Your Blessings

The relationship between gratitude and joy continues to be studied by doctors, psychologists, and counselors. The premise is pretty simple: when we're aware of all the good things we have in life, when we stop focusing on what we don't have and notice what we already have, we experience more joy. In other words, when we count our blessings, we realize how much God has blessed us and feel appropriately grateful.

In a culture that's focused on buying and spending to attain more and more, it's easy to overlook how much we actually have. Our health, our families, and our work should not be taken for granted. Food to eat, a roof over our heads, and clothes to wear are also gifts and not entitlements. Friends who care about us, reliable transportation, and a sense of humor—the list of blessings we tend to take for granted goes on and on.

Today, count your many blessings, especially giving thanks for the things you may take for granted.

—— DAILY INTERACTION ▼

 CONNECT: Share items from your "Top Ten" list with a friend in exchange for sharing theirs.

📅 **September 17**

> *[Jesus said,] "Whoever serves me must follow me; and where I am, my servant also will be. My Father will honor the one who serves me."*
> JOHN 12:26

A Life of Service

Sometimes we assume that being a servant requires us to be meek and mild, submissive and subservient, willing to take orders and do whatever anyone around us wants us to do. However, regarding biblical servanthood, nothing could be further from the truth!

It takes considerable strength, dedication, and humility to serve someone. You must be committed to obeying their wishes without questioning their judgment. You must trust them implicitly and want only what is best for them.

With these kinds of qualifications, it's easy to see why there's nothing passive or weak about serving God. He wants us to serve him as living sacrifices, as obedient sons and daughters who've been bought with a price and redeemed.

Serving is easy when we fully realize what we've been given.

 CONNECT: Stay unplugged during your free time today while you serve others, either in your neighborhood or at home.

JESUS HEALS

You need to persevere so that when you have done the will of God, you will receive what he has promised.

HEBREWS 10:36

▼ DEVOTION

Keeper of Promises

When was the last time someone promised you something but didn't deliver? In the business world, we often want our contractors and team members to "under promise and over deliver" instead of the other way around. Unfortunately, not everyone follows through and delivers what they say they will. They may even be well-intentioned, but if they can't provide what's expected, you will soon lose faith in their credibility.

God always over delivers on his promises. For thousands of years, he has maintained the hundreds of promises made in his Word. Numerous prophecies foretold the coming of Christ and various specific details about his birth, life, death, and resurrection, all of which were fulfilled.

Christ's promise to send his Spirit and always be with us reinforces his Father's promise never to abandon us. We have a God who keeps his Word and always delivers more than we deserve.

DAILY INTERACTION ▼

CONNECT: Reach out to a friend who's going through a challenging season and promise to help them through it. Check in with them each day for the next week.

— DEVOTION ▾ —

An Impact for Eternity

Our culture remains fascinated with life after death, the details of heaven, and what happens when we pass on. In movies and TV shows, characters consistently and miraculously seem to return from the grave. In soap operas, it's even become expected that supposedly dead characters will eventually return!

No matter how death and the afterlife are depicted in fiction, the reality remains that we will all perish. Our lives are finite here on earth. If we've trusted Christ as our Savior, we have the promise of eternal life with him and our Father in heaven. Without knowing what it will look or feel like, we're told that it will be a place without tears, sorrow, or time.

We never know how long our time here on earth will be. Whether we live a long life for decades to come or we are called home soon, we have the security of where we'll spend eternity. Heaven is our home forever. So make the most of the time you have today.

— DAILY INTERACTION ▾ —

CONNECT: Invite someone who doesn't know the Lord to have coffee with you, accompany you to church, or visit an upcoming outreach event.

> *In my integrity you uphold me*
> *and set me in your presence forever.*
>
> PSALM 41:12

JESUS HEALS

▼ DEVOTION

Integrated and Whole

When we are integrated, we are whole. All the various parts, pieces, roles, and responsibilities of who we are become grounded by the consistency of our character. As we follow Christ, all the different facets of our personality become transformed by God's Spirit working within us.

Much of the time, we concentrate on strengthening certain parts of our self and eliminating others. We want to emphasize our virtuous habits and disciplines and remove the weaknesses, mistakes, and vices. While there's  certainly merit in cultivating spiritual disciplines and resisting temptations, we must also remember that God loves all of us. He knows every facet of our being—after all, he created us—and nothing surprises him.

If we want to be integrated and whole, we need to be honest about all the parts of ourselves, not just the ones we like.

DAILY INTERACTION ▼

 CONNECT: Check in with a prayer partner or accountability partner at JesusDaily.com and renew your commitment to encourage each other.

🗓 **September 21**

> *[Jesus said,] "For where two or three come together in my name, there am I with them."*
> MATTHEW 18:20

DEVOTION ▼

Gathered in His Name

Most of us have had the experience of feeling lonely in a crowd at a big event. Even though we may be with people in close proximity, we remain disconnected, distant, and separate from them. We get lost in the crowd, wondering why we came.

On the other hand, sometimes we may feel as though we belong to an enormous cause with only one or two other people. Such is the Body of Christ. We don't have to be with a church full of people to know that we're part of something life-changing and history-making. We simply have to be with another believer, maybe a couple, who long to follow Jesus the way we do.

The original disciples were only twelve men. The early churches often met in homes with only a few dozen people. We can know God's presence in very intimate ways when we're part of a small group. We can help meet one another's needs, pray together, study the Bible together, and celebrate together.

DAILY INTERACTION ▼

 CONNECT: Reconnect with a Christian friend with whom you haven't communicated in a while. Let them know you're thinking of them and that they're not alone.

> *Blessed are those who have learned to acclaim you,*
> *who walk in the light of your presence, O LORD.*
>
> PSALM 89:15

JESUS HEALS

▼ DEVOTION

Walk in the Light

When the electricity goes out, when the flashlight doesn't work, when night falls faster than we thought on our hike, we experience darkness in an entirely new way. We may be tempted to panic and wonder how we'll see and be able to keep going. We may trip or stumble, groping around in the dark to find candles or fresh batteries. Even after our eyes adjust to the darkness, we may still struggle to see.

Sometimes we become so burdened with the cares of life that it feels as though the lights have dimmed around us. Circumstances seem bleak, and we can't see clearly as darkness seems to close in around us. We struggle for more light, for a clearer sense of what's going on.

During these periods of darkness, we must rely on God's light, trusting that it's there even if we can't see it the way we want. Like the sun or stars obscured by cloud cover, the light remains even though it's not visible. We simply have to wait for the clouds to pass in order for the light to shine brighter again.

DAILY INTERACTION ▼

CONNECT: Post a picture of a favorite source of light, whether it's the sun or moon, a lamp or lantern, candlelight or fireworks. Share a verse about God's light.

JESUS HEALS

📅 **September 23**

But the Lord is faithful, and he will strengthen and protect you from the evil one.
2 Thessalonians 3:3

You Can Handle It

Few people today are not affected by violence of some kind, either directly or through their loved ones. In addition, we often face the consequences of corruption in our offices, communities, governments, and, yes, sometimes even in our churches. Evil has many faces, and we may not always recognize it when it stares back at us. Nonetheless, we have to remain vigilant and strong in the power of the Lord. Our enemy is out to get us, to undermine our faith and take us out of the race.

When we face trials and temptations, we sometimes lose sight of what's really going on. We question God and wonder why he's allowing us to go through such hard times. During these moments, the enemy tries to use our feelings of doubt, fear, and anxiety to undermine our faith.

Faith requires us to not dwell on our emotions and allow them to control our decisions and actions. God will always provide the power we need to get through today's challenges. No matter how daunting it appears, you can handle what's ahead.

 CONNECT: Let others know you need their prayers, sharing as much as you feel led to reveal about your needs.

> *The LORD is faithful to all his promises*
> *and loving toward all he has made.*
>
> PSALM 145:13

JESUS HEALS

▼ DEVOTION

He Remains the Same

Despite the fact that weather can be unpredictable and change quickly, the four seasons remain constant. Some days may seem as though they include all four in one by starting out cool, growing warmer, blowing in a storm, revealing the sun, clouding up and turning chilly again, and ending with a few snowflakes. Depending on where you live, this may be more the norm than not.

However, over time, there are still characteristics of each season that remain consistent. In summer, on average the temperatures are higher. In winter, colder weather lingers more regularly. We learn that even though a particular day might be exceptional, the seasons on average remain consistent.

If the seasons, with each day's variant conditions, remain consistent, we can trust that God's faithfulness remains the same regardless of our life's circumstances. He's the same yesterday, today, and forever!

DAILY INTERACTION ▼

CONNECT: Post a photo or illustration of your favorite kind of weather. Pair it with a verse about God's faithfulness and unchanging nature.

For great is your love, higher than the heavens;
your faithfulness reaches to the skies.
PSALM 108:4

DEVOTION ▼

Higher Than the Heavens

How high above the earth have you been? If you've flown in a plane, you've probably been at least 30,000 feet above our planet. If you're one of the few people involved in space travel and exploration, you may have seen earth's surface from an even greater distance, one that the rest of us only see in photos and films.

Whether you've never flown or you're an accomplished astronaut, we can never know the limits of God's love. We're told they're "higher than the heavens," which appropriately seems like an infinite distance. We can't measure or quantify God's love because it's so immense, intense, and urgent.

He gave everything in order to win us back. He allowed his only precious Son to live as a man and die on a cross in order to pay for our sins. God's love is the only reason we, in turn, are able to love him.

DAILY INTERACTION ▼

CONNECT: Surf for images of earth taken from satellites. Post your favorite, sharing how much greater God's love is than the distance shown.

JESUS HEALS

> *[Jesus said,] "It is more blessed*
> *to give than to receive."*
> Acts 20:35

▼ DEVOTION

More Blessed to Give

How do you feel when someone gives you a gift? Grateful? Embarrassed? Curious about their motive? Obligated to give them one in return? We often give gifts because we want something from someone else, maybe even a gift in return. Sometimes we give gifts because it's the cultural custom, such as a housewarming or hostess gift. Other gifts are given because we want to express our sincere love for the recipient.

Regardless of our motive, it's clear that there's a blessing when we give. If you've ever received a gift you really needed or especially treasured, you know what a blessing such a gift can be. But Jesus tells us that it's even more blessed to give than to receive. The exercise of giving is one blessing and allows us to focus on God, not on attaining wealth or possessions. And the recipient's joy is at least one more blessing.

Today, practice the blessing of giving good gifts to those around you.

DAILY INTERACTION ▼

 CONNECT: Give someone you love an e-card of encouragement, letting them know how much you want to bless them with your love.

 **September 27**

JESUS HEALS

> *If your enemy is hungry, give him food to eat;*
> *if he is thirsty, give him water to drink.*
> PROVERBS 25:21

Reflect His Grace

Serving food and drink to people who intend to harm us can never be easy. Even as they oppose us, antagonize us, and injure us, God wants us to serve them in the most fundamental, vital way. Perhaps part of the reason may be that in serving them food and drink we're reminded of their humanity. Just like us, just like all people, they need to eat and drink in order to live.

Sometimes it's easy to dehumanize our enemies and dismiss them as villains to be hated or monsters to be destroyed. When we provide a meal for them, especially if we share in that meal with them, we cannot pretend that they are so different. They may even recognize our humanity and ask for forgiveness. But even if they don't, they will be shamed by the fact that we're returning their offense with kindness. We're not retaliating as they might expect, but reflecting the grace of God.

Surprise is often a key element in how God's grace sneaks up on us. Sometimes the best way to share his love with others is to do the opposite of what they expect, at least in the case of our enemies.

 CONNECT: Email or text someone who has opposed or hurt you in the past. Surprise them with your kindness and compassionate attitude.

*"My words come from an upright heart;
my lips sincerely speak what I know."*

JOB 33:3

JESUS HEALS

▼ DEVOTION

Transparency

What once seemed factual and objective now often emerges as subjective and clouded by the perceptions of various stake-holders. Journalists, scientists, attorneys, and engineers once relied on data to drive much of what they do; however, now they know that understanding the context of a problem and the various ways the information has a spin put on it makes a huge difference. In other words, many people often see what they want to see.

The truth of God's Word and the faithfulness of his promises are not subject to such fluctuating interpretation. We're told there is no shifting of shadows with God. He remains sovereign and his love remains constant. He always makes good on his promises.

Today, seek to be as honest, consistent, and faithful as God has been to you.

DAILY INTERACTION ▼

 CONNECT: Prayerfully and gently, talk with a close friend or loved one about a hard truth they need to know.

Therefore I glory in Christ Jesus in my service to God.
ROMANS 15:17

DEVOTION ▼

Use Your Gifts

When was the last time you felt the pleasure of God bubbling within you? Like you were doing something so significant, so personal, so sacrificial that you could just feel your Father smiling down at you? When you're doing what you were created to do, it's natural to feel his pleasure as you come into the fullness of your God-given potential.

Whether it's writing or nursing, teaching or singing, designing or counseling, we must discover those areas where God has gifted us to serve others. This is the way we also discover true contentment. When we know our purpose, we can let go of chasing empty pursuits for temporary pleasure.

You don't have to try to be happy when you're serving God through the gifts he has given you. Your joy will naturally be made complete as you live out your purpose, reflecting his glory and advancing his kingdom.

DAILY INTERACTION ▼

 CONNECT: At JesusDaily.com post a selfie doing something you know you were made to do; ask others to share the same.

Great peace have they who love your law,
and nothing can make them stumble.
Psalm 119:165

JESUS HEALS

▼ DEVOTION

Great Peace

When you're anxious and upset, your body reacts accordingly. If you're trying to run away from a perceived threat or imminent danger, you may literally lose your balance from fear, anxiety, and panic. Your heart will race and your breathing will become shallow and irregular. Adrenaline will course through your body as it prepares a "fight or flight" response to the threat before you.

When we know the peace of the Lord, however, our entire being experiences the calm tranquility of knowing our security is in him. Our body relaxes, we sleep better, and we aren't ruffled by the temporary storm clouds that appear on the horizon.

If we follow Jesus and obey God's commands, our feet will remain steadfast and sure. We will not stumble or fall victim to the many worries, fears, and anxieties that try to plague us. Our peace is certain. Today, don't let anyone or anything rob you of the security you have in the Lord.

DAILY INTERACTION ▼

 CONNECT: Email three friends and remind them that they have nothing to fear. Let them know you're praying for them to know the certainty of God's peace.

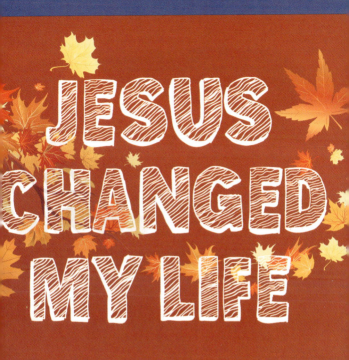

JESUS CHANGED MY LIFE

O**CTOBER**

*Now faith is being sure of what we hope for
and certain of what we do not see.*

Hebrews 11:1

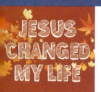

For with you is the fountain of life;
in your light we see light.
PSALM 36:9

A Wellspring Within

Underground springs often provide water for fertile areas even when there's no water present on the surface. Sometimes these areas become bogs or swamps, lowlands where the water bubbling beneath the ground doesn't drain away. Vegetation and animal life flourish there even though it might look surprisingly calm at first glance. Often, change and growth take place even when we can't see it.

The same is true with our spiritual lives. God's Spirit within us provides a wellspring of Living Water to nourish and sustain us. And while we may not feel as though we're becoming more mature or deepening our faith as we walk with the Lord, growth is taking place nonetheless.

Our Father provides everything we need to grow. His Spirit is at work even when we can't see what's going on.

 CONNECT: Post a picture of a fountain to accompany today's verse and encourage others to add it to their "likes."

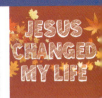

JESUS CHANGED MY LIFE

> *. . . whoever is kind to the needy honors God.*
> PROVERBS 14:31

▼ DEVOTION

Interdependent

We often think of "needy" people as being ones in tough situations with nowhere else to turn. Homeless people and those in crisis, caught up in domestic dysfunction or addictions, are obviously in need of help. But the truth is that we are all needy. No matter how hard we work to disguise our needs and appear self-sufficient, we need support, encouragement, and assistance from other people.

Whether it's money for groceries or encouragement to ask for a promotion, our sense of interdependency reflects the way God made us. He doesn't expect us to have everything together and take care of ourselves alone. He created us to be in relationships as part of a larger community.

Sometimes we must let our guard down and allow others to see how much we really need them.

DAILY INTERACTION ▼

 CONNECT: Browse the needs and prayer requests on a local church or community website and choose one that you feel led to fulfill.

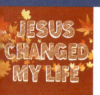

A cheerful look brings joy to the heart,
and good news gives health to the bones.
PROVERBS 15:30

———————————————————— DEVOTION ▼ ————

Share Your Joy

Most of us fear getting the proverbial phone call in the middle of the night, answering it with dread at the prospect of bad news. And we may cringe when we see certain subject lines in our email inbox or recognize certain return addresses on envelopes in our mail. However, the news is not always as bad as we think it is. In fact, sometimes the news is actually good.

With so many hard and challenging events all around us, and 24/7 media coverage of every moment, we often don't allow ourselves to hope for good news. We may even be guilty of having good news that we fail to share with those who would love to celebrate with us. Now more than ever good news is a prized commodity.

Let others know when you're giving thanks to the Lord for what he's done. Ask them to share in your joy and celebrate in your thanksgiving.

DAILY INTERACTION ▼ —————————————————

  CONNECT: Post some good news about your personal life or family for others to share and celebrate with you.

He himself bore our sins in his body on the tree,
so that we might die to sins and live for righteousness;
by his wounds you have been healed.

1 PETER 2:24

JESUS CHANGED MY LIFE

▼ DEVOTION

A Time to Heal

When we fell and hurt ourselves as children, it only took a hug from our mom or dad and a Band-aid to feel better. In a couple days, our scrapes usually healed and we didn't think about them again until the next fall, playground scuffle, or bike accident. We learned that our parents' attention comforted us and that time healed us.

As adults, our wounds and injuries often feel more complex and seem to require more time to heal. The scabs and scars last longer and remind us of the pain inflicted. Invisible injuries hurt even worse—the harsh words said, the devastating betrayals endured, the precious moments stolen.

Jesus knew what it meant to bear the pain of both visible and invisible injuries. He bore the burden of our sins through his death on the cross. We experience healing from all that hurts us because of his loving sacrifice.

— DAILY INTERACTION ▼

CONNECT: Encourage others to go for a physical exam or checkup, reminding them that October is breast cancer awareness month.

In his love and mercy he redeemed them;
he lifted them up and carried them all the days of old.
Isaiah 63:9

DEVOTION ▾

He Will Carry You

What's in your purse or briefcase right now? What items do you carry with you most every day in your backpack, pockets, or wallet? If you're like many people, you probably include cash, credit cards, I.D. cards or driver's license, pen, notepad, keys, and your cell phone. Throw in a few cosmetics such as lipstick or small cologne along with some breath mints or candy, and you have quite a bundle.

But these items are nothing compared to carrying another person on your shoulders. Parents know that even the smallest toddler soon seems to weigh like a ton of bricks after only a few moments. But our Father carries us with the greatest of ease, all of us, each and every one of us.

Sometimes we feel as though we can't continue forward carrying all the burdens that weigh down on us. Today, let them go and give them to the Lord to carry. He can put you on his shoulders as if you were a child. After all, he is your Father.

DAILY INTERACTION ▾

CONNECT: Shop for a new purse, bag, or wallet that will help you travel lighter. If you find one you like, purchase it. Give your current one to a friend or a local thrift store.

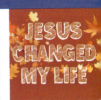

> *If the LORD delights in a man's way,*
> *he makes his steps firm.*
>
> PSALM 37:23

▼ DEVOTION

He Holds Us Firm

One of the greatest challenges during bad weather is maintaining your footing. Whether it's a rainstorm turning the ground to sloppy mud or a freezing snow that leaves the ground icy and treacherous, you have to take each step slowly if you don't want to fall and hurt yourself. Each year, regardless of the season but especially in fall and winter, thousands of people slip and fall. From sprained ankles to broken hips, such injuries leave strong individuals literally lying on the ground.

Even though life circumstances often make us feel as though we're trying to run uphill on slippery ground, we know that God holds us firm. We only have to take one step at a time, trusting that he guards each one, providing a firm foundation. We may fall occasionally, but our Father always lifts us up and helps us get back on our feet.

He leads us down a safe path on solid ground. Even when the weather is treacherous and the road seems slick, we can step out in faith and follow him.

───── DAILY INTERACTION ▼

CONNECT: Ask others to post their favorite verse about stepping out in faith. Choose one to illustrate and use as your wallpaper this week.

Do you not know that in a race all
the runners run, but only one gets the prize?
Run in such a way as to get the prize.
1 Corinthians 9:24

— DEVOTION ▼ —

Run for the Prize

Are you a competitive person? Do you enjoy being the first to complete a project at work or take special satisfaction in winning Monopoly during family game night? Do you find it impossible to avoid comparing your lawn to your neighbors' and need to try the latest electronic gadgets first?

Or maybe you're just the opposite. You move at your own pace and resent others who always seem intent on comparing and competing. You realize that God doesn't want us pushing and shoving others in order to get to the front of the line. Remembering that the last shall be first, you're content to let others pass you by.

Perhaps both ends of the spectrum get us in trouble. While we're called to be humble, selfless, and servant-minded, we're also called to be shrewd, vigilant, and dedicated. We're asked to give our best and compete with no one other than the potential God has created in us.

— DAILY INTERACTION ▼ —

CONNECT: Look at your status labels for the past month. Are you tempted to try and impress others with your latest purchase, prize, or product? Today, keep it humble.

*For it is by grace you have been saved, through faith—
and this not from yourselves, it is the gift of God—
not by works, so that no one can boast.*

EPHESIANS 2:8–9

▼ DEVOTION

Grace through Faith

Perhaps it's human nature to boast. Even the most humble among us want to be appreciated and valued for their contribution. We want others to notice what we bring to the group and affirm our unique skills and talents. Sometimes we might help others notice our efforts, either through direct bragging or the way many people disguise it as false modesty.

In either case, we're wanting to take credit for something that we've created, built, selected, achieved, accomplished, or won. With our salvation, there's no way we can take any credit whatsoever. All of us have sinned and fallen short of the glory of God. We can't earn his favor or save ourselves.

Jesus came to do what we could not. Through his sacrifice, we have eternal life simply by accepting his free gift. There's nothing we can do to buy it, win it, or earn it. We are all equal recipients of God's love and grace.

DAILY INTERACTION ▼

CONNECT: Send a Bible app to someone who needs to know the Lord. YouVersion is free, while others can be purchased and emailed as a downloadable gift for a small fee.

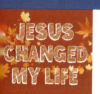

Now faith is being sure of what we hope for and certain of what we do not see.
HEBREWS 11:1

— DEVOTION ▾ —

The Invisible Bridge

As beautiful as they are, bridges can sometimes be frightening to cross. If you stop and consider that you're being supported thousands of feet above a deep, often dangerous, body of water, it can be disconcerting. Will the steel and concrete continue to hold? You can see the beams, columns, and cables reinforcing the strength of the bridge, but when it stretches for a great distance—miles even—it often causes concern.

But what if you had to cross an invisible bridge? "Just keep driving straight and don't look down if you're afraid of heights. Yes, it's a little scary to be so high above the water without being able to see the bridge that's supporting you, but it's there nonetheless." Can you imagine your response to such a recommendation?

And yet, in many ways, we're asked to cross an invisible bridge each day. God wants us to exercise our trust in him and his Word by stepping out in faith. We can be sure of what we hope for and certain of what we can't see.

— DAILY INTERACTION ▾ —

 CONNECT: Visit JesusDaily.com and post a picture of a bridge that you've crossed and ask others to share their own.

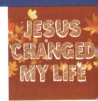

> *For a thousand years in your sight are like a day that has just gone by, or like a watch in the night.*
>
> PSALM 90:4

▼ **DEVOTION**

Beyond Time

Where has this year gone? Only yesterday it seemed that the new year had started, and you were beginning a fresh season of growing closer to the Lord. Then winter melted into spring, and you celebrated the resurrection of Christ at the Easter holiday. Soon the flowers pushed up through the ground and burst into color. Trees unfurled their green canopies, and suddenly you were basking in the joy of summer picnics, hikes, gardens, and holidays.

Then summer gave way to fall, and now here you are, enjoying the cool crisp air and the new season of glorious colors in the autumn art show of reds, golds, yellows, and browns. The holidays are just around the corner, and then before you know it, you'll be starting a new year again. Where has the time gone?

The speed of life seems to go faster and faster. Today, be thankful that you know where you will spend eternity, beyond the linear flow of time that currently confines you.

─ **DAILY** INTERACTION ▼

CONNECT: Construct a timeline of your life's major events and share with others how your relationship with God has shaped your life so far?

...the Lord knows how to rescue godly men from trials...
2 PETER 2:9

DEVOTION ▾

Power to Save

In so many movies and TV shows, comic books and novels, we're used to the powerful hero saving those imperiled from danger, death, and destruction. Whether it's a thrilling battle in space, hand-to-hand combat from centuries ago, or an imminent natural disaster, such calamities would surely claim numerous lives if not for the valiant efforts—often down to the nail-biting last second—of a superhero, space warrior, soldier, or resourceful everyman.

We admire and appreciate stories of heroes who can rescue us from danger. They give us hope that impossible odds can be overcome, unlikely solutions can work, and that last-minute rescues can happen. While this may not be realistic, we know there's one Savior who has already come through for us.

While we were yet sinners, Jesus left his Father in heaven and came to earth to live and die as a man—the ultimate "undercover" assignment. He bore our sins on the cross and defeated death through the power of the resurrection. We've already been rescued from the greatest danger to our souls.

DAILY INTERACTION ▾

 CONNECT: Share something about your favorite fictional hero with others, ask them to share theirs, and remind them that Jesus has the ultimate power to save.

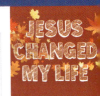

> *[Jesus said,] "In this world you will have trouble. But take heart! I have overcome the world."*
>
> JOHN 16:33

Live Unconditionally

It's so tempting to look over our neighbor's fence and think the grass is so much greener than our own. We think, *If only I had more money, I could be content. If only I didn't have so many responsibilities and demands from my family. If only I had chosen a different career. If only my spouse were the kind of person I want them to be. If only my kids were more obedient. If only I were free to pursue the kind of life I want to live.* If only, if only, if only . . .

We can live conditionally, suspending our awareness of the present and all the blessings we currently have in our lives. Or, we can live—and love—unconditionally, engaged with today as a gift from the Lord, another opportunity to enjoy the many gifts he's given us.

Today, remember that you have everything you need for now. You don't need to live conditionally, waiting until some future moment to be fully alive and present to your life. Jesus has overcome the world, including your own dissatisfaction and complacency.

CONNECT: Ask a friend or confidant to identify at least ten blessings in your life today. After you've done the same for them, share a prayer of thanksgiving together.

📅 **October 13**

You are my hiding place; you will protect me from trouble and surround me with songs of deliverance.
PSALM 32:7

A Safe Place

It's hard sometimes to find a safe place. Circumstances change, relationships deteriorate, and unexpected obstacles crash in on us. Where do we go when we're afraid, weary, anxious, and troubled?

You may not be able to have a home with walls and security surveillance or an isolated mountain cabin where no one can find you. But you can create a safe place within your heart by spending time with God and asking him to meet you there.

Throughout your day, numerous forces will disrupt your schedule, unravel your expectations, and frustrate your best laid plans. But you can remain calm and in control, knowing that you're grounded by the firmest foundation. God remains your hiding place, a safe shelter from the winds of change and the storms passing through today.

CONNECT: Share an image of your ideal "safe place" and ask others to do the same. What do you notice about the different ways we all want shelter?

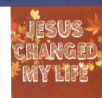
…for God's gifts and his call are irrevocable.

ROMANS 11:29

▼ DEVOTION

Your Divine Destiny

Some things you just know, and you can't "unknow" them no matter what happens. Once you love someone, it doesn't change, even if the nature of the relationship and circumstances force you apart. Once you've learned certain lessons about life, you cannot undo the wisdom you've gained from such experiences, nor would you want to. Similarly, once you experience a glimpse of who you're called to be, once you hear the whisper of your Father's voice revealing your divine destiny, there's no going back.

When you grasp the gift that God has given you, you know that nothing will satisfy you except living out your sacred purpose. You realize you're part of something bigger, something epic, that bears the redemptive design of your Creator. It's both exciting and frightening as you begin exploring this new territory of discovery. Like climbing a mountain, you can't look down—you must only look at the next step in front of you.

Today, live fully out of the call God has placed on your life, knowing that you're part of a grand story from the Author and Finisher of your faith.

DAILY INTERACTION ▼

 CONNECT: Help someone you know discover more of their divine purpose by giving them feedback about the talents, gifts, and skills you see in their life.

JESUS CHANGED MY LIFE

📅 October 15

> [Jesus said,] "Do to others as you would have them do to you."
>
> LUKE 6:31

DEVOTION ▼

The Golden Rule

You've probably heard the expression, "Walk a mile in my shoes." It's a saying often heard when someone feels as though their hardship or suffering is going unnoticed. It's that sense we all have at times that no one else understands how hard it is to be in our place.

And yet, if we allow ourselves, we can know almost exactly what it's like to be someone else. Human beings are more alike than different, more similar in the basic ways we reflect our Creator's image than in the uniqueness of our individuality. Although we may look different, sound different, or have different cultural lifestyles, beneath the colors of our skins, our languages, and our socio-economic differences, we are all spiritual beings. We all need food, water, sleep, and love to survive.

Some of the stories we love the most are ones about people who are different than we are. But the human condition and elements of the heart remain the same across time, across cultures, beyond differences of age, gender, education, and intellect. Today, remember to treat others with the same compassion you hope to experience from them.

DAILY INTERACTION ▼

 CONNECT: Surf the summaries of memoirs about characters radically different than you, choosing one to read that will broaden your understanding and compassion.

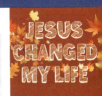
"For the LORD your God is the one who goes with you to fight for you against your enemies to give you victory."

DEUTERONOMY 20:4

▼ DEVOTION

He Stands by You

No one likes a bully. When someone takes advantage of others based on their size, authority, or power, we instinctively want to fight them. Many bullies use intimidation and emotional manipulation to prevent others from seeing their own insecurities. Sometimes it only takes someone with the courage to confront and expose a bully in order for them to back down.

Sometimes we can feel bullied by life's events and unfair circumstances. A less-qualified candidate gets the job. A friend's gossip betrays our secrets to the world. An accidental text reveals what a coworker really thinks of us. Our child gets sick with a serious illness. A loved one is unexpectedly taken from us.

But we have the ultimate backup on our side, even when life tries to bully us. God stands by us and empowers us to fight, to persevere, and to overcome. Today, the bullies of life will not be able to push you around with the Lord beside you.

DAILY INTERACTION ▼

 CONNECT: Visit JesusDaily.com and enlist others to help you minister to local people who have no resources or other advocates.

JESUS CHANGED MY LIFE

With God we will gain the victory,
and he will trample down our enemies.
PSALM 60:12

DEVOTION ▼

Victory Is Certain

As we go through the ups and downs of daily life, we often feel as though we're engaged in a battle. We struggle to maintain all the areas we're juggling—family, work, friends, church, and more. As we become more and more fatigued from the fight, we wonder how we'll keep going. Sometimes we may even feel as though we can't go on, that something has to give.

During these times, we must remember that our battle is already won. Yes, we continue to face certain challenges, but often the performance pressure we feel comes largely from our own sense of obligation. Circumstances may be less than ideal, but we have what we need for today. When we trust God with the future, we realize that we can begin living in the victory that Christ has already won for us through his death and resurrection.

We know how the war ends, even if a few skirmishes remain to be fought. Our confidence is not in how well we fight, but in the certainty of surrendering to our Savior.

DAILY INTERACTION ▼

 CONNECT: Post a favorite verse about Christ's triumph over sin and death, praying for others who need to remember this vital truth of our faith.

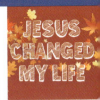
JESUS CHANGED MY LIFE

All hard work brings a profit…
PROVERBS 14:23

▼ DEVOTION

Dedicated Work

Some people naturally enjoy hard work. They like staying busy and always have several projects going at once. Their high energy level allows them to stay engaged in every environment, completing multiple tasks and remaining incredibly productive.

Others of us struggle to sustain our energy and wonder how others do it. We try to work hard but often wonder what we're working for. We feel trapped in our circumstances, afraid that what we're doing doesn't have meaning or matter in the long run.

When we dedicate our work to the Lord, however, we can know that what we do always matters. God wants us to give him our best efforts, whether hard work comes naturally for us or requires more discipline. Even when we can't see the results, he uses our efforts to further his kingdom and to reveal his glory for all to see.

DAILY INTERACTION ▼

CONNECT: Remain unplugged today in your free time, using the occasion to catch up on your work and check items off your to-do list.

> *. . . now is the time of God's favor,*
> *now is the day of salvation.*
> 2 Corinthians 6:2

Be Fully Alive

Where is your heart right now? What preoccupies most of your mental energy today? How would you describe your relationship with God at this very minute? We often have a hard time engaging with the present, being fully alive and aware of our hearts, minds, and bodies. It's much easier to remain focused on the past—what happened, what didn't happen, what we wished had happened. Or, on our future—our hopes, dreams, expectations, and goals.

But today is what you have before you. Right now is the present moment. What will you do with this extraordinary gift that the Lord has given you? What have you been putting off that needs attention? What happened in the past that you need to release and relinquish to God's healing? What do you want to happen in the future that requires you to begin today?

Use today as an urgent opportunity to do what the Lord calls you to do.

 CONNECT: Encourage a friend to make the most of their day, letting them know that you're praying for all their endeavors.

> *For the LORD will not reject his people;*
> *he will never forsake his inheritance.*
>
> PSALM 94:14

▼ DEVOTION

A Priceless Inheritance

We've all heard stories about people who receive legacies left by relatives whom they did not know they had. Maybe you've even received such an inheritance yourself. But for most of us, these kinds of stories remain the plot devices of fiction and fantasy. We may have received a legacy, but it came with the steep price of losing a loved one such as a parent, guardian, or partner.

However, the most valuable inheritance we have comes as a free gift. And as the saying goes, salvation is free but it is not cheap. Our inheritance was secured by the ransom paid when Jesus died on the cross for our sins. We had an unfathomable debt we could not pay; God became man to fulfill our payment once and for all.

As a result, we are heirs in an eternal reward. We have a priceless inheritance that comes in the fullness of joy—evidence of our Father's passionate pursuit and unconditional love for us.

DAILY INTERACTION ▼

 CONNECT: Email or text a loved one, telling them how much you appreciate what they have contributed to making your faith stronger.

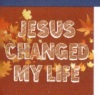

Let us not become weary in doing good, for at the proper time we will reap a harvest if we do not give up.
GALATIANS 6:9

— DEVOTION ▼ —

Daily Diligence

If you've ever raised your own vegetables, herb garden, or flower bed, you know how challenging it can be to maintain. Even the smallest gardens require constant tending—watering, weeding, pruning, shaping, and guarding. In order to reach a harvest, we have to invest the hard work of vigilance and dedicated effort throughout the preceding season.

We grow in faith the same way. In order to reap a harvest, we must practice the disciplines of daily diligence. We must spend time in prayer, Bible study, and service to those around us in order to become more intimately acquainted with our Father and more familiar with the perfect ways of his Son, Jesus.

What daily disciplines do you practice in order to grow stronger and produce fruit in your life?

— DAILY INTERACTION ▼ —

 CONNECT: Check out the Bible study guides and reference works available to you online. Ask others for recommendations of the sources they've found most helpful.

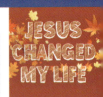
I will praise the LORD, who counsels me;
even at night my heart instructs me.

PSALM 16:7

▼ DEVOTION

Shine On

As the days grow shorter and the sun sets earlier each day, it can be hard to face the darkness. After the glorious light of the summer months, the prospect of a cold dark season can be tough to face. However, we don't have to despair or resign ourselves to hibernating, no matter how short the days or how dark the approaching season.

Our Father's light and life reside in us all year round. Even when the daylight seems to disappear before we've even gotten home from work, we can know that the light in our heart remains constant and bright.

The days may grow shorter, but the Light of the world ignited inside you by God's Spirit will never dim. Today, let others see God's light shining through each word you speak and every action you take.

DAILY INTERACTION ▼

 CONNECT: Visit JesusDaily.com and encourage someone who's going through a dark period with the light of your compassion.

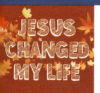

 October 23

> *Let your gentleness be evident to all.*
> *The Lord is near.*
> PHILIPPIANS 4:5

Gentle Strength

We often think of gentle people as ones who are sensitive, quiet, reserved, and tentative in the way they approach and interact with those around them. However, the kind of gentleness to which we're called is one grounded in strength, compassion, and service. Gentleness is based in love and remains slow to anger. It does not use power unnecessarily but instead humbly serves others in need.

It takes a remarkably strong person to speak and to act with gentleness. You must know who you are and Whose you are in order to let go of having to prove yourself, exercise power over others, or demand the attention of entitlement.

Today, exercise the strength necessary to be gentle in all you do and all you say. Let others see the Father's tenderness and toughness through you.

 CONNECT: Reach out to someone who models the gentleness of Christ and let them know how much you appreciate this trait in their life.

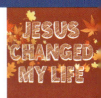

> *"I will give them an undivided heart and put a new spirit in them; I will remove from them their heart of stone and give them a heart of flesh."*
>
> EZEKIEL 11:19

▼ DEVOTION

A Healthy Heart

Without exercise, our muscles atrophy. They stiffen and become weaker at the same time. Without the stress of regular use, our muscles deteriorate until they cannot support us or the regular functions they once maintained. We must remain in motion, actively stimulating them in order for them to remain healthy and grow stronger.

Our heart muscles, both literally and figuratively, require regular exercise as well. When we're not praying, giving, serving, and loving on a daily basis, it becomes harder and harder to feel connected to God, to relate to other people, and to feel the purposeful joy that comes from serving.

Our hearts don't harden overnight. They gradually atrophy until we find ourselves with a heart of stone, as cold and calloused as a slab of granite. Regular exercise allows us to love more deeply and serve more humbly. It keeps our heart tender and compassionate, alive and grateful.

DAILY INTERACTION ▼

 CONNECT: Post a picture that depicts God's compassionate heart toward us. Ask others to respond in kind.

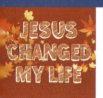

JESUS CHANGED MY LIFE

📅 **October 25**

…I know whom I have believed, and am convinced that he is able to guard what I have entrusted to him for that day.
2 Timothy 1:12

—————————————————— DEVOTION ▾ ——

He Know Your Secrets

Who knows your secrets? Who is the person with whom you share your hurts, hopes, heartaches, and happiness? When we tell a spouse, friend, or family member something "in confidence," we are exercising our trust in them. We're telling them because we're confident in their discretion, their love for us, and their commitment to our relationship.

But even the most trusted friend, partner, or confidant can betray your confidence and destroy your trust. Even as we forgive them and try to rebuild the relationship, we're also reminded that Jesus knows our secrets and guards our hearts better than anyone. He will never betray us, condemn us, or belittle us.

We never have to worry about telling the truth—the whole truth—about our feelings, failures, and fumbles with God. He holds all of us, the good and the bad, close to him, loving us as his precious child.

——————— **DAILY** INTERACTION ▾ ———————

CONNECT: Touch base with someone you know who struggles with an ongoing bad habit or addiction. Let them know that you're praying for them.

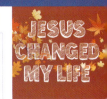

"For who has known the mind of the Lord that he may instruct him?" But we have the mind of Christ.

1 Corinthians 2:16

▼ DEVOTION

Like Jesus

It's truly difficult to fathom that Jesus could be fully human and fully God while he was here on earth. We're told he knew the same temptations that we know and yet did not sin. He loved his parents and friends and got angry at his enemies. He ate and drank, worked and slept, wept and walked just like you and me. His hair grew, his fingernails grew, and he bled when cut.

And his body suffered the blows of the Roman guards. He hung on two crossed pieces of wood until his mortal body expired. Then he was buried.

But because he was also God, Christ did not remain dead. He did what no one else could do—defeat sin and death once and for all. And when he ascended, he promised the gift of the Holy Spirit, which descended upon his followers ten days later and continues to indwell us today when we invite Christ into our lives.

Once the Spirit lives in us, we begin the process of becoming more like Christ. This includes our minds. We can think the same thoughts and condition our minds to focus on our Father's love and grace in all that we do.

—— DAILY INTERACTION ▼

 CONNECT: Start a discussion among fellow believers about what it means to have the mind of Christ in our daily lives.

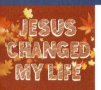
JESUS CHANGED MY LIFE

📅 **October 27**

Now this is what the LORD Almighty says:
"Give careful thought to your ways."
HAGGAI 1:5

Carefully Consider

Do you give "careful thought" to your ways? Or do you usually just go with the flow, follow the crowd, and do what's expected of you? God calls each of us to live a life that's characterized by the way we love and serve those around us. He wants us to lay aside the selfish pursuits and personal pleasures that entrap and ensnare us in sin. God wants us to enjoy the freedom that comes from following the example of his Son, Jesus Christ.

It's quite easy, however, even when we're firmly rooted in a church or other community of believers, simply to do what everyone else is doing. We end up not seeking the ways we're called to live our life to please God, and instead just doing what it takes to fit in, conform, and be accepted by the majority.

Sometimes we have to break away from the herd and follow the path God has for us, not the wide road that everyone else continues to travel.

 CONNECT: Connect with an accountability partner and let them know you're making a change in your daily habits.

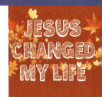

> *...you are no longer foreigners and aliens,*
> *but fellow citizens with God's people*
> *and members of God's household.*
>
> EPHESIANS 2:19

▼ DEVOTION

Fellow Citizens

As travel and technology continue to shrink the world into a global community, now more than ever we have the ability to explore, to understand, and to accept the hundreds of diverse cultures that comprise our planet. As we go to share the good news of Jesus to every nation and to love and serve those who are different than we are just as much as those who are like us, we realize that we are all brothers and sisters in the same royal family.

God created us as men and women in his image, no matter if we're born in India or Indiana. As we accept the free gift of salvation and commit to following Christ, we share as joint heirs in eternal life. We're called to work together in love as the Body of Christ, to appreciate our complementary differences instead of allowing our contrasts to divide us.

Prejudice and bigotry may always tempt us to fear and to judge those who are different than we are. But in the family of God, no one is an outsider, alien, or foreigner. We are all God's children.

DAILY INTERACTION ▼

CONNECT: Research a country, culture, or people group that you find intriguing. Try to find a fellow believer with direct knowledge and start a conversation about them.

When the storm has swept by, the wicked are gone, but the righteous stand firm forever.

PROVERBS 10:25

DEVOTION ▼

Storms

Storms come and go regardless of the season. This is true in life as well as in nature. Autumn often brings windstorms and even hurricanes in coastal regions. Winter welcomes snowstorms, blizzards, and even avalanches. Spring showers can quickly become thunderstorms and tornadoes. Summer squalls drench us and send us running for cover from lightning. But the beauty of each season remains undeniable, nonetheless.

Our life circumstances seem to fluctuate the same way. We struggle to become independent from our families and pursue our education as a way to become established. Then we begin to create a life for ourselves, a home, a community, and perhaps marriage and children. Career and financial strains may exert pressure on us as we seek to balance our lifestyle needs with our priorities. As our lives reach a midpoint, we look ahead at enduring empty nests, slowing down, and sometimes starting over.

Storms come and go, but God's promises, his Word, and the truth of his love through Christ remain bedrock in our lives. No matter what circumstantial weather passes through, we can cling to our Solid Rock of salvation.

DAILY INTERACTION ▼

CONNECT: Seek out a fellow believer who's ahead of you in life and has already been through your current season. Ask them for their prayers and wisdom.

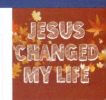

JESUS CHANGED MY LIFE

> *You open your hand and satisfy the*
> *desires of every living thing.*
> Psalm 145:16

▼ DEVOTION

Deep Satisfaction

A restful night's sleep. A delicious meal. A restorative vacation. It's good when both our expectations and our needs get met. We end up satisfied, satiated both by what we need, such as food and rest, but also contented by the enjoyment of the process. Many meals can provide the nutrition we need and fill up our stomachs, but not every meal satisfies us. Many nights we sleep until morning, but don't awake as rested and refreshed as we'd like. We return from many vacations, grateful for the time away, but still agitated and anxious about our life's responsibilities.

Only God provides us with a deeper satisfaction, a peace that passes understanding, throughout all our endeavors. Whether we have our expectations met or get what we hoped, we can still give thanks and trust that God has provided all we need. We can rest easy, enjoy our meal, and feel our spirits lifted regardless of our circumstances.

This is the essence of contentment. This is the joy of the Christian life. This is soul satisfaction.

DAILY INTERACTION ▼

CONNECT: Unplug today and use the time to rest in the security and contentment of the Lord.

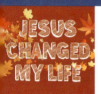

JESUS CHANGED MY LIFE

Test everything. Hold on to the good.
Avoid every kind of evil.
1 Thessalonians 5:21–22

DEVOTION ▼

Test Everything

At this time of year and particularly on this day, many people enjoy dressing up, focusing on the supernatural, and celebrating things that frighten us. Whether to participate, or to what degree, with the cultural customs and events around us often perplexes many believers. We want to be culturally engaged and relevant to all people while at the same time honoring God and obeying his commands in all that we do.

Perhaps this is why we're told to "test everything" so that we can "hold on to the good" and "avoid every kind of evil." When we bring our decisions before the Lord, we can trust that his Word, his Spirit, and the example of his Son will guide us. Together with the wisdom of other believers and the needs of those who don't know Christ, we can act with confidence, whether we're in costume or not.

Don't condemn cultural customs as situations to be avoided at all costs. View them as opportunities to experience God's guidance as you continue sharing his love and the good news of the gospel with everyone around you.

DAILY INTERACTION ▼

CONNECT: Visit JesusDaily.com and let others know that you're praying for them as they make their own decisions about engaging in cultural practices.

I NEED JESUS

NOVEMBER

Come, let us bow down in worship,
let us kneel before the LORD our Maker.

Psalm 95:6

Give me a sign of your goodness, that my enemies may see it and be put to shame, for you, O LORD, have helped me and comforted me.

PSALM 86:17

DEVOTION ▼

Signs of His Goodness

Most days we go through our routines and barely notice all that's around us. Sometimes we get stuck in a rut and end up running on autopilot, coasting through the day until something forces us to change. And other times, we may be so preoccupied with a problem or stressed by challenging circumstances that we lose sight of what's right in front of us.

God gives us signs of his goodness every day. We don't always notice them, but if we remain engaged with the present—not consumed by past worries or future uncertainties—we realize that the Lord's faithfulness is constant.

Sometimes the signs of his goodness may be small—a friend's text of encouragement, an unexpected kindness, the sight of a bird at our window. Other signs may be larger and more dramatic: test results that confirm our good health, reconciliation in a relationship, provision for bills, a new job or promotion. Regardless of whether the signs are large or small, you will find them today if you only look.

DAILY INTERACTION ▼

 CONNECT: Post a comment at JesusDaily.com about one of the signs of God's goodness that you spotted today.

Since we live by the Spirit, let us keep in step with the Spirit.

GALATIANS 5:25

▼ DEVOTION

Walk with the Spirit

If you've ever been on a hike or gone running with a group, you know how challenging it can be to remain together. Some companions may have long legs and a quick gait, while others move slower and take their time. Even walking with someone who has a different stride than your own can be frustrating as you work to keep up or wait for them to catch up.

It's comforting to know that God's Spirit is always with us, step by step and stride for stride. We don't have to worry about going too fast or too slow. We can move forward confident that our Father always keeps pace.

Today, walk in the fullness of the Lord, trusting him for your sense of timing.

DAILY INTERACTION ▼

CONNECT: Send a picture to a friend as you check in to see how their walk with the Lord went today.

> *For God did not call us to be impure,*
> *but to live a holy life.*
> 1 Thessalonians 4:7

— DEVOTION ▼ —

Be Renewed

Have you checked your pantry lately? What about your fridge? Many times we reach for a jar of sauce or container of milk only to discover that the "sell by" date was passed a long time ago. The food has spoiled and is now no good for consumption. You can't use it and have to throw it out and replace it.

Some of our habits often work the same way. They may have served us for a time, but now we've outgrown them and they may be getting in our way or preventing us from adopting necessary changes.

Part of living a holy life, one free from impurities, is being willing to adapt to change. God calls us to remain obedient no matter what changes we encounter, but he also promises to give us wisdom and power when we ask him. Sometimes we feel as though we don't have what we need, not because God hasn't provided it, but because we cling to outdated methods.

— DAILY INTERACTION ▼ —

 CONNECT: Encourage others to clean out their pantry and send unwanted canned goods and dry items, still good of course, to local community food banks.

> *Be very careful, then, how you live—*
> *not as unwise but as wise.*
>
> EPHESIANS 5:15

▼ DEVOTION

Wise Living

How can a wise person continue to live as someone who is unwise? At first glance, it seems impossible, but when you stop to consider it, we're all guilty at times. We know what is true, good, and righteous, and yet we don't practice it. We're aware of God's commands, and yet fail to obey them on a daily basis. Perhaps we're even willing to obey and practice them, but without action and consistency, our good intentions only make us unwise.

Wisdom requires action to be complete. We must do more than draw on truth from God's Word and our experiences; we must live according to this powerful knowledge. Put what you know to be true to practice.

DAILY INTERACTION ▼

CONNECT: Connect with a friend whose life is characterized by wisdom and let them know how much you appreciate their witness.

> *"Act with courage, and may the LORD be with those who do well."*
> 2 CHRONICLES 19:11

Act with Courage

We often think of *courage* as a special word reserved for war heroes, valiant survivors of injury or disease, and extraordinary people who beat the odds and achieve greatness. However, we all have opportunities to exercise courage most every day.

It takes courage to stand up for our faith when it's easier to remain silent. It takes courage to help someone in need. It takes courage to admit the truth about a problem we have or a habit we're overcoming. It takes courage to ask for help. It takes courage to live by faith when you're uncertain of how you'll keep going tomorrow or the next day.

Courage is a gift from God that enables us to overcome our fears and receive his strength, power, stamina, and fortitude.

 CONNECT: Find a song, video clip, or interview that illustrates godly courage in action and post a link at JesusDaily.com.

> *But Christ is faithful as a son over God's house.*
> *And we are his house, if we hold on to*
> *our courage and the hope of which we boast.*
>
> HEBREWS 3:6

I NEED JESUS

▼ DEVOTION

We Are His House

What's your dream house? If you could live in any structure in the world, what would your home look like? Maybe your imagination conjures up images of grand mansions or even ancient castles. Or perhaps your ideal house is a cabin on a mountain, a beach bungalow, or a loft in the city.

No matter what the style or size, the house you long to live in cannot compare to the house of the Lord. Christ rules over God's house, and we sustain it through our courage, faith, and hope. As we serve others, we're strengthening our Father's kingdom and glorifying him for others to see.

Today, be thankful for your earthly dwelling but praise God for your eternal home!

▼ DAILY INTERACTION

 CONNECT: Post a pic of your dream house and trade ideas with friends and family.

DEVOTION ▼

Control Your Anger

Maybe it's people who cut you off on the highway. Or it could be people who talk or text when you're at the movies. People who constantly complain, certain reality TV shows, and automated customer service phone systems do it for most people.

Regardless of your pet peeve, we all have things that set us off and get our blood boiling in a hurry. Whether it's the rudeness of others or inefficient methods of completing tasks at work, we all have experiences that push our buttons and ignite our anger. Sometimes we're tempted to retaliate, to return rudeness with rudeness, insult with injury, and the anger of others with our own.

But God calls us to a different standard, a different control on our anger's thermostat. He wants us to be slow to anger and to resolve issues quickly so that we don't give our enemy a foothold or opportunity to create jealousy, resentment, or bitterness. Because once our anger bleeds into those areas, we'll probably act on it.

Today, don't let anything or anyone cause you to lose your temper.

DAILY INTERACTION ▼

 CONNECT: Ask others how they control their anger and how they respond in situations that provoke them.

> *Hatred stirs up dissension, but love covers all wrongs.*
> PROVERBS 10:12

Through His Power

When we forgive other people, we're displaying a response that often defies logic. After all, some wrongs just seem too big to be forgiven: murder, rape, genocide, on and on. However, God forgives all sins—there's not one that's any worse than another, although some sins certainly have larger, more devastating consequences.

But all have sinned and we all fall short of the glory of God. When we choose to hate instead of love, we're basically saying that only some sins are forgivable. However, that's not what God tells us and shows us through his grace. He sent Christ to live among us and die on the cross for our sins. Our Father wanted us to see his love in action in an irrefutable, irrevocable way.

Christ's death and resurrection changed everything. We aren't limited by our own hatred or inability to love. Through God's power, we can love even those who hurt us with unimaginable betrayals and injuries.

CONNECT: Research the relationship between fear and anger and hatred. What emotions and experiences usually lead to hating someone?

Make every effort to keep the unity of the Spirit…
EPHESIANS 4:3

───────────────── DEVOTION ▼ ─────────────────

Togetherness

What brings you together with people? For most of us, we often gather for birthdays, holidays, and celebrations. Weddings and funerals also cause us to unite as we celebrate or mourn together. Family dinners also bring everyone together to fellowship around a meal, but those are often rare and infrequent. People's schedules pull them in opposite directions, and it becomes harder and harder to feel connected.

In the family of God, we should make extra effort to remain connected to one another in the unity of the Spirit. Our Father brings us together with other believers so that we can build up one another's faith, encourage one another, bear one another's burdens, and celebrate our joys.

Sometimes we allow petty differences and personal preferences to divide our unity. With the catch-all excuse of being busy, we dodge the hard conversations and avoid the opportunities to forgive and extend grace. But the Lord calls us to serve as one body, the Body of Christ.

───────────── DAILY INTERACTION ▼ ─────────────

CONNECT: Send out an e-vite to at least a dozen believers and plan a time of worship, prayer, and fellowship together in the coming weeks.

> *...for the LORD will be your confidence and*
> *will keep your foot from being snared.*
>
> PROVERBS 3:26

▼ DEVOTION

Guard Your Heart

Have you ever seen an animal in a trap? Whether it was a mouse trap or a hunter's trap hidden in the woods to catch small game, it can be a painful sight even when necessary. Most traps feature some kind of bait to attract the creature to the snare. When the animal attempts to take the bait—SNAP—the trap captures them if not kills them.

We assume we're too smart to get caught in such simple snares that we've seen used on animals. However, we fall into other kinds of traps just as easily as a mouse eats cheese. Too often we don't take precautions to avoid the temptations that so easily ensnare us. We dodge the truth when others question us and even lie when loved ones try to hold us accountable.

If you're going to escape from the snares of sin, you must be wise and guard your heart. You will need people to help you keep going and occasionally to pull you out of a trap. And God gives you all the power you need to escape the enemy's snares and avoid his temptations.

DAILY INTERACTION ▼

 CONNECT: Have you been visiting any websites that lead you to temptation and sin? Should you consider a filter or other means of accountability?

I NEED JESUS

> *"The LORD himself goes before you and will be with you;*
> *he will never leave you nor forsake you. Do not be afraid;*
> *do not be discouraged."*
>
> DEUTERONOMY 31:8

———————————— DEVOTION ▼ ————————————

He Goes Before You

Historically, new territories often required scouts to go ahead of the main party of settlers. These forerunners would advance as quietly and discreetly as possible and assess the new terrain, noting potential dangers and predators as well as determining sources of food, water, and shelter. Many times scouts would be charged with eliminating adversaries prior to the arrival of the followers to come.

In new territories where the landscape was unknown, scouts would also blaze a trail, making a clear path that indicated where it was safe to walk and make camp. Instead of large groups being ambushed or overtaken in densely wooded areas, the spies sent ahead would make sure it was safe for the others.

In many ways, God serves as our scout—going ahead of us, clearing a path for us to follow, and eliminating danger. He knows what's ahead of us and carefully uses what's behind us to equip us for the future. When we can't see what's ahead, when the new frontier appears hostile, we can take comfort in the strength of our Lord.

———————————— DAILY INTERACTION ▼ ————————————

 CONNECT: Read a few accounts from early scouts, such as Lewis and Clark, in the history of our country. What was the greatest danger they faced?

> *The goal of this command is love, which comes from a pure heart and a good conscience and a sincere faith.*
>
> 1 TIMOTHY 1:5

▾ DEVOTION

An Attitude of Love

We don't often think about recipes being in the Bible, but there are at least a few. Certainly, the ingredients needed to fulfill God's command to love is spelled out quite clearly: a pure heart + a good conscience + a sincere faith = LOVE. While this may seem simplistic or even trite, there's great truth as well.

A pure heart is one devoted singularly to loving God and obeying his commands. Someone with this kind of devotion isn't perfect, but they know the source of life and remain focused on serving others and sharing this love. Their purity is not perfection but their wholeness is dedicated to their Father.

A good conscience is both one that works to prompt us when we sin as well as one that's clear and washed clean by God's grace. A person with a good conscience is attuned to the Holy Spirit within, aligning their thoughts, words, and actions with God's instructions and commands.

A sincere faith requires trust motivated by belief, anchored by conviction, and fueled by hope. There's no pretense, pride, or self-righteousness in a person whose faith is sincere. Together, it's elementary: these three work together to reflect God's love in our lives.

DAILY INTERACTION ▾

 CONNECT: Post a favorite verse about God's love at JesusDaily.com and memorize one posted by someone else.

Love must be sincere.
Romans 12:9

— DEVOTION ▼ —

Love Sincerely

We're all aware of the way the word *love* gets thrown around quite carelessly. We love the new restaurant that just opened in our neighborhood. We love crazy cat videos on YouTube. We love the taste of chocolate. We love our best friend. We love Disney movies. We love sunsets and mountains.

And then there's the way we love God and experience his love. One word that often comes up to describe this kind of spiritual love is *sincere*. We usually think of sincere as a way to describe someone who's genuine, earnest, unpretentious, and open about their feelings.

While it's uncertain, many scholars believe the word *sincere* might come from two Latin words, *sine* meaning "without" and *cera* meaning "wax." Apparently, in ancient Rome sometimes slaves and builders would gloss over imperfections in marble and building stones by filling them with wax. Therefore, someone who was "without wax" could be trusted as a scrupulous, dedicated craftsman of the highest standards.

When we love sincerely, we build our relationship with God, day by day, committed to a rock-solid faith.

— DAILY INTERACTION ▼ —

CONNECT: Repair a blemish on a piece of furniture by using a piece of wax, then post a picture of your "repair" and ask others to share their "insincere" attempts as well.

> *Therefore, prepare your minds for action; be self-controlled; set your hope fully on the grace to be given you when Jesus Christ is revealed.*
>
> 1 PETER 1:13

I NEED JESUS

▼ DEVOTION

Prepare Your Mind

When you're learning a new sport, physical exercise, or skill, many teachers will tell you to visualize yourself going through the motions of your new endeavor. They encourage students to imagine themselves successfully performing the motions in hopes that their bodies will naturally follow. These instructors know that mental preparation is a significant part of anything requiring action.

If we are to obey God and live according to his commands, we must also practice mentally. We have to be committed to living a life of purity, honor, and integrity. Many times we succumb to temptation because we get caught in the heat of the moment, blinded by the emotional pull. But if we've thought ahead about how to avoid and resist temptations, we've already started the process of growing stronger.

Today, prepare your mind for potential areas of struggle. Imagine yourself obeying God and resisting temptation, remaining strong in your faith.

DAILY INTERACTION ▼

 CONNECT: Research the way that mental preparation and visualization techniques are used by athletes, doctors, and physical therapists.

I will lie down and sleep in peace, for you alone,
O LORD, make me dwell in safety.
PSALM 4:8

— DEVOTION ▼ —

Enjoy His Embrace

Babies often like to be held until they fall asleep because of the sense of security they feel in their parent's arms. They know they're safe and can feel the presence of someone keeping watch over them, protecting them from harm.

We have the same assurance as our Father watches and guards us. We have nothing to fear because he is with us all night long. When we feel restless and anxious, we can experience his peace by praying and reminding ourselves of his Spirit within us. When our mind spins with worries, fears, and "what if"s, we can calm ourselves by remembering that he's in control. There's nothing that he can't handle, no matter how scary or threatening it may seem to us.

Today, take comfort in your Father's arms, enjoying the embrace of the One who created you and loves you the most.

— DAILY INTERACTION ▼ —

CONNECT: Encourage someone who needs a long-distance hug by sending them an e-card or favorite verse reminding them of God's love.

*Through Jesus ... let us continually offer to God a sacrifice
of praise—the fruit of lips that confess his name.*

HEBREWS 13:15

▼ DEVOTION

A Sacrifice of Praise

The last crops have been harvested and the fields now lie fallow.
The bare branches of many trees wave at us in the wind, and
the remaining leaves cannot linger much longer. Morning frosts
etch their icy signature across the landscape out our window. The
holidays are quickly approaching, and plans are already in motion
for family dinners, office parties, church programs, and community events.

Now, before the festive season of busy celebration descends, it's
good to focus on praising and thanking God for this past year. He's
given you so much and brought you so far. Think about how this
year began and all the obstacles that you didn't anticipate. You've
hit a few bumps in the road, but the Lord has remained faithful to
lead, guide, and direct your paths.

Give him praise for the many blessings of family, friends, work,
home, and church in your life. Before you start rushing and get
caught up in the bustle, think through what you've been given. Ask
God to give you a calm center from which you can approach the
coming weeks, giving him thanks and praise for all that's ahead.

DAILY INTERACTION ▼

CONNECT: Post a favorite autumn landscape or other photo
from the past few weeks on your personal page. Let others
know you're thankful.

> *...the righteous are as bold as a lion.*
> PROVERBS 28:1

Lionhearted

As Christians, we sometimes feel we should be meek and mild, nice and quiet, reserved and even passive in how we interact with others around us. However, nothing could be further from the truth! Jesus tells us to be salt and light, flavor and illumination to the bland darkness of the world. We're told to be bold in the way we love others, letting our light shine rather than hiding it away.

Even if you don't think of yourself as a bold person, you can rely on God to empower you and give you the courage needed to take action. With nothing to fear, you can proceed with the same fierce determination and confident strength as the king of the beasts. Christ was called the Lion of Judah, and like him, we can move with calm authority through our day.

Today, be a lion in the way you pursue loving others, fierce and determined, regal and majestic.

 CONNECT: Post an illustration or photo of a lion and ask others to share their favorite animals, explaining the traits they have in common.

God made him who had no sin to be sin for us, so that in him we might become the righteousness of God.

2 CORINTHIANS 5:21

▼ DEVOTION

Our Substitute

In most theater productions, understudies prepare to take the lead roles when the regular cast members portraying them cannot perform. In sports, some team members serve as replacements or substitutes for key players, allowing them to rest or to recover from an injury. In many professions, when someone must take time away or call in sick, they find a substitute. Substitutes are usually not quite as talented, strong, or experienced as the person they're replacing. They can do the job at hand but not as effectively.

However, there's one person who substituted himself in our place in a way that's far superior to anything we could do in the role. Weighed down by our sin, we could not maintain a relationship with our Father and his utter holiness. We had to pay for our sins, but didn't have the power to pay for them once and for all. Like only paying interest on a financial debt, we were trapped by our constant need for a sacrifice to atone our sins.

So Jesus took our place. He bore the penalty that we deserved so that we could be forgiven once and for all. His substitution opened the door to eternal life.

DAILY INTERACTION ▼

 CONNECT: Direct a new friend to JesusDaily.com, sharing with them how it strengthens your faith and blesses you.

> *…you know that the Lord will reward*
> *everyone for whatever good he does.*
> EPHESIANS 6:8

DEVOTION ▼

The Greatest Reward

How often do you do something and expect to get something in return? Maybe it's a matter of attention or financial gain. It could be the affection and appreciation of other people. It might be a transaction in which we gain something in exchange for something we have that others need. Much of our lives operates on this principle of cause and effect, action and reaction, sowing and reaping, service and reward.

While our Father often blesses us with good gifts, we have already received the assurance of the greatest reward imaginable: spending eternity with him in heaven. If we've accepted Jesus into our hearts, we don't have to earn God's favor because we've already been forgiven and welcomed as his cherished son or daughter.

We will get our heavenly reward after we pass from this life. But today, we can live with the confidence that our Father has already bestowed his grace upon us, adopting us as joint heirs with his Son, Jesus.

DAILY INTERACTION ▼

 CONNECT: Post a picture or image that reminds you of heaven. Ask others to do the same, explaining their selection.

[Jesus said,] "And if anyone gives even a cup of cold water to one of these little ones because he is my disciple, I tell you the truth, he will certainly not lose his reward."

MATTHEW 10:42

▼ DEVOTION

Demonstrate Grace

While there's nothing we can do to earn God's favor, it's clear in Scripture that our actions reflect our faith. What we say we believe and what we actually do must be in alignment if our faith has legs—literally. Without the behavior to back up our beliefs, we're only giving lip service. How we live, on the other hand, reveals something about our priorities and what we value most.

If we say we want to be loving, gracious, and generous, but don't practice these traits when given opportunities each day, we're liars. If we claim we love Jesus and follow him as our Master, but we spend all our time and money on ourselves, our commitment has little substance.

In order to reflect our Father's love, we must accept what he's done for us. To the extent that we embrace grace, we can then express it to those around us. When we give a cup of cold water to a thirsty child, we're demonstrating the tenderness of the Lord and the compassion of Christ.

DAILY INTERACTION ▼

 CONNECT: Find a need or prayer request that's been posted and connect with the person in need, offering what you can to help.

> *...give thanks in all circumstances, for this is God's will for you in Christ Jesus.*
> 1 Thessalonians 5:18

A Spirit of Gratitude

Often around the Thanksgiving holiday, we're encouraged to be especially mindful of the many blessings in our lives. Many family gatherings include testimonies around the table about what we're particularly grateful for this year. While this wonderful practice allows us to pause and thank God in a celebration of his goodness, we must also remember that our hearts should be attuned to praise him year-round.

It's good to list our many blessings and reflect on them at this time of year. Our families, our friends and loved ones, our health, our jobs, and our homes should not be taken for granted. All the more reason that we should make Thanksgiving a year-round holiday.

With a spirit of gratitude in our hearts, we recognize all that God gives us and lose sight of what we think we want but don't have.

CONNECT: Post a favorite Thanksgiving recipe and ask others to share theirs. Let friends and family know how thankful you are for their presence in your life.

> *. . . just as you received Christ Jesus as Lord, continue to live in him, rooted and built up in him, strengthened in the faith as you were taught, and overflowing with thankfulness.*
>
> COLOSSIANS 2:6–7

I NEED JESUS

▼ DEVOTION

Overflowing with Thankfulness

Sometimes it takes a season of hardship, loss, and suffering to remind us of all we have been given—and to appreciate how God provides. Certainly, the early Pilgrims to our country faced struggles far beyond what they imagined in the new, untamed wilderness. Without the help of Native Americans willing to share food and to teach them how to farm and to hunt, the first colonists would have likely perished in only a few months.

But God prepared a way and brought others into their lives who could help them discover methods of survival. Their new lifestyle certainly wasn't as easy as they may have hoped, but the Lord strengthened them and provided for them nonetheless. Many of those early European settlers came to America so that they could have religious freedom and worship God independently.

As the celebration of Thanksgiving begins a season of feasting, celebrating, and partying, let's not lose sight of worshipping together, thanking our Creator for the many ways he has blessed each of us as well as our ancestors.

DAILY INTERACTION ▼

CONNECT: Read an historical account of the first Thanksgiving and the history of our country celebrating it as a national holiday.

> *But thanks be to God! He gives us the victory through our Lord Jesus Christ.*
> 1 CORINTHIANS 15:57

—————————————————————— DEVOTION ▼ —

The Ultimate Prize

What are the most prestigious awards you can think of? Perhaps the Nobel Peace Prize or a Pulitzer. Maybe a Super Bowl title or the Master's. It could be a Purple Heart or Congressional Medal of Honor. Regardless of what your "highest prize" might be, it still cannot compare with the achievement that Jesus secured for us. The victory he won was something that only he and he alone could win.

It wasn't a matter of skill or ability, not even goodness or power. Jesus victoriously rose from the dead because of God's love for his people. His victory trumps all the awards and accolades our world has to offer.

When we invite Christ into our lives, we get to share in his victory. Our sins are forgiven and we win the ultimate prize—eternal life.

— **DAILY** INTERACTION ▼ —————————————————

 CONNECT: Create an award for someone you love and let them know that they're the "Best Sister" or "Funniest Friend."

Come, let us bow down in worship,
let us kneel before the LORD our Maker.

PSALM 95:6

▼ DEVOTION

Come and Worship

It's not easy to humble ourselves, especially to get on our knees and acknowledge our powerlessness and respect before someone in authority over us. We may have negative associations of slaves bowing before their masters or commoners bowing before kings and queens. But God is the King of all creation and the only One worthy of our praise, worship, and adoration.

The Bible tells us that every knee will bow and every tongue confess that Jesus Christ is Lord. Everyone will ultimately recognize the holy divinity of God. As we learn to acknowledge his authority and humble ourselves before him, we can experience the fulfillment of our deepest longing.

God is not only our King but our loving Father. Yes, we bow down and worship him, but he also chose to humble himself in human form and die for us. It's not about acknowledging our powerlessness before him that compels us to kneel. It's our love, gratitude, and devotion.

—— **DAILY** INTERACTION ▼ ——

 CONNECT: Video conference with a friend or loved one and spend some time praying and worshipping together.

Grace and peace be yours in abundance through the knowledge of God and of Jesus our Lord.
2 PETER 1:2

———————————— DEVOTION ▼ ————

True Abundance

In our consumer culture, we're often encouraged to buy in bulk. Big box stores offer low prices on products that can be sold in multiple units. As a result, many people stock up on staples and end up with a year's worth of paper towels, canned tomatoes, or apple juice. We even have TV shows about people who excel at using coupons to save money and acquire even more products. And taken to an extreme (as if it's not already), we see cases with people who hoard things that they will never use, acquiring more and more out of compulsion.

True abundance, of course, is not about having more stuff. It doesn't rely on stockpiling canned goods, paper products, or enough emergency candles to light up a stadium. True abundance is not about the quantity of material possessions you have but the quality of your heart and soul.

When we dwell on our knowledge of God and his Son, we experience an abundance of peace and grace. We don't have to have more in order to experience the satisfaction and joy that only our Lord can provide.

———————————— DAILY INTERACTION ▼ ————

CONNECT: Unplug today as you clean out your excess and give it away to others who can use it.

And God is able to make all grace abound to you,
so that in all things at all times, having all that
you need, you will abound in every good work.

2 CORINTHIANS 9:8

▼ DEVOTION

Abounding Grace

Most home improvement projects take twice as long because the homeowner has to make at least four trips to the hardware store. The first time is to buy the wrong things. The second time is to buy the wrong size. On the third trip, the homeowner buys one of everything in every size. And the fourth trip allows them to return all the stuff they didn't need.

What would it be like to have exactly what you need for all things at all times to do your work? We can't even imagine! Yet God promises that when we are doing his good work, the work that he has given us to do, we will have everything we need.

It's called *grace*. It's not something that we can earn or buy or conjure. It's free from a loving God who wants to give us gifts to do his will. He will surprise us as we do his good works. We might not recognize ourselves, but we will recognize him.

DAILY INTERACTION ▼

 CONNECT: Find an online resource to help you with your times of prayer and Bible study. Ask others for recommendations of their favorites.

The LORD is my light and my salvation—whom shall I fear?

PSALM 27:1

— DEVOTION ▼ —

Rest in His Arms

As children move into new developmental stages, they go in and out of irrational fears characterized by disquiet and difficulty expressing their feelings. They are afraid to go to sleep and to leave their parents. They don't want to go to unfamiliar places. This can be trying for parents as they try to deal with unreasonable thoughts and heightened feelings. We tell our children, "Just trust me. I won't let you get hurt or lost." We want them to put the full weight of their fear in our hands and rest in the fact that we will handle whatever comes up.

Adults have issues around these fears too. We are afraid to lose our way. We are afraid for our safety. Often these fears are multiplied because we have the responsibility for others. Just like children, we have difficulty letting go because we don't believe that God is bigger than these fears.

But we need not fear. God is our light—we are never lost because he always knows where we are. God is our salvation—we are in his safekeeping. He saves us. Our hearts can proclaim this as we rest in his arms.

— **DAILY** INTERACTION ▼ —

CONNECT: Message someone who needs to be reminded of God's ability to carry them through their present trial. Let them know you're praying for them.

I will listen to what God the LORD will say;
he promises peace to his people, his saints…

PSALM 85:8

▼ DEVOTION

His Promise of Peace

"Know God, Know Peace. No God, No Peace." So reads the church sign that you pass everyday on your way to work. It's easy to ignore such signs because sometimes they can seem trite. However, they also carry a simply profound truth: if you want peace in your life, get to know God.

You may be thinking, *But I thought I would feel more peaceful when I have more money, or get married, or have children, or get well.* Those are the things you may be telling yourself, the conditions you may be placing on your future peace of mind.

But spending time getting to know your Father is the way to have more peace. Ask questions and tell him what's on your mind. Write letters to him and read his mail in return. Find out what's important to him. Spend time with him. Introduce him to your friends and family. Look at Jesus. Do things he likes to do. Go places he likes to go. In other words, invite God to be a part of your life and he will honor your request. You will learn that he is good and loving and trustworthy and kind. Peace will abound.

DAILY INTERACTION ▼

CONNECT: Visit JesusDaily.com, post a picture that depicts tranquility to you, and pair it with your favorite verse about God's gift of perfect peace.

> *The Word became flesh and made
> his dwelling among us.*
> JOHN 1:14

The Word Made Flesh

The gift of language is one of the greatest God has ever given us. Through language, we can speak, sing, communicate, write, read, learn, and grow. We can compile information for future generations and learn from what once happened to our ancestors. We can tell stories and entertain one another, teaching lessons and revealing truths about human nature and God's character. We can teach, encourage, inspire, and motivate one another.

Jesus is the Word made flesh, the holy breath of God the Father brought into human form in a manger in Bethlehem. Christ grew and made his dwelling among us before revealing himself as Immanuel, "God with us," and Messiah, "the Savior of his people."

When we consider Christ as the Word made flesh, we're reminded that our faith is one of word as well as deed, of sentences as well as actions. When we step out in faith, we live from the center of our beliefs. We become more like Jesus, redeemed by his blood and saved by faith.

CONNECT: Choose a favorite word related to your faith, such as *sacrifice* or *devotion* or *commitment*, and study its origins online.

*Whatever happens, conduct yourselves in
a manner worthy of the gospel of Christ.*

PHILIPPIANS 1:27

▼ DEVOTION

The Next Right Step

All too often, we come to a point in our lives, and we just don't know what to do. We wake up in the morning, and without a specific agenda for the day, we know that if we don't move in some specific direction we will waste our day.

Or, we have so much to do in one day that we cannot possibly get it all done. On a much larger scope, we have big decisions to make and we don't know the best way to go, or we have sudden disastrous circumstances and we can't see beyond this moment. It is not unusual at all to find ourselves on a road with no map guiding the way.

Perhaps you've heard the saying, "Do the next right thing." Though this is easier said than done, it seems to bring the next step down to the present moment. It reminds us that we are on a path that leads somewhere and our present decisions affect where we end up.

Today, you need to do something but you don't have to do everything. Just take the next right step.

DAILY INTERACTION ▼

 CONNECT: Ask a trusted friend and mature believer how they make hard decisions. Ask them for prayer regarding one of the hard decisions you're currently facing.

WHICH IS WORTH MORE?

DECEMBER

*"Glory to God in the highest, and on earth
peace to men on whom his favor rests."*

Luke 2:14

*"Therefore the Lord himself will give you a sign:
The virgin will be with child and will give birth
to a son, and will call him Immanuel."*

ISAIAH 7:14

DEVOTION ▼

Signs of His Presence

How often do we wish that God would just give us a sign—something that would point to his presence in the world and, more specifically, in our lives! We have a tough decision to make, or we don't know what to do next, or we feel so alone. These are daily states of mind and heart that we experience, and we wish for *something* to nudge us to the direction of hope. We need a light at the end of the tunnel.

The children of Israel were looking for a promised savior, but it had been so long, and so much had happened to cause them to lose heart. They needed to know that God was with them. Then God himself spoke these words through Isaiah: "the Lord himself will give you a sign . . ." In other words, he told them, "I haven't forgotten you! Keep looking for me. Have hope!" How gracious of God to remind us of his presence and point to a time in the future when we would have a flesh-and-blood reminder that he is with us.

Today, look for reminders and signs that God is with us.

DAILY INTERACTION ▼

 CONNECT: Make a list of the signs of God's presence in your life. Send the list to someone who needs to know a message of hope and of God's presence today.

> *"She will give birth to a son, and you are to give him the name Jesus, because he will save his people from their sins."*
>
> Matthew 1:21

▼ DEVOTION

Our Savior

God told Mary and Joseph to name Mary's baby Jesus. *Jesus* was not an uncommon name at that time and was a derivative of the name *Joshua*, which means "to rescue" or "to deliver," in other words, to save. This name also described Jesus' mission among us. He was to save his people from their sins. Everything was clear from the beginning. Right?

But did Mary and Joseph understand what that name would ultimately mean? The Jewish people were looking for a savior, but they had in mind a king to provide freedom from their oppressors. How confusing it must have been for Mary, thirty-three years later, as she stood at the foot of Jesus' cross. What happened to the baby who was to be the king? It felt like a loss of a dream, a promise.

We have the gift of the whole Bible to give us the complete picture of this story. However, often we misinterpret the messages we hear from God, and we are confused and perplexed. We need to remember that God's promises to us are always right, but we don't always have the information to see God's whole picture.

DAILY INTERACTION ▼

 CONNECT: Post a favorite picture from a past Christmas and ask others to share theirs. How have your views on Christmas changed over the years?

📅 December 3

But the angel said to her, "Do not be afraid, Mary, you have found favor with God. You will be with child and give birth to a son, and you are to give him the name Jesus."

LUKE 1:30–31

DEVOTION ▾

In His Plan

Mary was a young teenage girl going about her daily routine when an angel appeared to her and said, "Do not be afraid." Of course she was surprised and fearful, and maybe these words put her at ease. But the next part? "You will conceive and give birth to a son . . ."

That "favor" she received from God must have been powerful from the beginning. God gave her what she needed to stand in the presence of an angel and receive a message that would not only change her whole life, but change history. He revealed to her the unique role that she would play in God's purposes. And she embraced that role, even though it would come with a great personal cost.

As we go through the routines of our day, we assume that God fits into our story. Christmas is a reminder that our story, including all of the difficult parts, is never really understood until it's seen in the light of the larger story that is God's. His gift to us is that favor that includes us in his plan.

DAILY INTERACTION ▾

 CONNECT: Research the word *favor*. Record your observations of God's favor in your life.

> *The angel answered, "The Holy Spirit will come on you, and the power of the Most High will overshadow you. So the holy one to be born will be called the Son of God."*
>
> LUKE 1:35

▼ DEVOTION

Beauty in Surrendering

"How will this be?" Mary asked an understandable question to the angel after his announcement to her of the incredible task God had asked of her. The angel does not really explain the manner. His answer involves clouds and spirits and shadows. He doesn't want Mary (or us) to get bogged down in the mechanics of a virgin birth. He only wants to lead Mary to contemplate the power of the Holy Spirit and to surrender herself silently and calmly to his guidance.

We often spend so much time and energy trying to figure out how something will happen. If we can't explain it or imagine it, we don't believe it can be done. Sometimes we refuse to participate in God's plans because we can't see the next step, or steps, and how they would lead to an outcome. We don't want to live in a shadow and rely on the power of the Holy Spirit to accomplish his work.

There is beauty in surrendering to the mystery of God and saying, "I don't know."

DAILY INTERACTION ▼

 CONNECT: In your online journal, make a list of situations in your life right now that you cannot explain.

"I am the Lord's servant," Mary answered. *"May it be to me as you have said." Then the angel left her.*
LUKE 1:38

— DEVOTION ▼ —

Say Yes

Mary was a young, inexperienced girl, and as the angel described what her son's purpose would be as the Son of the Most High and the great mission being entrusted to her, it must have frightened her. She probably did not know what her son's "reign" would look like. No doubt she could look ahead and see the lack of understanding, hurt, and ridicule that awaited her. She would have to tell Joseph, her fiancé, and he would surely reject her and send her away. The future did not look good.

So, with surprise, we read her response. "I am the Lord's servant. Let this happen to me as you say!" Mary, obviously, could see something more. She had a glimpse of the Bigger Picture. She was prepared to say yes to this task. She had been listening to God's voice and knew how to recognize it. Therefore, when she heard him say something that didn't quite make sense, she was ready to obey because she knew it was from God. Her deepest desire was to do his will.

What is your deepest desire? Can you say yes to God no matter what he asks?

— DAILY INTERACTION ▼ —

 CONNECT: Visit JesusDaily.com and pray for someone to be obedient to God's direction as they pray the same for you.

"...do not be afraid to take Mary home as your wife, because what is conceived in her is from the Holy Spirit. She will give birth to a son, and...he will save his people from their sins."

MATTHEW 1:20–21

▼ DEVOTION

Courageously Obey

Engaged to be married, Joseph had big plans for his life ahead with Mary. But Mary became pregnant. He did not know how, but he knew that he was not the father of her baby. He was hurt, and in order to avoid embarrassment, he decided to break it off with Mary quietly. An angel came to him in a dream and told him to go ahead with the marriage because Mary's baby was the Son of God by the Holy Spirit. He probably did not understand all of what he heard, but he went ahead with the marriage.

Joseph's story tells of a change in life plans. This happens to all of us. We all have stories of disappointment and heartbreak. We thought we were going one way, and we end up somewhere else. Sometimes we can see God's leading, but often we are not given a reason. We have to move on and do the best we can, knowing that God's plan might be different from ours.

This requires courage and trust. We call upon God to redeem and use our new circumstances, knowing he loves us and knows best. Even with the inside information from the angel, Joseph faced ridicule, loss of reputation, and ostracism. It took courage for him to take on his new family and his new mission in life. Joseph courageously obeyed God.

DAILY INTERACTION ▼

 CONNECT: Make a list of people who have helped you in your disappointments. Send them a thank-you message.

… she exclaimed: "Blessed are you among women, and blessed is the child you will bear!… Blessed is she who has believed that what the Lord has said to her will be accomplished!"

LUKE 1:42, 45

DEVOTION ▼

Live in the Moment

Did you ever feel blessed by something you didn't understand and maybe even didn't particularly want? It must have taken Mary a while to believe that an out-of-wedlock pregnancy and shot-gun marriage were good things. However, in her visit to Elizabeth, God gave her the encouragement to believe in her strange calling. God gave her the faith that she would need to bear the Son of God.

Often we think that we do not have the faith to do the wonderful, courageous acts that we see in others' lives. How did they get so strong? Why can I not accomplish these great things for God? The answer is living in the moment.

God is never early with his gifts to us. He has promised that we will have exactly what we need in the moment that we need it. Mary took the next step, and God was there to provide all of the courage and the faith and the grace to bear that moment. He will do that for you, too.

DAILY INTERACTION ▼

 CONNECT: Research others' stories of greatness for God. Identify the common threads in these people's lives.

December 8

▼ DEVOTION

Songs of Praise

Mary is visiting her cousin Elizabeth, and the two women are
overwhelmed by the gifts that God is giving to each of them.
Mary breaks forth into song about how wonderful God is and her
gratitude toward him for the great things he has done for her. She
is starting to understand the amazing work he is doing through
her. She has been chosen to carry the Son of God! She rejoices even
though she refers to herself as a humble servant. Despite her humble
position, she will be honored by all generations. Generations will
see her as an example of a simple human touched by divine power
and presence.

How many times have you felt unworthy of a blessing or a gift?
This Advent season delivers an opportunity to reflect on the many
gifts with which we have been blessed and to rejoice in God. Take a
few moments to read Mary's Song of Praise for yourself. Reflect on
God's blessings in your life. Are you rejoicing in them?

The only people whose soul can truly magnify the Lord are
people such as Elizabeth and Mary—people who acknowledge
their lowly estate and are overwhelmed by God's choosing them
for his work.

DAILY INTERACTION ▼

CONNECT: Connect with friends or family members who
live far away. Let them know you're thinking of them and
missing them during this Christmas season.

📅 December 9

The Spirit of the Sovereign LORD is on me, because the LORD has anointed me to preach good news to the poor. He has sent me to … proclaim freedom for the captives and release from darkness …

ISAIAH 61:1

— DEVOTION ▾ —

Set the Captives Free

The good news foretold by Isaiah and other Old Testament prophets came to life in the manger in Bethlehem. Jesus became human and was born of a virgin. He came to start a revolution, not the political kind like many of the Jewish people hoped, but the kind that releases us from the tyranny of sin and the punishment of death. Christ gave up his throne in heaven in order to experience what it's like to be a man—to live as one, to love as one, and to die as one. Only he was also God. He defeated death and set all the people who had been held captive by its power free.

We no longer have to dwell in darkness or remain shackled to the sinful habits and selfish addictions that so frequently bind us. Because a baby was born in little more than a cave-like stable where animals were kept over 2,000 years ago, we have new life— eternal life.

— DAILY INTERACTION ▾ —

CONNECT: Shine the light of God's love on someone who may be struggling in darkness right now. Send them a favorite verse, e-Christmas card, or online gift card.

> *"Therefore keep watch, because you do not know*
> *on what day your Lord will come."*
>
> MATTHEW 24:42

▼ DEVOTION

Keep Watch

Many a mother wishes she would know the exact time when her baby would be born. There is so much preparation that needs to be done for a newborn. Doctors can give an estimated time of birth, which is helpful, but sometimes parents are caught off guard and unprepared. The key is to be ready.

At the time of Jesus, many thought the end of the world was close at hand. Today, many people think the same thing. Since no one knows the exact date and time, what does it mean to "keep watch"? Just as with a new addition to the family, we need to make room for Jesus in our hearts and lives.

As parents grow in knowledge and love, wanting to know all they need to care for their child, so we can learn as much as we can about God and how to be his son or daughter. God has given us work to do, and we need to seek and serve him and care for those who represent Jesus in out midst. We need to open our eyes and diligently watch, so that when Jesus comes, we are pleasing to him.

DAILY INTERACTION ▼

 CONNECT: Ask others to post their favorite Christmas traditions and personal ways to celebrate the season. Borrow one and try it out for you and your family.

An angel of the Lord appeared to them, and the glory of the Lord shone around them, and they were terrified. But the angel said to them, "Do not be afraid. I bring you good news of great joy…"
LUKE 2:9–10

—————————————————————— DEVOTION ▼ ——————

The Best News

Can you imagine what it must have been like? You're out doing your job, trying to keep warm from the chilly desert winds, watching for predators that might try to snatch your sheep, when suddenly the entire night sky explodes with light. The brightness blinds you, outright terrifies you, and then you hear a voice telling you not to be afraid. The voice claims to be a messenger from heaven bringing you the best news imaginable. The Messiah, the long-promised One who would come to free his people, has been born!

The story is familiar to us and therefore difficult for us to imagine with the intensity and surprise of that original encounter on a Judean hillside so long ago. But the shepherds responded as so many of us respond—fear and confusion transformed into awe and worship and unfathomable joy.

The good news may be old, but it's still the best news you'll ever hear.

—————————————————————— DAILY INTERACTION ▼ ——————

 CONNECT: Instead of online shopping for others' gifts, look for trips, classes, and experiences that you could share together.

> *For to us a child is born, to us a son is given, and the government will be on his shoulders. And he will be called Wonderful Counselor, Mighty God, Everlasting Father, Prince of Peace.*
>
> ISAIAH 9:6

▼ DEVOTION

Our Mighty God

Have you ever wondered why God seems to have so many names? Or even why he's comprised of three distinct dimensions—Father, Son, and Spirit? The Jewish people often gave God names or descriptive phrases that reflected their experience of him. Therefore, some emphasize God's ability to provide while others stress his righteousness.

As God's prophet, Isaiah foretold the nation of Israel that God was going to send a Savior, a baby born of a virgin who would be God's own Son. It's curious, though, that the prophet Isaiah lists three names here that would all apply to God. In fact, we usually think of the Holy Spirit as our counselor and comforter. Everlasting Father is clear enough and reminds us of our Abba's love. Prince of Peace seems to reflect Jesus' role as the King's Son, royalty sent to end strife and heal wounds. Together these three indeed comprise the fourth name Isaiah mentions, Mighty God.

Father, Son, and Spirit—God remains ever present in our lives, demonstrating his love, grace, and power in limitless ways.

DAILY INTERACTION ▼

CONNECT: Choose one of the names for God from your list, read at least one commentary on its usage and significance, and share it with others.

...during the time of King Herod, Magi from the east came to Jerusalem and asked, "Where is the one who has been born king of the Jews? We...have come to worship him."
MATTHEW 2:1–2

DEVOTION ▼

He Is Our King

Not all that many years ago, people believed that the earth was the center of the universe. All of the planets were thought to be in orbit about the earth. Modern astronomy has shown this to be in error. This historical view of the universe tells us a great deal about the mentality of mankind. As people, we want to believe that everything revolves around us—what we want, what we need, what we can control and attain. We want to be at the center of what is happening.

King Herod knew the ancient prophecies about the birth of the Messiah, and it terrified him to think that somewhere a child was being born who would take his place. And yet that's what the visitors from the East inquired about—they were aware of this infant king's birth and seemed intent on finding him there in Israel. So Herod tried to seize control and protect his future by murdering the baby boys in Bethlehem. Such cowardice and fear, let alone such violent slaughter of innocent children, repulses us.

Nonetheless, we sometimes respond the same way Herod did—with fear, uncertainty, and anxiety. Instead of looking for Jesus, we work hard to maintain our identity apart from him.

DAILY INTERACTION ▼

CONNECT: Remind someone close to you that they aren't responsible for making everyone else happy this time of year. Let them know how much you care.

December 14

▼ DEVOTION

Worship the King

We often try to escape the hustle and bustle of the holiday season—the crowded shopping malls and busy stores, the obligatory office parties and professional gatherings. Even our family dinners and church programs can leave us feeling frazzled, weary, and jaded. Sometimes we long for just a quiet moment of calm serenity, time to step back from all the busyness and simply to reflect on the marvel of Jesus' birth.

The shepherds who found the baby lying in a manger might have felt the same way. They had been busy tending their flocks by night when the heavenly host crashed through the darkness and announced news that sent them hurrying to discover the truth for themselves. Breathless, tired, excited, confused, and uncertain, they must have approached the quiet couple in the stable with trepidation. But then they saw the baby, wrapped in swaddling cloths just as the angel had told them. It was true!

The shepherds went from being frantic to bowing in worship to the newborn King. We are called to do the same during this busy time of year.

DAILY INTERACTION ▼

 CONNECT: Visit JesusDaily.com and post a picture of something calm, soothing, and unexpectedly peaceful.

"Glory to God in the highest, and on earth peace to men on whom his favor rests."
LUKE 2:14

DEVOTION ▼

Sing His Glories

Music is a vital part of Christmas. From sacred hymns and carols to popular and historical favorites, almost everyone enjoys the sounds of the season. We go caroling to share our joy and holiday spirit with friends and neighbors. We download classics from beloved performers and tune in to radio stations devoted to playing nothing but Christmas music around the clock. We sing in choirs and perform classical cantatas and sacred music that has been sung for hundreds of years.

But none of it can compare to the sounds of the heavenly host as they announced the birth of Christ to the shepherds and rejoiced in songs of jubilation the likes of which have never been heard. We're privileged to enjoy beautiful music this time of year and to use it to worship the birth of our newborn King.

Today, let the song in your heart emerge from your lips in praise of Christ's birth!

DAILY INTERACTION ▼

CONNECT: Attach an audio file or link on your personal page with a favorite song or piece of music that inspires you to worship.

We have seen his glory, the glory of the One and Only,
who came from the Father, full of grace and truth.

JOHN 1:14

▼ DEVOTION

He Is Here

At some point in our lives we have experiences or sightings of incredible things or people, and the best we can testify is that we saw it "in the flesh." We mean to say that we saw it with our own eyes. In some cases the occurrence is far better than we would have expected, but often we are disappointed. We imagined how it would be and the reality just didn't live up to our imagination.

Imagine that you have heard and read about Jesus your whole life. The stories and expectations surrounding him have become legends of brilliance. And then one day, he is here before us, in the flesh. All of the words that have been told of him are embodied in one person. We realize that he came from God to give us a picture of his glory and to act out his grace and truth as he walks among us. That would be something to see with your very own eyes, wouldn't it?

God wants us to experience the ongoing, living truth of his Word made flesh.

DAILY INTERACTION ▼

 CONNECT: Surf the many pictures, paintings, and illustrations of the nativity scene throughout history. Choose one to use as your Christmas season wallpaper.

*But Mary treasured up all these things
and pondered them in her heart.*
LUKE 2:19

DEVOTION ▼

Treasure in Your Heart

During the Christmas season, we often receive numerous gifts from coworkers, friends, colleagues, and, of course, our family. They often range from small tokens such as candy, fruit, or homemade goodies to items such as books, DVDs, and gift cards. From there, the list of gifts usually becomes more personal—clothing, perfume or cologne, practical items we need, and beautiful items that the giver knew would delight us in some way.

Usually, after all the presents have been received, opened, and put away, one or two linger in your mind. Perhaps they stand out because they were unexpected or due to the pleasant association with the person and event, the context in which they were received. Or maybe some presents just speak to us and emerge as favorites.

Mary sorted through all her memories and precious moments with her newborn son as if exploring a museum of priceless art. Perhaps she simply couldn't choose one special scene or indelible memory over another. She treasured them all, aware of the miracle that had taken place in her own life, and for all mankind.

DAILY INTERACTION ▼

CONNECT: Post one of your favorite childhood Christmas photos as your status on your personal page.

> *The shepherds returned, glorifying and praising*
> *God for all the things they had heard and seen,*
> *which were just as they had been told.*
>
> LUKE 2:20

▼ DEVOTION

The Greatest Party

Have you ever overheard coworkers or friends at church talking about the great party they all attended the night before? They're joking and reminiscing, recounting the highlights of what was clearly a good time. There's one problem, however: you weren't invited.

It's not fun being left out while others celebrate, feeling overlooked and ignored, unimportant—or worse—unwanted. However, the greatest party in history is one that's still going on and one that you're most certainly invited to attend. In fact, you're not only invited but you can bring as many friends and family members as you want!

The good news of the birth of Christ continues to be for all people. Not for the elite, or the hip, or the wealthy or successful. But for everyone. Our Father loves us all. Jesus was born and died and rose again for everyone. The party is just getting started.

DAILY INTERACTION ▼

 CONNECT: Post a favorite verse about the Christmas story on JesusDaily.com and "like" as many others posted as you can.

> *… they saw the child with his mother Mary, and they bowed down and worshiped him. Then they opened their treasures and presented him with gifts of gold and of incense and of myrrh.*
> MATTHEW 2:10–11

It's Not the Price Tag

It's often difficult to remain within your budget when shopping for Christmas presents. Sure, there are some presents that you need to give just to show your thanks and appreciation to clients, coworkers, bosses, and acquaintances. Other presents are more fun to shop for as well as to give. You know you want to give something personal, something special and meaningful, something that will surprise and delight your recipient.

The wise men from the East gave incredibly expensive and luxurious gifts, the kind literally fit for a king. The spared no expense or difficulty in finding and bringing the three most famous presents at that first Christmas. Their respect, adoration, and belief were clear by what they gave, not because of the price tag but by the thoughtful care behind their selection.

It's not a matter of how much you spend on someone's gift that matters. It's how much heart you put into what you give them—both at Christmas and throughout the year.

 CONNECT: Share the memory of a favorite childhood Christmas gift with others at JesusDaily.com.

Thanks be to God for his indescribable gift!
2 Corinthians 9:15

▼ DEVOTION

His Indescribable Gift

What are the best gifts you've ever received at Christmas throughout your entire lifetime? Did you get a pony when you were growing up? A new bicycle that you dreamed about? A favorite doll, drum set, or iPod? Or maybe you've been blessed to receive some presents as an adult that have left you speechless: perhaps an engagement ring, a new car, a precious family heirloom, or a surprise vacation.

Regardless of your best gifts, none of them can compare with the ultimate gift—the indescribable gift of grace and eternal life! God gave us his most precious, most beloved Son, knowing that his time on earth would not be easy. And yet, our Father knew that this was the only gift that could bridge the gap between our sins and his holiness.

It's always memorable to give and to receive larger-than-life, breathtaking gifts. But the most dazzling gift of all has already been given.

DAILY INTERACTION ▼

 CONNECT: Share a memory about one of the silliest or "worst" gifts you've ever received. What makes this particular gift stand out in your mind?

📅 December 21

*Every good and perfect gift is from above,
coming down from the Father of the heavenly lights,
who does not change like shifting shadows.*

JAMES 1:17

DEVOTION ▼

Be a Gift

For all of its holiday spirit, Christmas cheer, and joyful celebrations, this time of year can also be one of the loneliest, most painful seasons. There's enormous pressure placed on us to be jolly, happy, and merry all the time. We see movies, TV shows, cards, and stories with large happy families. We watch eager shoppers scramble for bargains, excited to buy whatever they choose without seeming to worry about their budgets.

But what if your family lives far away? Or you don't have many people in your life? What if your budget can't accommodate even the smallest gift or tiniest ornament? What if you're not sure how you'll pay the rent or afford groceries or cover the heating bill?

If you're serious about reclaiming Jesus as the reason for the season, you must be willing to be Christ to those who need him most. Look around you and see how you can meet the needs of others as a Christmas gift to the Lord, a thank-you present for the indescribable gift of his precious Son.

DAILY INTERACTION ▼

 CONNECT: Connect with someone online and make a date to get together before the holidays pass.

> *"Here I am! I stand at the door and knock.*
> *If anyone hears my voice and opens the door,*
> *I will come in and eat with him, and he with me."*
>
> REVELATION 3:20

▼ DEVOTION

The Door of Your Heart

Most of us relate this passage in Revelation to the time of our initial salvation experience with Jesus. The door of our heart has a handle that can be opened from the inside to allow entrance to Jesus, or anyone. It is often said that Jesus is a gentleman, and he will not barge into our houses uninvited. That was true on the day of your salvation, and it is true today.

Have you ever considered that Jesus is still knocking at the door of your heart? He still desires entrance, not as a stranger but as a friend or a neighbor. He wants to spend time with you. He sees that you need help with household chores and offers to assist you. He asks about your family, friends, and loved ones. He wants to know how work is going. He wants to listen to what's truly on your heart.

Look, he's even brought you a meal and wants to share it with you. You are hurting, and he just wants to sit with you. Even though you are a part of God's family, you still have the choice of what you allow God to do in your life. He wants to do it all.

DAILY INTERACTION ▼

 CONNECT: Write a letter to a hurting friend and remind them that Jesus is with them all of the time.

> *On this mountain the L*ORD *Almighty will prepare a
> feast of rich food for all peoples, a banquet of aged wine—
> the best of meats and the finest of wines.*
> ISAIAH 25:6

DEVOTION ▼

A Taste of Heaven

In almost every culture, special foods are prepared and enjoyed to help celebrate the Christmas season. Everywhere we turn it seems that someone has homemade cookies, peppermint candy, fruitcake, fudge, or gingerbread. Then there are parties and dinners, not to mention our own family gatherings with favorite dishes and grandmother's secret recipe.

While we have to watch our waistline during this calorie-laden season, it seems fitting that we celebrate with such delicious tastes and distinct holiday dishes. With the many festive flavors, we remember that God's gift is incomparable.

Many people anticipate that in heaven we will enjoy a banquet beyond our imaginations, a feast in which the food and fellowship is literally out of this world. At Christmas time, perhaps it's only fitting that we get a little taste of heaven.

DAILY INTERACTION ▼

 CONNECT: Trade holiday recipes on your personal page, reminding friends and family of God's presence at our holiday feasts.

> *For he remembered his holy promise*
> *given to his servant Abraham.*
>
> PSALM 105:42

▼ DEVOTION

His Holy Promise

At Christmas, we celebrate the birth of Jesus in many ways. Among them, we incorporate family traditions and bring out heirloom ornaments and special decorations. Many of these traditions and items have been passed down from generation to generation, all the more special as we realize that our parents, grandparents, and great-grandparents enjoyed the same special elements of their Christmas celebration.

Just as we enjoy the unique family elements handed down at Christmas, we're reminded of our eternal inheritance. God promised his people that he would make a way to save them from their disobedience and bad choices. He promised to send them a Savior, his Son, Christ the Lord.

Our Father always keeps his promises, and the greatest one of all remains our most precious gift, a baby in a manger wrapped in swaddling cloths.

DAILY INTERACTION ▼

 CONNECT: Unplug and encourage others to do the same and spend uninterrupted time with family and friends.

"For God so loved the world that he gave his one and only Son, that whoever believes in him shall not perish but have eternal life."

JOHN 3:16

DEVOTION ▼

Celebrate Him

Today, celebrate the birth of Baby Jesus over 2,000 years ago! Amidst all the presents and festivities, the meals and the memories, take time to thank God for the greatest present you'll ever receive.

DAILY INTERACTION ▼

 CONNECT: Remain unplugged as you focus on quality time with family, friends, and your Savior.

> *Teach me your way, O LORD, and I will walk*
> *in your truth; give me an undivided heart,*
> *that I may fear your name.*
>
> PSALM 86:11

▼ DEVOTION

An Undivided Heart

After the holidays, it's sometimes difficult to regain our footing and get back to a normal schedule. We have to clean up the aftermath of our parties, pick up all the boxes and wrapping paper, deal with the leftover food, and figure out how to pay for the places where we went over budget.

The letdown after an emotional high is normal, but we don't have to lose any of the wonder, joy, and peace that comes with the celebration of Christ's birth. How do we avoid a post-holiday sadness?

Our hearts remain whole and singularly focused when we concentrate on loving God and serving his kingdom. We don't have to crash after the wonderful celebration of Christ's birth. His Spirit dwells in our hearts, and he has promised to be with us forever.

DAILY INTERACTION ▼

 CONNECT: Post some pics of your Christmas celebration, highlighting the people and not the presents.

> *For he has not despised or disdained the suffering of the afflicted one; he has not hidden his face from him but has listened to his cry for help.*
>
> PSALM 22:24

He Remains Constant

Jesus came for the people who needed him the most, not for the ones who thought they had life figured out. Even from his entrance into this world, Christ lived in a way that was humble, understated, and without fanfare. He could have been born into the grandest palace and worshipped by world leaders for his entire life.

Instead, he was born in a feeding trough in the outskirts of a little village called Bethlehem. Rather than royalty heralding his arrival, shepherds came along with three wise men. He even had to flee in exile from his homeland because of the life-threatening edict that King Herod issued.

From the beginning, Jesus knew what it was to be an outsider. He would grow up to mingle with fishermen, tax collectors, and prostitutes, and be rejected by the religious and political leaders of his day. Christ relates to our pain because he experienced it.

 CONNECT: Let others know how much you enjoy their pictures from Christmas as you begin to reconnect with your online community.

*Great is the Lord and most worthy of praise;
his greatness no one can fathom.*

PSALM 145:3

▼ DEVOTION

More Than Worthy

As the year begins to wind down and you begin to reflect on all that's happened in the past twelve months, notice the ways God has been faithful to you. Consider the moments when you didn't know how you'd keep going or if you could get out of bed in the morning. Remember the sleepless nights and long days on the job when you didn't think your work would ever end. Reflect on the ways your Father has been there for you, every step of the way, each and every day.

He is more than worthy to be praised. We truly cannot fathom his greatness. Not even if we spent an entire year trying.

DAILY INTERACTION ▼

 CONNECT: Share a favorite verse from this year on JesusDaily.com and see how many people also like it.

December 29

When my spirit grows faint within me,
it is you who watch over my way.
PSALM 142:3

DEVOTION ▼

Count on His Presence

As the new year looms on time's horizon, you may already have started worrying about what's ahead. There are certainly plenty of problems that you know will be waiting, as well as unpleasant surprises that are bound to pop up along the way. But even amidst your worries and concerns, hold fast to the peace of the Lord.

Looking ahead may always cause us to be anxious and fearful. But we must remember that our Father watches over us at all times. We've made it through another year because of his faithfulness and goodness. His sovereignty doesn't change just because our calendar does.

We can count on God's presence to go ahead of us and walk alongside us into the new year ahead.

DAILY INTERACTION ▼

 CONNECT: Ask others to share any New Year's resolutions they may be making and share one of yours as well. Agree to pray and hold one another accountable.

May the God of hope fill you with all joy and peace as you trust in him, so that you may overflow with hope by the power of the Holy Spirit.

ROMANS 15:13

▼ DEVOTION

Overflow with Hope

Some years are characterized by hardship and loss, struggle and unfathomable devastation, illness and financial troubles, unemployment and divorce. Other years seem more pleasant, filled with new arrivals, well-deserved promotions, and unexpected blessings and provisions. We tend to think that just because the numbers change on our calendar that somehow our circumstances will automatically change, too.

While such a neat ending and new beginning rarely happens, we can trust God with every area of our lives. In the year to come, his peace will continue to ground us, his joy will continue to satisfy us, and his hope will continue to sustain us.

You have everything you need to begin a new year of walking with the Lord.

—— **DAILY** INTERACTION ▼

 CONNECT: Send thank-you notes to individuals who have especially blessed you with their kindness this past year.

📅 December 31

> *He put a new song in my mouth, a hymn of praise to our God. Many will see and fear and put their trust in the LORD.*
>
> PSALM 40:3

A New Song

Regardless of how you choose to ring out the old and ring in the new, whether it's a watch party at church or a loud party with friends and family, make your first moments in the new year filled with praise and thanksgiving.

God is doing a mighty work in your life. He's started something new inside you, and he will not abandon you now. He's with you for the long haul, for this year and all the years to come.

Amidst the parties and resolution-making, the toasting and kisses at midnight, spend some time today reflecting on your year and giving thanks. Ask God to strengthen and bless you throughout the year ahead, no matter what it may hold.

 CONNECT: Visit JesusDaily.com and let others know you'll be praying for them throughout the new year to come.

NOTES ▼

NOTES ▼